1746

IG MT

STO·PRO·VERITATE

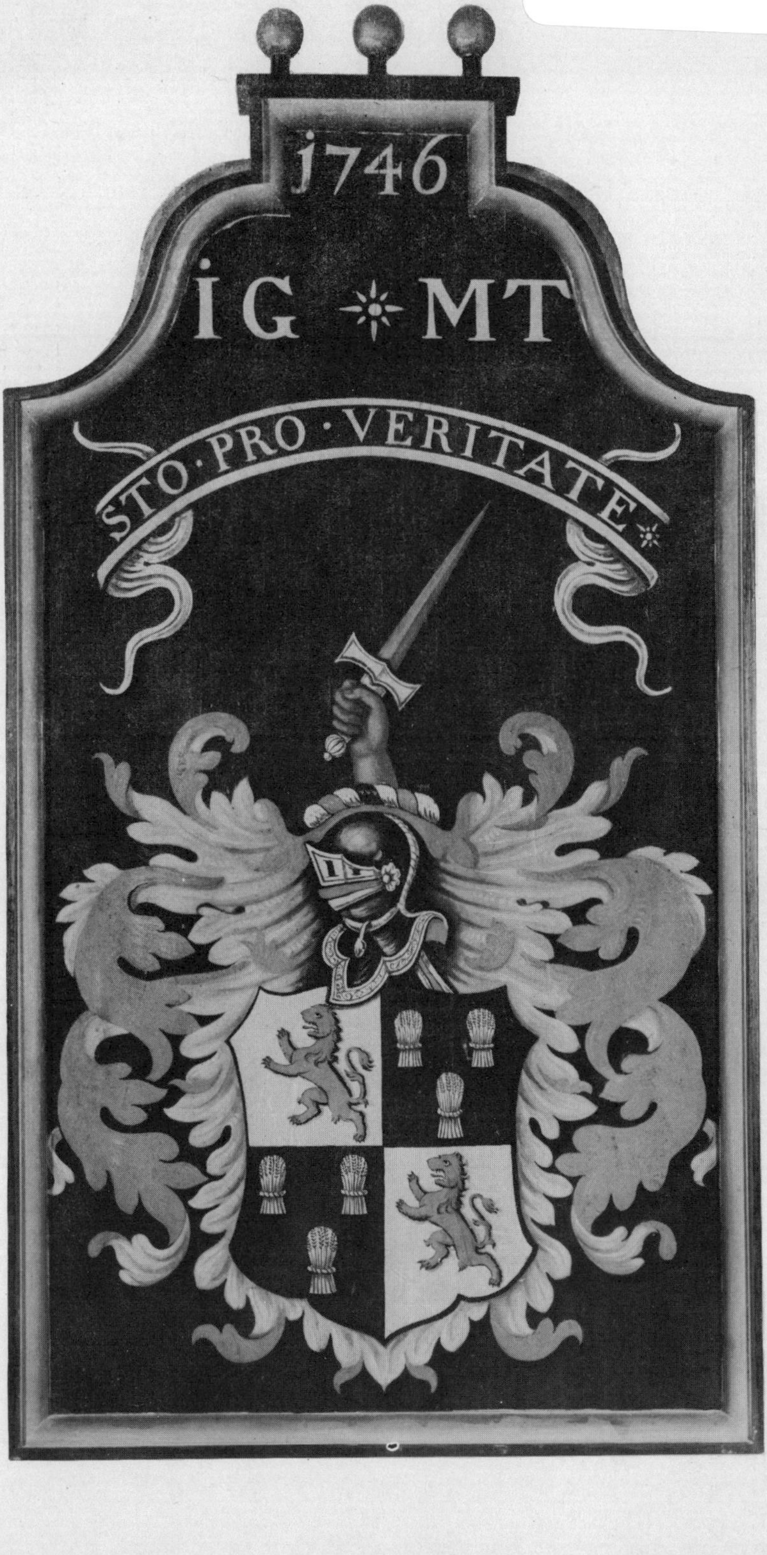

THE TRADERS

THE TRADERS

A STORY OF
BRITAIN'S SOUTH-EAST ASIAN
COMMERCIAL ADVENTURE

SJOVALD CUNYNGHAM-BROWN

NEWMAN NEAME

First published in 1971 by
Newman Neame Limited, London, for
Guthrie & Company (UK) Limited
52–54 *Gracechurch Street, London* EC 3
Printed in Great Britain by
R. & R. Clark Limited, Edinburgh

© *Guthrie & Company (UK) Limited, 1971*

Library of Congress Catalogue Card Number 70–150490

SBN 08 017413 2

To the Merchants and the Factors and the long-forgotten Writers;
Who sowed the Seeds of Empire in a rudely-furrowed sod;
The race of Trader-statesmen and the clan of Trader-fighters
Who laid the lines of order by the Grace and Will of God;
The Sons of these descended with the people in their keeping;
The men who bear the burden of this heritage today;
Each toiler in the noonday with his heart amid the reaping –
To these and those that watch them do I dedicate this lay.

(*Anonymous dedication found in the original copy of* An Anecdotal History of Old Times in Singapore, *by Charles Burton Buckley, printed in Singapore by Fraser and Neave, Limited, in 1902, to which work I am deeply indebted for various details in this book.*)

I meant neither to embellish nor disfigure, but
solely to give as just a resemblance as I could.

(*Lord Macartney's Journal of his Mission to China 1783–5*)

CONTENTS

ILLUSTRATIONS

INTRODUCTION

The British have always been traders. It was trade, their own personal profit, not national ambition, that lured British adventurers into so many far corners of the earth – that lured them there, sometimes against their own government's settled policy, to fend for themselves in distant lands. In doing so, and by eventually persuading Britain to intervene in their support, it was these same traders who often provided the means of bringing order and progress to many a race of oppressed and struggling peoples.

Yet so much that one reads today gives a very different picture.

In some parts of the world, Britain's tenure of office as overlord has left an aftertaste of bitterness. Not unnaturally, in their understandable joy at being at last their own masters, some 'newly emergent' nations have been apt to forget the vast prosperity brought to them by British enterprise; and by the machinery of government designed for their use by generations of British administrators which alone has made their independence possible.

We do not hear enough of what these countries were like before the British came. We are seldom told of the distresses that had generally been suffered as a normal condition of existence in such lands; nor do we often read the simple story of how the traders – the 'Box-wallahs' – went in first and of what they did; of their affections and generosities; or of how they frequently impelled their government to take action in the cause of humanity as much as in that of their own purses.

To tell such a story would be worthwhile; for 'the evil that men do lives after them; the good is oft interréd with their bones'.

But to write a mere eulogy of such a history's characters, as they emerged over the years, would not do at all. These traders must be shown for what they were – tough and hard-headed business men determined to succeed, who realised that the only path to riches lay through the success of their firm, which they therefore forced forward in every way they knew; whilst fighting on the one side to 'keep the business in the family' and on the other to take over the leading position in it for themselves.

Their inner lives and struggles would be as vital to the story as the progress of their business itself; for they are the two sides of one coin.

To treat these traders as Men rather than as lay figures – to describe their personal ambitions, their heart-burnings and failures as well as their grit – would add salt to a tale of Britain's trade in South-east Asia.

Guthries', the oldest East India merchant firm, with its fine motto of the Guthrie clan, *Sto Pro Veritate*, ('*I stand for Truth*'), would be taken to represent all the business houses of Britain that took root in Stamford Raffles's small trading colony of Singapore. The story would be told of the merchants' clashes with a reluctant government in their efforts to safeguard their position, to promote Britain's interest in the East and to bring development to the empty island of Singapore as well as to the 'Native States' on the mainland of the Malayan peninsula.

The 'Flag', in short, would at last be shown in its correct position of following, not leading, 'Trade'.

The goodwill between Britain and the two new nations of Singapore and Malaysia reflects the greatest credit on the good governments and kindly people of all three of those countries; and is proof, if any were needed, that the merchants and administrators touched on in this story built honestly and built well.

With Guthrie and Company standing at the forefront of its own romantic history, yet in itself representing the whole of Singapore's enterprising 'East India' trading community over the last hundred and fifty years, I decided to call this book *The Traders*, a story of Britain's South-east Asian commercial adventure.

SJOVALD CUNYNGHAM-BROWN

BOOK ONE

IN THE BEGINNING

CHAPTER I

ALEXANDER GUTHRIE

Alexander Guthrie was born on the 30th of December 1796, on land that had been worked by his forefathers for generations.

The Scottish county of Angus stretches from Dundee on the Firth of Tay, across the Vale of Strathmore and then north again up the glens into the heart of the Highlands. Throughout it all, those of the ancient family of Guthrie have spread themselves as landowners and farmers for more than a thousand years – embroiling themselves in the troubles of Scotland; amassing money as bankers; gripping the soil with the tenacity of their race, and harking back in thought and story to the centre from which they all sprang, the great old Guthrie Castle on the Lunan.

There at the time of Alexander's birth, lived old John Guthrie of Guthrie (of 'that ilk', as they say in Scotland) and his gentle wife Ann – a typical eighteenth century couple in the finest tradition – to be followed, when Alexander was eight years old, by young John Guthrie, a dark and tousle-haired sporting squire with a face like Alan Breck in Stevenson's *Kidnapped*. But, of them all, it was little William Guthrie whom Alexander most resembled. Fifteen years our hero's junior, there young William stands today, halfway up the stairs of Guthrie Castle in his uniform of an Ensign of the 42nd (later the First Battalion of the Black Watch) – all seventeen years of devil-may-care spirit and youthful zest gazing from a portrait that still strikes the heart after the lapse of a century and a half.

These were Alexander Guthrie's people. These were the normal, quiet old country families, scattered throughout England and Scotland, whose younger sons and cousins habitually sought their fortunes overseas; who were to be found in the military cantonments of India, on the South American pampas and in the seaports of all the world.

They were the central reservoir of Britain's nineteenth century power; and of its glory.

Alexander Guthrie's birthplace was the farm of Burnside, about three miles north-west of the market-town of Brechin near the foot of the glens. He was the youngest child of the farmer, whose first name was also Alexander and who had married a wife whose maiden name had been Guthrie. (Following the prudent fashion of that time the said Margaret Guthrie may no doubt have been very willing to marry her own cousin for the good reason of 'keeping the *sillar* in the family'.)

Old Alexander had inherited Burnside from his father, great grandson of the laird of Guthrie Castle. He had had several elder brothers, who might have inherited the land rather than he, but they had all died young.

Alexander the farmer had also a younger brother Thomas, who had gone away to sea as a boy and never come back to the land. The Fox-Maules, a powerful Brechin family who were related to the Guthries, had found a place for this young Thomas as an apprentice in the East India Company's marine service when he had reached twelve years of age; and away he had gone.

Throughout the period of the Peninsular War, the farmer's youngest son, Sandy – as Alexander was always called – grew into a tough and lusty lad on land that flourished during those rich years. Farming paid handsomely and life in the country was good.

* * *

Among the many cheerful events in the family was the regular arrival of news from Thomas Guthrie, young Sandy's sea-going uncle.

A close friend of this uncle Thomas, about whom he frequently used to write, was one Thomas Talbot Harrington, who had become quite a legendary hero with Sandy. Tom Harrington, a Wiltshireman born in Salisbury on 19th September 1778, was one of the many sons of a certain John Harrington and his wife Rachel. He had entered the East India Company's marine service at the same time as Thomas Guthrie; and when this story opens was midway in a career that would seem nowadays to be astonishingly precocious and successful.

When fourteen years old he had sailed on a two-years voyage to the Coromandel coast in the East Indiaman *Manship* as one of her midshipmen. From sixteen to nineteen, still a midshipman, he did a three-years trip to China and back in *Canton*. Then back to China in *Rose* as fourth mate, followed by *Duke of Buccleugh* and *Dorsetshire*, also to China, as second mate. Finally, at the advanced age of twenty-six, he had found himself in 1805 in command of the Company's fine East Indiaman *Ganges*, bound for Bengal.

Aboard that vessel, and adding to the responsibilities of Harrington's first command, were Thomas Raffles (later the famous Sir Thomas Stamford Raffles, founder of Singapore) and his first wife, Olivia; Raffles being on his way out East for the first time as a young writer in Sir Philip Dundas's Presidential government of Penang.

These passengers Harrington landed safely at Madras, where they joined the East Indiaman *Warley* for the final stage of their voyage; *Ganges* then proceeding north to Calcutta.

However, in spite of this connection with the renowned Raffles, later to be Britain's greatest figure in South-east Asia, Harrington's claim to the hero-worship of a nine-year-old Sandy arose not at all from his acquaintanceship with historical personalities, but solely from the fact that on his return voyage his ship went down off the Cape of Good Hope.

The story of that sinking – of the month-long struggle of exhausted men and the final desperate decision of her captain to abandon ship – may still be read in *Ganges's* salt-encrusted log in the India Office Library, where it may perhaps have been glanced at once or twice during the last 160 years. It is still possible to decipher the painstaking entries regarding wind, sea and increasing depth of water in the well; written in until the last by a hand numbed with cold and fatigue, but one evidently belonging to a man with a clear head and a faithful attention to detail.

The incident does Harrington credit; and the East India Company were apparently of the same opinion, for he was soon once more posted as Captain, this time of *Charles Grant*, before becoming Commander in 1811 of what was to prove his last ship, *Scaleby Castle*, a new vessel and one of the Company's finest.

But the sea now ceased to be the fortune for ships' officers that it had until recently been. From 1796 onward, members of the East India Company's Marine Service had been allowed to trade on their own account. The free carriage of goods outward bound and back, not to exceed a total of ninety tons each way, had been granted them for that purpose; the only restriction being on 'woolens and warlike stores' on the outward passage and on 'musk, camphire, arrack and China raw silk' on the way home.

Unfortunately for them, in 1813 an Act was passed throwing the East India trade open to private competition. Realising that their officers could now no longer be expected to gain much profit from buying and selling, the Company decided to grant them a fixed rate of pay – which was very distasteful to the ambitious – and from then on forbade them to carry on any trade of their own.

This being altogether too much for Captain Harrington, he handed in his papers immediately *Scaleby Castle* reached Blackwall dock on 18th November 1813; and the following year took ship, as an independent merchant, to his most familiar port of call en route for India, the flourishing Cape Town.

Here his friend John Pringle had been East India Company's agent ever since the place had been taken from the Dutch by Sir George Elphinstone and Sir Alured Clarke in 1795. To Cape Town therefore Harrington had sent forward his own son just after the place had finally been ceded to Britain, after years of chopping and changing, by the Congress of Vienna; and within a few months he went out there himself.

By mid-1816 Harrington was well installed at the Cape. He had rapidly become a man of business with large commercial interests in the trade with India – the owner of a fine house at Kaizersgraght near the centre of the town and the proprietor of landed property out at Simonstown. He was also a tenderer for naval contracts in addition to his own business as exporter of Cape wheat and flour.

* * *

But Alexander Guthrie, the fifth and last son of a Scottish farmer already beginning to feel the cold hand of want

John Guthrie of Guthrie **Ann Guthrie**

John Guthrie **William Guthrie**

Guthrie Castle

with the ending of the Napoleonic Wars (a strapping lad of eighteen with little chance of making a career for himself at home), what was to become of him?

The answer lay ready to hand. Let uncle Thomas give him an introduction and he would go out and join the successful Harrington in his prosperous business at the Cape.

So it came about; and thus Alexander Guthrie left his home in Scotland and embarked upon his chosen career.

In 1816 Alexander Guthrie found himself in the office of Thomas Talbot Harrington of Cape Town; and on the 15th December 1817 he is to be observed signing, on behalf of 'T. T. Harington', a document headed 'The memorial of Thomas Talbot Harrington, Merchant', requesting His Excellency the Right Honourable Lord Charles Henry Somerset, Governor and Commander in Chief at the Cape, 'to permit the shipment by the vessel *Marquis of Wellington* of 2,000 pounds of flour to St Helena, to the order of Messrs Balcombe and Co, Purveyors to General Buonaparte'.

Here the reader has for the first time the satisfaction of regarding young Sandy at work and of examining his signature. He may allow himself not only to smile that two different spellings of the name 'Harrington' should appear in one document, but to wonder whether that Scottish face of his did not break into a grin at the choice of vessel fated to feed poor Napoleon in his exile.

No. 407
[illegible]

His Excellency the Right Honorable Lord Charles Henry Somerset Governor & Commander in Chief &c &c &c

The Memorial of Thomas Talbot Harrington of Cape Town Merchant

Most respectfully sheweth

That Memorialist has received orders from Messrs Balcombe & Co Purveyors to General Buonaparte for the Shipment of two thousand Pounds weight of Flour to Saint Helena.

That the Ship Marquis of Wellington is now about to proceed to Saint Helena and ready to take on board said Flour as soon as the requisite Permission can be obtained

Wherefore

Wherefore Memorialist prays that Your Excellency will be graciously pleased to grant permission for the Shipment thereof

And Memorialist as in duty bound shall ever pray

For T. T. Harington
A. Guthrie

Cape Town
15 Decr 1817.

His Excellency the Right Honorable Lord Charles Henry Somerset Governor & Commander in Chief etc etc etc

The memorial of Thomas Talbot Harrington of Cape Town Merchant Most respectfully sheweth

That memorialist has received orders from Messrs Balcombe & Co Purveyors to General Buonaparte for the shipment of two thousand Pounds weight of flour to Saint Helena.

That the Ship Marquis of Wellington is now about to proceed to Saint Helena and ready to take on board said Flour as soon as the requisite permission can be obtained. Wherefore memorialist prays that Your Excellency will be graciously pleased to grant permission for the shipment thereof

And memorialist as in duty bound shall ever pray.

For T. T. Harington
A. Guthrie

Cape Town
15 Decr 1817

CHAPTER 2

EASTERN CHALLENGE

On the 6th February 1819 Sir Thomas Stamford Raffles took formal possession of Singapore. Behind that simple statement of a transaction between Raffles and two Malay Chiefs known as their 'Highnesses the Sultans Hussein Muhammed Shah of Johore and Dato Temenggong Sri Maharaja Abdul Rahman of Singapoora' lies a wealth of history with which this account need not concern itself.

It is sufficient to recollect that the said Thomas Raffles was last encountered in 1805 aboard Captain Harrington's fine ship *Ganges* en route for Madras as a young writer in Sir Philip Dundas's Ministry at Penang; and to note how often the threads cross and re-cross each other in forming the pattern of this story.

More than two years had passed since Alexander Guthrie had become installed as a junior merchant at Cape Town; years in which he would be maturing from a raw youth to an enterprising man of business.

The East Indiamen, calling in for stores and water on their voyages to and from India and China, would bring news not only from London but also from Canton and Calcutta. Ships' captains, their cocked hats flung on the table as they smoked their Manila cheroots, easing a tight cravat with a horny thumb, would ask each other by what possible folly Britain could ever have been induced to sign that damned Settlement of 1815.

Did they wish to strangle Britain's Eastern business? Look at that great commerce, the China Trade. How, they asked, could that be conducted other than by ship and through the Eastern Seas – down the Malacca Strait or through the Sunda Strait, it didn't matter which, but through the very centre of the East Indies whichever way, – and did not Britain have full control of those same Indies throughout the war, ever since Holland fell to the French, even sending that clever shrimp of a fellow Thomas Raffles to govern Java with his squint eye and strangely sweet-natured face?

Some thirty-two years before, in 1786, Francis Light, by his founding of the Settlement of Prince of Wales Island, Penang, had staked the first British claim to a share in South-east Asian commerce (Bencoolen, though established in 1685 being out of the trade route and of small account). Penang had also proved of little value, being away north up the Strait and too far from that vital South-east Asian corner – now deeply inset into the renewed Dutch sphere of influence – that every ship must pass on its way to and from China.

'And it is not only Britain that is interested in this affair', would say one, a Commander on the run to the Coromandel coast, 'but Calcutta too. Surely London knows that China will accept no payment in exchange for teas but silver from India, or opium by the back door? Let the Dutch grow stronger in the Far East and see what will happen to John Company's holdings nearer home, in India. The Dutch, forsooth – and "His Britannic Majesty's desire to afford lasting testimony of his friendship and attachment to the House of Orange"! It is all very well to try to build up Holland as a buffer against the French, but let "His Britannic Majesty" look indoors before peering out o' window.'

So it would go, Harrington the old sea captain taking his share in the talk and Alexander Guthrie listening with mouth shut and ears wide open.

How often, sitting there at the Cape and watching the run of trade as it streamed by – woollen goods and manufactures one way and teas the other – must young Guthrie have daydreamed of those far eastern Isles that lay like a barrier across the path; a challenge to be taken up and fought for one of these days if trade was to continue to run freely, as it should.

* * *

But now at last, in mid-1819, exciting news reached the Cape by a succession of returning East Indiamen.

Sir Thomas Stamford Raffles, purloining a plum out of the jaws of the Dutch, spiriting up an exiled claimant to the throne of Johore, had by some means established himself, with every appearance of legality, on that country's southern extremity – on a small marshy island, said to be uninhabited but with facilities for an excellent harbour, known locally among the Malays as Temasik or Singapoora.

Raffles had been to Calcutta the year before and had been encouraged by the Governor-General, the Marquis of Hastings, to form a settlement on the main trade route through the Eastern Isles, provided he was careful to do nothing that might offend the Hollanders – and now captains outward bound from home were full of tales circulating London coffee houses of the English Secretary of State Lord Castlereagh's rage at what Sir Stamford had been about; and of the Dutch Ambassador, Baron Fagel's, bleatings to the Hague at what he called 'this new extravagance – this prank – of Sir Raffles'.

Even Colonel Bannerman, the Governor of Penang, was inflaming his friend the merchant prince Palmer in Calcutta against every action of Raffles, the ambitious thruster whom he sneeringly referred to as 'the Golden Sword'. Raffles was a man whom he disliked, both on personal grounds and because of his 'outrageous trespass' into an area which should clearly, he felt, fall under Penang's sphere of influence.

Hastings was on the horns of a dilemma. He could not show support to his young protégé without antagonising his chief Home authority; he could not agree with Castlereagh without injustice to Sir Stamford.

It merely remained to be seen whether by force of words or brilliant strategy Raffles himself could weather the storm; and, in so doing, shield the minute settlement he had founded in the interests of the China trade and of the growth of British influence in South-east Asia.

A 'war of paper' had broken out which was to hagride and bedevil Singapore's very existence – to say nothing of its growth – for the next four years.

Tom Harrington and Alexander Guthrie were both adventurers, or they would not have been where they were. Both were as ready to take a chance as the next man – readier than most – though as merchants there were necessary problems to be weighed. Here was an opportunity to strike out afresh, into new fields further East, right on the route of the China Trade and into unexplored country in the heart of the far eastern lands of spices, where primitive populations, possibly large, would trade tin and coconut oil, gambier, pepper and cloves for English cloth and manufactured goods of all descriptions.

Here a well financed undertaking could underwrite enterprises of endless kinds, become shipping and general agent for who knew how many different lines of commerce in a newly opened colony.

But, – and it was a big 'but', – who knew whether this Singapore they spoke of would live and grow or be no more than a flash in the pan? What was best to do in such a case?

It did not take them long to decide. Strike now, whilst the iron was hot. Sandy packed his bags and was off to Singapore, taking with him aboard the East Indiaman a cargo of trade goods from Harrington's warehouse. Captain Harrington himself was to follow as soon as he could, by another ship with his wife and his daughter Marianne – first to stay a while in Penang and Malacca with friends and then to continue by sea via Singapore right through to Macao, in search of a chance to grip the root of trade at its eastern point of origin.

* * *

'The Golden Chersonese' of the Greeks, drawn on Ptolemy's map as a peninsula jutting out toward the south-east from the continent of Asia, had been shown by later geographers to be the extremity of the Himalayas as the diminishing tail of that range curves down toward the equator – a fifteen-hundred-mile-long chain of mountains, swamp and equatorial vegetation, thrusting its mass into the midst of the islands of the South-east Asian seas.

The Greeks had visited it in search for gold, as well perhaps as for the peacocks and ivory associated with it in the story of the Queen of Sheba; leaving behind them a few amphorae, but little else to awaken the curiosity of later ages or to evoke a human interest in the enormous journey they must have undertaken.

When the Greeks arrived the land was probably only inhabited by primitive 'food-gathering' man; a naked wandering shadow, flitting darkly through the mountainous forests with blowpipe and wild negroid eyes in search of birds and fish and jungle roots, as he does to this day. The Greeks would also have met his coastal counterpart the 'Seletar'; an amphibious Caliban along Malaya's shellfish-abounding shoreline.

Secondly, scattered here and there in their close-built stick villages surrounded by crops, they would encounter a race of neolithic people who had come wandering in from the north some two thousand years before; a brown-skinned folk with curly hair and open features, retreating under pressures of population from their home in the plains around the eastern Himalayas – a prolific and clever race with knowledge of boatbuilding, who had overrun much of South-east Asia, occupied the Eastern Archipelago, Borneo, the Philippines, and spread boldly east across the Pacific to form the matrix of many of the South-east Asian and Pacific Ocean peoples of today.

Later on, a commerce had grown between the east coast of India and the western shores of Sumatra, Java, Bali, and even the mainland of the Malayan peninsula itself. This Indian contact had tinctured the blood of the brunette Himalayan-type peoples with Dravidian or Arian infusions, to provide a second, Sanskrit, root to their language and to form a race – or rather a series of ethnologically allied races – who might be regarded as the first beginnings of the present-day Malays.

Such, gross simplification as it is, may have been the information gleaned by Alexander Guthrie as he neared Malaya's shores.

He would be told too, not only of the Chinese, who had worked and traded in Malaya since pre-Christian times and had settled in Malacca as merchants in 1400, but also of the great Cylendra dynasty of Java as well as the Majapahit and Sri Vijaya kingdoms of Sumatra, which had held sway over southern Malaya whilst Arab traders based in Sumatra ruled the north, causing Malays as different in thought and speech as the Scots and English to inhabit the two halves of that land today. But all Malays, except in far-away Bali, since about 1400 had abandoned their old Hindu faith for the simpler and more vigorous religion of Islam.

As they rounded the north of Sumatra and sighted the sands of Balohan Bay on Pulau Wey, Alexander had his first glimpse of that East that was to be his home, and could not fail to have thought back to the old days of the Portuguese caravels.

Sequeira in 1509 and two years later Albuquerque himself had sailed these very seas to the taking of Malacca. An exhausted St Francis Xavier had stopped to take in water at nearby Penang Island on his way to China in 1542. The Hollander, Admiral Matalief, had beaten the Portuguese fleet off this very point in 1606, so that Malacca fell like an over-ripe fruit into the hands of the Dutch in 1641.

Now, after Thomas Raffles's bold stroke of the previous year in 1819, a wedge was to be driven into Dutch pretensions – and Alexander Guthrie, as far as trade was concerned, was at the forefront of the adventurers.

CHAPTER 3

SINGAPORE

Degrees back and days ago, coming down on the long swell from the Bay of Bengal, the East Indiaman had driven forward into a new wind system. The north-east monsoon, which hereabouts follows the coastline and tends to curve round and blow from the north-west, had gradually faltered. Now the land had closed in upon them. A series of small islets, densely infested with vegetation and looking like green velvet pincushions floating, through refraction, high above the water, had swum up from the sea to surround them on all sides and to usher them forward to an anchorage half a mile from the shore. It was the 27th of January 1821.

There in front of them stretched some rather muddy sand, through which a small river seemed to disembogue; much mangrove to right and left; a very few roofs of houses, all palm-thatched, sheltering in a coconut grove close to highwater mark; and an abrupt hillock, back a little from the sea, in the process of being cleared from standing jungle. Singapore, such as it was, clustered round a rather large flagstaff (the top-gallant mast of an East Indiaman clearly) set up on the sandspit at the river mouth.

In those days the East India Company were careful whom they allowed to take up residence in any part of their possessions. Before his departure from the Cape, Guthrie had successfully obtained his 'Indenture', dated the 10th April 1820, from the Marquis of Hastings, Governor-General of India, allowing him 'to proceed to any part of the principal settlements in the East Indies, there to reside for the transaction of the business of the house of Messrs Harrington & Company . . .'

A copy of this document still exists among the Guthrie archives, with its irregular upper edge where it was separated from the original. These copies were sent to the port of destination in the official bag, the original being kept by the intending resident and the two being carefully 'married' together once more by the local Government authority, in order to prevent 'unindentured settlers' (of which there were many) arriving under false colours.

It needs little imagination to conceive how Alexander Guthrie, having gone ashore with Captain Flint the Harbour Master (Raffles's brother-in-law) at some hour of mid-morning, must have been torn with desire to present this bulky parchment to the Chief Local Authority, and so be rid of its bulging discomfort as it distorted his heavy black riding coat; nor of how, at the same time, he must have longed for the cool verandahs of the large thatched bungalows that lined the shore to the east of the river mouth.

The landing stage of one, belonging to a Mr A. L. Johnston, was almost certainly where Alexander first set foot in Singapore. This great rambling residence-cum-warehouse seems to have been the favourite morning meeting place for the town's élite, just as the Battery immediately opposite, or 'Scandal Point', as it came to be called, was soon to grow into the turning point of every evening walk and the ideal site for the relaxing sundown cigar and quiet tête-à-tête.

* * *

Coming in from the glare outside and his eyes growing accustomed to the cool shade, Alexander took the measure of Johnston, his host; a lean, clean-shaven man of Dumfriesshire, whose every word and movement betokened the shipowning sea captain he had so recently been.

Alexander was introduced to David Napier and his Penang-born partner Charles Scott – both of whom had arrived three months after the founding of Singapore in 1819 and had been the first to set up in business together. People liked Napier and Scott; and they were often to be seen with Johnston and later on with his new assistants Andrew Hay and Christopher Rideout Read, either at Johnston's place on the sea-front or at the 'Napier-Scott' godown* on the river, just by the first bend upstream.

Captain Flint introduced him to a strange, swarthy, squat bundle of a man with a blue jowl – rather gone to fat and

* Warehouse.

mopping his brow. 'Claude Queiroz', whispered Captain Flint, 'watch out for him – he is that Calcutta banker Palmer's Portuguese by-blow. Anything you say will go back to father. He's smart as a whip, in spite of being so fat. Arrived in February last year with his large family and has now got himself well established – living in Prendergast's house, the army surgeon, whilst Prendergast, with his wife and children, are away on furlough in India. He has a piece of land along the foreshore here and hopes to get permission to build a godown on it. You'll see everybody here that's in business – they are all traders; and out for what they can get.

'There's one you won't see though – John Morgan. He came out with Johnston in July last year, making the fourth freelance to arrive here if you count Johnston as third. He is a lawyer, and has everyone's back up against him already, cantankerous brute. You watch out. Johnston and he hate each other. We shall have him sent packing if there is much more of it.

'And here is the fifth gambler to arrive in our den of thieves – Graham Mackenzie – Guthrie.'

The casual introduction effected, Alexander Guthrie ran his eye over the great frame and blond features of another east-coast Scotsman – and one who, judging from his loud voice and emphatic manner, was used to saying exactly what he meant and being listened to.

'Cathcart Methven', Mackenzie boomed out in a Scottish burr that would have done credit to Arbroath, 'Cathcart Methven – what is the man anyway? Friend of Sir Stamford Raffles – comes here as an officer of the Honourable Company, living in the Mess and putting on the airs of a prince – and all the while he is running a wee shop at the back of the barracks, undercutting the lot of us and will sell you a sack of rice or a ball of twine as quick as a Hindoo street hawker. Did you ever hear the like of that? Guthrie, are you listening? If the whole of us here have not enough spirit to put a stop to this now, we'll be out of business in a month. What charter has Methven as a trader? I demand an immediate inquiry – and if you'll not all sign to that now I shall take it up with Farquhar today and by myself.'

* * *

Guthrie was beginning to absorb the atmosphere of his surroundings. Here, gathered together before him were the men who were to be his companions over the years; with whom he was to combine in battling against many a future policy of Government; and against whom he was now to set himself up in active business competition, as the sixth indentured trader to establish himself and gamble his all on the hazardous future of that precarious adventure known as 'Singapore'.

How many of these small firms, in that fever-ridden, gambling 'Tom-Tiddler's-ground' between East and West, between competing Dutch and British claims and between the warring interests of Calcutta and their own local community, would survive a decade – would see the end of the century – would develop into a worldwide concern as the type-pattern of the 'Eastern Trader'?

Alexander Guthrie would ponder, not only on how they and their many successors certain soon to come would succeed, but also what fortune the years might have in store for that great busy, struggling mass of labouring men he had seen upon the beach as he came ashore – the Hindoos, the Chinese, the Malays; and the army of Portuguese-Eurasian clerks and tallymen who had swarmed in from Burma, from Penang and from Malacca in the wake of Thomas Raffles and who were already forming a respectable hardworking middle class in the growing settlement's economy.

Raffles, when he had left Singapore more than a year before, after his remarkably short and dynamic tenure as the settlement's Founder,* had appointed Major William Farquhar, formerly the East India Company's Resident in Malacca, as Chief Local Authority. Massive instructions were left upon that ageing man's never very adequate shoulders as to free port status for the settlement; and of the need for the most tactful handling of the two Malay Chiefs who, though afforded opportunities for entering effectively into the new administration, were now no more than a couple of pensioners. Last but not least, the argument raged over Raffles's instruction to plan the town with its business quarter to the west of the river and its residential area to the north and east, due regard being given, nevertheless, to the observation throughout of the strictest economy . . . model instructions

* Raffles returned to the British possession of Bencoolen, a coastal strip of land in south-west Sumatra, of which he was Lieutenant-Governor.

from a now distant perfectionist chief; the instructions undoubtedly of a genius; but ones which would require for their carrying out either a similar genius or another such as Raffles himself, with enough courage and independence to disobey instructions when he felt inclined, together with sufficient weight with the authorities to expect his conduct to be condoned.

Farquhar, a rather 'sticky' old officer in his demeanour and outlook, possessed none of these attributes, but was merely a hardworking administrator with old-fashioned ideas who was loyally endeavouring to comply with the orders of a much younger superior, and one with whom he was already beginning to suffer a sensation of considerable pique. Raffles was getting all the credit for the founding of the Settlement. It had, after all, been a shared enterprise, and Farquhar had mentioned Singapore as an ideal site before Raffles had probably even heard of it. Also there was the unfortunate affair of the White Ensign, which should of course have been set to fly over the Residence of the Chief Local Authority, but which, on appeal to Raffles, was permitted to be flown only over the Port Office – or over Master Flint's House, whichever way you liked to look at it.

* * *

No, it was not an altogether happy atmosphere in which Alexander Guthrie found himself that hot morning of his first arrival.

There was first of all the question of business accommodation. According to Raffles's plan, every warehouse was to be built either away out on the 'East beach', which was quite unsuitable for handling cargo, being an open coastline with shallow, muddy shore, or on the western river bank and the flat land immediately behind it. But the latter place was a swamp and, as it stood at present, utterly unsuitable. Government had intended to fill it with rubble from an adjacent mound, but labour was short, wages high and the whole project apparently connected with the construction of the Battery on the sandspit, progress on which was lagging abominably.

Farquhar had been sensible enough, realising that Singapore's very reason for existence was trade, to permit warehouses and business premises to be erected on the east side of the river; but these were only to be of a temporary nature, with no security of tenure and without the issue of any form of title. 'There is the rub – no title! How can we do business that way? Everything having to hang in the wind not only for Castlereagh and Baron Fagel to fight it out and decide whether we or the Dutchman are to have the place; but also, even in such small matters as the siting of a warehouse, we now have to await a decision from his distant nibs the "Golden Sword"!'

'And as for free port status,' said Mackenzie, 'would Guthrie have seen that great Chinese Choon, or Junk, as the sailors miscall them, lying in the outer harbour as he came in this morning? The first one that has ever called in at our precious "Free Port" of Singapore, enticed here at word of British protection against every form of duty and exaction. All the way from Amoy she comes, with what could be the beginnings of an excellent trade. And have you seen the captain of her, "Taikong" or what you will? Lying there in the stocks for having taken the British at their word and failed to bring "presents" to their Sultanic Highnesses Tungku Long and the Temenggong! What sort of a "free port" is that, I should like to know. There's a fine way to start our Eastern commerce!'

Guthrie could not fail to have pondered these things, nor is there any great likelihood that he refrained from making mention of them on his visit that afternoon to Major William Farquhar with Mr Alec Laurie Johnston; for it is a truism that a newcomer seldom venerates the local chief or fears his thunder as does the old hand – and as he too will learn to do when he has found his humble niche in the hierarchy of the Court.

However that may be, Farquhar not only accepted the young man's Indenture with good grace, but caused immediate action to be taken to release the Chinese skipper and rebuke the Temenggong – a juxtaposition of events that was certainly not lost upon the Chinese, to judge from Guthrie's future trade. However, as rebukes were the order of the day, Major Farquhar found it necessary to indite a highly bureaucratic note to the merchants in reply to a letter on the same subject they had just submitted. 'Not without feelings of Surprise and Regret . . . Subject which in no way required the Interference of the Body of European Merchants . . . cannot for a moment admit the Propriety or Expedience of interposing uncalled for their collective Voice in any measure having a Political Tendency . . .'!

* * *

Fortune was apparently smiling upon Sandy Guthrie from the moment of his arrival in Singapore. Through the friendship of Laurie Johnston (and as a result too, perhaps, of a certain good-natured regard on the part of Farquhar for a pleasant young countryman of his own on the threshhold of his career) an empty warehouse – that rarest of commodities in the Settlement at that time – was offered him on a temporary licence to occupy. Mr Dunn, an uncovenanted servant of the East India Company who had been sent to Singapore to collect botanical specimens, had made very little use of it. The Company had had it especially constructed for him of bricks brought down to the new port by one of the ships in the original convoy with Stamford Raffles from Calcutta; and now here it was, the first answer to his hopes, standing four-square beside the track already called 'Hill Street' that led from the shore to the small hill in process of clearance.

Alexander accepted this windfall immediately and signed, in the name and on behalf of Captain Thomas Talbot Harrington, his agreement to occupy Mr W. Dunn's godown at the Company's pleasure and without issue to him of any title deeds.

Those who know Singapore today may find it hard to understand what Alexander Guthrie was faced with, in pure physical difficulty, upon his first arrival; . . . intense exertion; a low diet of poor food; relentless humid heat; a blazing sun interspersed with torrents of equatorial rain; and duck-boards laid across a muddy clearing, where every pool bred clouds of anopheline mosquitoes that hovered in front of the eyes and settled on face and arms, making rest by day or night impossible as they fed on fresh blood and paid for their meal in the pallid coinage of an aching, bone-shaking ague.

But youth and enthusiasm overcome all. At dawn, coat off and with streaming sunburned face, Alexander Guthrie stood

PERSONS TO RESIDE COVENANT, 1816.

Cox and Son, Printers, Great Queen Street.

Recital of the Party's Application for Leave to go to India there to reside.

This Indenture, made the Tenth Day of April, in the Year of our Lord One Thousand Eight Hundred and Twenty Between the *United Company of Merchants of England Trading to the East-Indies* of the one Part, and Alexander Guthrie of the other Part, **Witnesseth**, That at the Request of Alexander Guthrie, the said *United Company* have given, and granted, and by these Presents do give and grant, full and free License, Power, and Authority, unto the said Alexander Guthrie, during the Pleasure of the said *Company*, and until this License shall be revoked by the said *Company*, or their Court of Directors, or the Governor General, or Governor of the Presidency where the said Alexander Guthrie shall from Time to Time be found, to proceed to any of the principal Settlements belonging to the said *United Company* in the *East-Indies*, there to reside for the transaction of the Business of the House of Messrs Harington and Company at the Cape of Good Hope according and subject to the Provisions and Restrictions contained in an Act of Parliament made and passed in the fifty-third Year of the Reign of His Majesty King George the Third entitled "An Act for continuing in "the *East-India* Company for a further Term the Possession of the British Territories in *India*, together with certain exclusive Privileges; for establishing further Regulations for the Government of the said "Territories, and the better Administration of Justice within the same; and for regulating the Trade to and from the Places within the Limits of the said Company's Charter;" and subject to all such Provisions and Restrictions as are, or hereafter may be in Force, with regard to Persons residing in *India*, and also subject to the Covenants and Agreements of the said Alexander Guthrie, hereinafter mentioned.

He covenants:

Provided always, and these Presents are upon this express Condition, that in case of Breach or Non-observance of any of the Provisions, Restrictions, Covenants, or Agreements, subject to which this License is granted, and on the Part of the said Alexander Guthrie, to be observed and performed, then and from thenceforth the License hereby granted shall be and become absolutely null and void, and of no Force or Effect whatsoever, and the said Alexander Guthrie shall be deemed and taken to be a Person residing and being in the *East-Indies* without any License or Authority for that Purpose. And the said Alexander Guthrie, for himself, his Heirs, Executors, and Administrators, doth hereby covenant, promise, and agree, to and with the said *United Company*, in Manner and Form following, that is to say:

— To submit himself to the Regulations of the Local Governments there.

(First) That he the said Alexander Guthrie from the Time of his Arrival at any of the principal Settlements aforesaid shall and will behave and conduct himself, from Time to Time, and in all Respects, conformably to all such Rules and Regulations as now are, or hereafter may be in Force, at the said Presidency, or at any other Presidency in the *East-Indies*, where he, the said Alexander Guthrie may happen to be, and which shall be applicable to him or his Conduct, and which he ought to obey, observe, and conform to:

— Not to trade contrary to Law.

(Secondly) That he the said Alexander Guthrie shall not nor will, by himself, or in Partnership with any other Person or Persons, or by the Agency of any other Person or Persons, either as Principal, Factor, or Agent, directly or indirectly engage, carry on, or be concerned in any Trade, Bank, Dealings, or Transactions whatsoever, contrary to Law:

— To make Satisfaction to Natives or Foreigners and Native States, for Oppression, Wrong, and Offences.

(Thirdly) And that, in case the said Alexander Guthrie shall be guilty of any Violence, Oppression, or Wrong, to any Person or Persons, not being an European-born Subject, or European-born Subjects of His Majesty, his Heirs, or Successors, or shall commit any Offence against any King, Prince, Government, State, or Nation, within the Limits of the said *Company's Charter*, or shall be charged with any such Violence, Oppression, Wrong, or Offence, then, and in such Case, the said Alexander Guthrie shall and will submit himself therein, in all Things, to the Decision of the said *United Company*, or their Court of Directors, or of the Governor-General in Council, or Governor in Council, of any of the Presidencies of the said *Company* in the *East-Indies*, if they, or any of them, shall see fit to interfere therein; and that he, the said Alexander Guthrie, his Executors or Administrators, shall and will pay and make good all such Sum and Sums of Money, and do and perform all such Acts, Matters, and Things whatsoever, as a Reparation of the Injuries which he shall have occasioned, or the Offence he shall have given, as he shall be required by any such Decision to pay, make good, do, or perform; and on Failure thereof, it shall be lawful to and for the said *Company*, or their Court of Directors, or any of their Agents, to pay, or cause the same to be paid, made good, done, and performed, and thereupon the said Alexander Guthrie, his Executors or Administrators, shall and will reimburse to the said *Company*, their Successors or Assigns, all such Sum and Sums of Money as shall be so paid, and all Costs, Charges, and Expenses, which may be incurred thereby:

— Not to quit India without satisfying all Debts to the Company, Natives, and Foreigners, before Departure.

(Fourthly) And that, before he the said Alexander Guthrie shall return to *Europe*, or remove from, quit, or leave the Presidency or Settlement where he shall reside or shall be found, he, the said Alexander Guthrie shall and will pay and satisfy, and perform all such Debts, Sums of Money, Duties, and Engagements, as he shall owe or be liable to perform to the said *Company*, or any Person or Persons, not being an European-born Subject or European-born Subjects of His Majesty, his Heirs, or Successors, or for any Injury or Offence he may have done or committed, as herein-before mentioned; and that, in case of any Breach of this Covenant, he the said Alexander Guthrie, shall and will pay unto the said *Company* and their Successors, for the Damages in respect of the Breach thereof, such Sum of Money as he shall have owed, and which he shall have omitted to pay, as herein-before mentioned, or such Sum of Money as shall be equal to the Damage actually sustained by any Person or Persons, by Breach or Non-performance of any Duty or Engagement which, under the Covenant herein-before contained, he ought to have satisfied or performed, before such Return or Removal, to the End that the said *Company*, if they shall see fit, may pay over such Damages to the Creditor or Creditors, or injured Party or Parties, for his, her, or their own Benefit, or may apply them to any other Purpose, or keep them for the Use of the said *Company*, their Successors or Assigns. **In Witness** whereof, to one Part of these Indentures, the said *United Company* have caused their common Seal to be affixed, and to the other Part the said Alexander Guthrie has set his Hand and Seal, the Day and Year above-written.

~~Sealed and delivered (being first duly stamped) in the presence of~~

Alexander Guthrie's Indenture from the Marquis of Hastings, 1820

Singapore from Government Hill, 1846

knee-deep by the rough lighter as sweating coolies, Chinese and Malay, off-loaded his stock-in-trade of goods onto their bare backs and jogged rhythmically away with them along the planks to the brick godown that from now on was to be his home. Splendid people – and most of them no more than youths – boys almost. Their laughter warmed his heart already; and sowed the seeds of a dedication to the East and to the poor and struggling inhabitants of Singapore that reflected the religious fervour of his ancestors, and was to dominate his future life.

Young people crowded round him, fascinated with the Malay he had learned at the Cape, and rejoicing to find someone so obviously interested in their affairs.

Hanyut, the 'castaway', a sixteen-year-old orphan who seemed to have appeared from nowhere, had already installed himself in the godown as his watchdog, houseboy and faithful slave.

In common with many others, his practical and benevolent heart had become absorbed in the happiness of association with young and simple people – in helping the neglected and needy – and was to remain so to the end of his days.

A newcomer, young Andrew Hay, assistant in Mr Alexander Laurie Johnston's warehouse, had soon become Guthrie's close friend.

When the chaos in the godown had been reduced to some sort of order, they had spent days together exploring a track that led due north, past the east side of the hillock and through marshy jungle beside a small stream, right inland about two miles, to where three round-topped jungle-covered hills stood up from the surrounding swamp. On the westernmost of these Claude Queiroz was already beginning to open a clearing with the intention of planting a spice orchard. And now, in such little spare time as they had, they themselves were both throwing all their energies into doing likewise – Hay clearing the eastern hill and Alexander Guthrie the middle.

No sooner done than Sandy, inspired by the abundant enthusiasm of a pioneer, set his heart upon a large tract of jungle south-west of the Settlement, on a promontory of land named 'Tanjong Pagar', where a narrow, fiord-like arm of the sea insinuates itself between that headland and the island of Belakang Mati to form a 'back door' into Singapore harbour. This he speedily acquired from the helpful Major

Farquhar and proceeded to have trees felled and land planted.

And now too, at last, it was possible to lead a life not altogether devoid of grace and amenity. Not long after occupying the godown, Guthrie was able to invite Andrew Hay and a personable stranger named Walter Scott Duncan, three years Sandy's junior, to dine with him in some slight atmosphere of elegance; as a result of which the three young men struck up a friendly acquaintance together and were frequently to be seen visiting each other's thatched houses, taking boats up river or tramping about the now rapidly opening clearings at the far end of what was already becoming known as the 'Orchard Road'. This 'will be a valuable and beautiful spot', as Walter Scott Duncan wrote in his diary after having dropped in there one afternoon and been given by Guthrie a glass of brandy and water. Hot arguments broke out too, over the new track's construction, 'making a needless ascent which a single horse will find a difficulty in getting over both in coming and going' in order not to make inroads into the hard-headed Sandy's land – for which, Duncan says, Hay 'promises Mr Guthrie a devil of a scolding'!

CHAPTER 4

THE CHINA TRADE

But to work. Trade first; and the pioneering fun of jungle-clearing as a mere pastime. After his Cape Town experience it had not taken Alexander Guthrie long to find his feet and learn the ropes; vastly different as they were in this far eastern settlement from the stately progress of the settled European-type commerce at the Cape.

Here, in this entirely new environment, one would obviously be wise to follow the procedure already beginning to be employed by the firm of A. L. Johnston and Company.

With the opening of Singapore eighteen months before, a large number of Chinese had poured into the new Settlement in search of work, many from Malacca, some from as far away as Penang, a few from across the Strait or from small Chinese tin workings in the forest clearings of Johore. These were now being augmented by the first arrivals of hungry immigrants by junk from Amoy, Canton and other ports along the Chinese coast – a noisy, bustling, energetic community; whose grass huts, or 'chukias', as they called them, were growing like mushrooms under the coconut trees, among the mangrove and along the jungle edges, in a wide and untidy suburban periphery known loosely as 'Chinatown'.

These newcomers, who already formed the majority of the population, jostled for work at the waterfront and the clearings. They were bound together by guilds and societies of their own; made the night hideous by their lurid flares, the clanging of gongs and the vast explosions of their fireworks; obeyed – or at times disobeyed – the orders of their headmen and spoke no form of language understood by the British or the Malays.

Contact between them and 'The Government' was therefore conducted through their Malay-speaking 'Kapalas' or headmen, with results generally satisfactory on both sides.

In matters of Trade and Commerce however, no such

simple arrangement on the part of the British merchants – say by translated conversations between them and the owners of the great number of shops that were now springing up – could possibly have accorded with the complexity of the enterprising and ingenious Chinese mind.

Here in Singapore the British were for the first time encountering a business intellect as sharp as, or sharper than, their own.

'Why – trade, certainly;' the Chinese said in effect. 'What could be more delightful! But not with the shopkeepers direct. That would never do. You would only be cheated and get into difficulties. No, no. Let there be another rung inserted into the commercial ladder, an entirely new storey built in the edifice of commerce in accordance with good Chinese architecture. An army of competent "middlemen" or "commission agents" will take your British goods on credit (six months or so should suffice for settlement) and will place these with the many shopmen of their acquaintance, either "on consignment", in which case they will remain on the British merchants' stockbooks until sold, or for cash down in "Spanish dollars". And naturally, to make matters of business easier and happier on both sides, you would be wise to employ an intelligent young English-speaking Chinese on your payroll – there are many well educated persons of that type to be found in Singapore hailing from the good English schools of the Reverend Mr Hutchings and of Dr Morrison at Penang and Malacca (indeed I have a nephew who would suit you admirably) – who will become your "Compradore", keep in touch with the activities of your "middlemen" and relieve you of all your worrying burdens.'

Guthrie followed, therefore, the lead of A. L. Johnston, unaware that the two of them together were setting the pattern of an Anglo-Chinese participation in commerce that was to outlive their century, create an array of Malayan-Chinese millionaires and secure Britain's future in South-east Asia as a new type of European flexible enough to share profits and be a reasonable partner. Alexander Guthrie's only course, faced with this shrewd Chinese urbanity, was the puzzled smile of bewildered acquiescence.

He wished to trade with the Chinese and in agreeing with these suggestions had taken the only course open to him. As can be seen from a position of 150 years later, he had also taken the wisest possible course for his firm, for the people of

Singapore and for Britain's good name in Asia. Whether he quite saw the matter in that light however in the year of 1821, is certainly open to question!

Thus Alexander Guthrie was able, within a few weeks of his arrival, to begin spreading his goods – his woollen cloth and cotton twist, his barrels of nails, his Sheffield axes and knives, his clocks and stationery, to say nothing of his brandy and sherry – throughout a wide range of shops in Chinatown and the European quarter. All these were rapidly distributed by his busy commission agents, some 'on consignment', a few for cash down and most as barter; in exchange for pepper, gambier, nutmeg, cloves, tin and gold dust (all for shipment to Britain or India) which were to be delivered at 'Mr Guthrie's godown' within three, or in some cases six, months of entering into the contract.

The wheels were beginning to turn; the warehouse was filling up; and Guthrie was able to write by home-going East Indiaman to Messrs W. & J. Burnie, Harrington's faithful agents in London, that goods of such and such description and quantity were to be dispatched to them by the next available vessel, 'for disposal please on the London market at best rate obtainable; proceeds, after deduction of their usual commission, to be employed in the purchase and consignment to Calcutta for trans-shipment to Singapore of further goods as separately specified'.

The Singapore Branch of the firm Thomas Talbot Harrington and Company had come alive; and already its linkage, its umbilical cord, with the maternal body in the distant Cape was shrivelling and becoming tenuous.

* * *

But this domestic import-export trade was by no means Alexander Guthrie's only preoccupation as he waited with some impatience for the arrival of the good Captain Harrington himself; and of the dark-haired little Marianne.

In Guthrie's view this local trade in imports and exports should be, in effect, no more than an interesting sideline. From it, he hoped, would certainly grow a flourishing business for his firm as agent for producers and manufacturers in Britain, who would send him their woollen and cotton piece goods, for example, on consignment, for him to dispose of through his commission agents in Singapore and pay for in, say, six months in 'long bills' to be discounted in the London money market. Even better, he hoped they would accept payment by purchase of his coffee, sugar, pepper and tin. But when it came to the making of real fortunes there were much more profitable avenues awaiting him.

The abolition of the East India Company's monopoly of the British 'China Trade', which had thrown Captain Harrington on his beam ends in 1813 and had been the cause of his leaving the Service shortly afterwards, had resulted in a heavy increase in privately owned trading ships, as may be imagined. Fleets of vessels, 'country' craft built in Calcutta or in one or other of the Coromandel coast ports – brigs, snows, barquentines, a few small barques and even an occasional open-decked old 'Gurab' – now plied here and there about the Eastern seas with Singapore as their home port. These now vied with the lumbering Chinese junks for their trade in produce from Canton down to the new port of Singapore.

This 'country trade' to and from China was highly popular with all senior grades of the East India Company, if not with old 'John Company' itself. The former could now ship cargoes of their own in private 'country' vessels from China down to Singapore, where they would be re-shipped in Company's ships for London. The restrictions prohibited their participation in cargoes carried in 'Company's bottoms' to or from the China ports, not ports in South-east Asia. Hence Singapore, where private cargoes could be loaded aboard East Indiamen with legality wherever they might have come from, was already proving itself, even if of doubtful benefit to the Company, at any rate a godsend to its officers!

Fortunes were beginning to be made by yet another generation of 'Nabobs'. A crowded harbour seethed with lighters bringing ashore nankeen raw silk in bales, bundles of cassia and gunnysacks of ginseng root for storage, till they could be shipped forward to London or Bengal and sold to the credit of some Company's officer in faraway Calcutta or Madras – or even transhipped direct from the heavily laden 'country' vessels into the holds of an East Indiaman which had sailed down from Whampoa (the point of origin of the cargo) unprofitably and half empty!

Here then, in this brisk entrepôt trade now growing to

massive proportions, was Guthrie's chance. Trans-shipment, storage, insurance of cargo, local forwarding and general agent for a hundred distant shippers; and – why not? – purchasing agent too, as soon as Captain Harrington had set himself up in Macao, with long term financial accommodation when necessary, (at good discount of course) to those who wished to take part in this exciting and most profitable 'China' enterprise.

* * *

When Captain Harrington and Marianne arrived in June 1821 – sailing down from Penang in leisurely fashion aboard Sahib Jee Hormus Jee's comfortable old barque *Fessel Kerrim*, after a long stop at Malacca where Harrington's wife had relatives living – they were met by a Sandy who had difficulty in restraining his enthusiasm. There was the godown to display, his future plans to discuss and a whole range of questions to be hammered out and settled concerning the return cargoes – mostly tin, birds' nests and opium according to Sandy's way of thinking – that should be loaded aboard the empty country vessels bound for China.

Opium, though strictly speaking illicit, was a perfectly safe cargo of course, as Captain Harrington knew very well. This was brought down to Singapore from Calcutta in Company's ships, much of it being off-loaded there for trans-shipment to non-Company vessels and distributed by them to various ports along the China coast with the connivance of the local Chinese mandarins – who were making as fine a fortune out of that trade, against their Government's policy, as many individual members of the East India Company were making to the detriment of theirs!

Already young Mr Guthrie was becoming a person of some consequence in the growing European community of the town.

He had just sat, in March that year, as member of a Committee to recommend on the matter of policing the new Settlement.*

* A. L. Johnston had been in the Chair, Charles Scott and Claude Queiroz were fellow members, and Mr F. J. Bernard (Farquhar's brother-in-law), represented the 'Police Force' of which he was in charge – if such an exalted term could be

The regard from sweet Marianne's dark eyes as she drank in these tidings reduced Sandy's thoughts to a very complicated condition indeed – and there is little doubt, as her father mentioned one day to his old friend Billy Moffat, his successor as commander of *Scaleby Castle* (to which vessel they were now transferring to complete their voyage to China) that had Fate intervened to the extent of a loose pintle or a sprung foremast, young Mr Guthrie's branch in Singapore would soon be connected with Messrs Harrington & Co of the Cape by stronger links than purely commercial ones.

But the pintles of that fine vessel were beyond reproach. Her foremast showed no trace of a spring in any part of its handsome length. And in five days they had loosed their gaskets, clewed out all standing sail to the yardarms, shantied tops'ls, t'gallants and royals home, and were away out through the eastern entrance into the China Sea.

Perhaps for the first time, but certainly not for the last on that far eastern shore, a young man swallowed a lump in his throat; turned his eyes away from what might have been his future and threw himself into the work at hand; too proud – and too sensitive – to take on shallow local liaisons and sublimating his emotions in care for those whom he could help and who stood in need of his energy and his affection.

---

applied to one Malay clerk, one gaoler, an Indian ex-army sergeant and eight ordinary Bengali policemen, or 'Peaders' as they were called. The result was that Government had been asked to approve the institution of a 'Night-watch' fund to be collected from the business community as well as from the Malays, together with all the householders of Chinatown.

CHAPTER 5

DEUS EX SUMATRA

Now, in 1823, all was confusion and bustle.

Sixteen busy months had gone by since the Harringtons had left and Singapore had grown to a pulsating, ramshackle Chinese town spreading everywhere in a disordered jumble of thatched-roofed 'Hongs', 'Chukias' and 'Bungsals'*, with a total population of some ten thousand people.

Guthrie had already suffered one severe misfortune in the loss of his fine godown, which had suddenly been sold over his head by Mr Dunn to a new-come firm of Armenian merchants. Uncomplainingly, Alexander had sought the advice of old Farquhar, who had first offered him a plot of land on the 'East Beach' at Kampong Glam, to which Guthrie had demurred as being 'unsuitable for commercial purposes', and had then very obligingly reserved for him instead a handsome plot of broad dry land in the middle section of the High Street, the best portion of the town where dwelt the officers and high government officials. This Sandy immediately purchased for four thousand Spanish dollars (a very large sum in those days) and on it had built another excellent large warehouse.

Now Guthrie flourished again and his godown was a hive of activity.

Suddenly, like a stick thrust into this prosperous ant-heap, emerging unannounced from the obscurity of Bencoolen to drop anchor in the roads and take up his residence in Captain Flint's house, ignoring poor old Farquhar's proffered hospitality, came the flaming 'Golden Sword' in person.

A shattered wreck, lean-shanked and yellow as a guinea, his second wife Sophia desperately ill, his children (all but little Ella, who had been sent home separately) dead and buried; his friends Chaplain Charles Winter and even Doctor Jack (his closest colleague ever since his first wife

* Storehouses and sheds.

Olivia and poor Leyden, his bosom friend, had died in Java) gone of the fever and their bones rotting in the graveyard at Marlborough Fort at Bencoolen, he had only one thing left to do, only one last imperative necessity to complete before his greatest life's work was achieved; and that was to bring order, law and a just administration to the chaos of Singapore.

The need was too great, time was too short and he was too far gone in sickness and fatigue to consider the niceties of conduct. If Farquhar opposed him, Farquhar must go. Whoever stood in his way must be removed.

Everything was wrong. The town had not been built according to his plan; and he had no patience with excuses. The Land Office records were inaccurate, ill-kept and in a general mess. Adjacent hills had apparently been given out to Farquhar's 'friends'. No constitution or code of law for the settlement had been drawn up. Nothing had been done about education. The question of slavery among the Malays had not been tackled. And not only were the defences incomplete but the very swamp itself on which the business quarter was to stand had not even begun to be filled in.

Raffles, mad with frustration, was struck down by a brain-storm – the forerunner of the cerebral tumour which later killed him – and lay vomiting and blinded with headache for days in a darkened room; whilst Farquhar, having vainly protested his inability to obey his superior's orders without either funds or adequate staff, was finally compelled to write for justice to Calcutta.

Both men are to be equally admired and pitied. Farquhar continued loyally to carry out his chief's instructions however much he disagreed with his attitude and resented his demeanour to him personally; and Raffles, despite his sickness, was able to call together a Captain Salmond and Dr Lunsdaine, both of whom had accompanied him from Bencoolen, to meet one Dr Wallich on sick-leave from Nepal, in order that together they should form a Committee to advise upon re-siting the whole town according to the original plan.

The Committee first sat exactly a week after Raffles's arrival; and were able to submit him a comprehensive report in another seven days.

Then began a stupendous work of demolition and rehousing, such as was not to be seen again throughout the land for another hundred and twenty-six years, when the great 're-settlement' schemes of 1949 to 1953 resited many tens of thousands of families in Malaya and stemmed the Communist tide.

Vast gangs of labour – Malay, Indian and Chinese – lured by the fantastic offer of one rupee per day (which was later to be increased) dug up and carried away in baskets an entire hill for earth to reclaim the swampy land west of the river. A strong stone 'bund' or sea wall was constructed along the riverside. Roads were made in an organised rectangular network. Markets were laid out. Huge compensations were paid for the resettlement of the Malays and Chinese in a replanned Kampong Glam and Chinatown. An adequate land office staff was engaged and trained for the issue of proper titles to the new holdings; and in short all those miracles performed that rely for their success upon ruthless action and a cornucopia of gold.

* * *

Caught up in the maelstrom with Johnston, Queiroz, Mackenzie, Methven and all the rest, Alexander Guthrie was summarily ejected from his new godown and left to his own devices.

A weaker man might well have thrown in his hand at this juncture and sat passively waiting for the storm to blow over, or have begged A. L. Johnston to buy him out. Johnston had secured one of the few pieces of dry land on the western river bank; and on this was now building his new warehouse and home – a large establishment soon to be known as 'Catch-all-the-trade-point' (Tanjong Tangkap), named after its highly desirable position. The temptation to sell out to him, or go into partnership, must have been very real.

An intriguer, on the other hand, would certainly have joined forces with Claude Queiroz and Cathcart Methven in their campaign of slander, obstruction and sniping at Raffles; and in their sudden support of a Farquhar to whom they would not seem to have shown any particular attachment until that time.

But Guthrie was made of different stuff. Refusing to knuckle under to this second blow of Fate; scorning to allow his name to be tarnished in a battle of mud-slinging led by Cathcart Methven, who had once been Raffles's own friend and brother officer in the taking of Java, Guthrie quietly set about leasing a patch of swamp and partial reclamation on the west side of the river.

Thus it came about that for the annual payment to the Government of thirty-six Spanish dollars – 'each containing 370 grains and 95/100ths part of a grain of pure silver of the standard weight of Great Britain' – Guthrie became the owner of a 999 year lease of 27,922 square feet of sandy bog and clay, richly overlaid with a liberal deposit of slimy rain-soaked red mud, on what had now just been named 'Boat Quay'. It must have amused him to discover, when he eventually received the title to it, that this also endowed him with all rights over such 'woods, trees, underwoods, ways, paths, passages, waters, water courses, profits, commodities, advantages and appurtenances' as might be found in or on the said bog-smitten wilderness.

A large rickety atap-roofed structure, accessible by plank paths and raised gantries over the mud, eventually took shape. The goods were moved in. And the firm of Messrs Harrington and Guthrie were able to issue on the 1st February 1823 a circular to all intending clients for the first time officially advertising the fact of their existence.

Whilst all this had been going on, Guthrie – busy in his spare time with committee and welfare work on behalf of the regrowing town and of the many needy people in it – was informed that Sir Stamford Raffles wished to gazette him, in company with A. L. Johnston and several others, as Magistrate; a highly onerous appointment carrying with it all the status and, more to the point, the responsibilities and duties, of a nineteenth-century Justice of the Peace.

Now there could no longer be any thought of continuing to live in the godown like a beachcomber. He must have a house; and a respectable one at that.

Hence, on his former warehouse site in the High Street, throughout the rains of January and the fine sunny days of February and early March, when every tree puts on a fresh glory of its own, a busy Alexander superintended the erection of his future mansion. A large house of local wood soon took shape, riding high on square brick pillars some seven feet clear of the damp ground; with airy verandahs, wide doors, three excellent bedrooms, a fine big dining room and an elegant reception hall. A great palm-thatched roof threw dark shade around the walls; and from it young Guthrie's handsome head was frequently to be seen emerging as the final layers of palm-frond (the 'ataps') were laid on.

Alexander moved in at once, little realising that he was to be visited – and by the Chief Local Authority – in quite extraordinary circumstances and almost immediately.

* * *

On return from the godown on the evening of 11th March he discovered his house in an uproar.

Forcing his way upstairs through a gesticulating mob of Sepoys and 'Peaders', Guthrie found, lying on the sofa, with Montgomerie bending over him and a white-faced and shaken young Andrew (Farquhar's son) at his side, no less an unexpected guest than the old Colonel Farquhar in person, stabbed and apparently dying from a great wound in the chest, from which blood throbbed upon his open tunic and torn shirt to drip in a growing pool upon the floor.

From Farquhar's two distracted daughters (and from that notable young Malay named Abdullah bin Abdul Kader, the 'Munshi' or Malay teacher attached to Raffles's personal staff from whose excellent account of the incident these facts are taken) Alexander learned that Colonel Farquhar had been brought in by his son Andrew and by Abdullah himself, immediately after an affray at Syed Omar's house just across the road, in which the Colonel had been stabbed with a 'kris' by a certain Syed Yassin from Pahang, an outraged litigant in a civil suit before Mr Bernard, the Magistrate, that very afternoon.

Farquhar's son Andrew had immediately drawn his sword and sliced Yassin's head through from the mouth to the back of his ears; whereupon the Sepoys had thrust the Syed through and through with their bayonets.

At this distance of time the scene stands out crystal clear, like a vignette, from the fog of history; still carrying with it its own terrifying undertones of expectant tragedy. The dark night; a minute British community among ten thousand possibly hostile Asians; the guns dragged tearing forth by half-clothed Sepoys in the light of smoking flambeaux to surround the Temenggong's stockade, on Captain Davies's mistaken belief that this was a Malay plot; Raffles's fury and refusal to let them open fire; his promise to hang Bernard if Farquhar died, for letting Yassin loose; and the grim exposure ordered by him of Yassin's mutilated body in an ox-cart around the town and for two weeks hung in an iron cage on a mast at Telok Ayer Point – horrors upon which there is no need to dwell, other than to mention that brave old Farquhar recovered from his wound; and that, had it not been for Raffles's restraining order to Captain Davies, Britain's tenure of Singapore might well have been a short and very bloody one.

Even as it was, the exposure of the holy Syed's body cost Britain much goodwill, and Yassin remains to this day a martyr and his grave a place of Muslim pilgrimage.

* * *

Let the dead past bury its dead. Many better and more cheerful things occurred in those first busy years than mistakes and intrigues and fears – the angers and distresses that were the growing-pains of Britain's eastern adventure. Whilst the clash of temperament between Raffles and Farquhar had reached such boiling heat as to cause poor sick Raffles to dismiss Farquhar from office on 1st May 1823 – for which act he was later censured – Surgeon John Crawfurd, Farquhar's successor, arrived on the 27th of the same month in the East Indiaman *Hero of Malown* and immediately took up his new office of Resident of Singapore.

Alexander Guthrie attended to his business – planting his orchards and assisting in a committee set up by Raffles for arranging the official opening of an 'Institute' for the education of local children – and occupied such time as he could spare in preparing his house for the return from China of Captain Harrington and Marianne.

Sandy now had a horse and buggy; and with smart little Hanyut up behind him in his cocked hat and breeches, a brave sight they made among the assembled gentry, as they crowded to the shore on 9th July to bid farewell to Raffles.

A great man – for one of Britain's greatest sons he undoubtedly was – Raffles looked his last on a town which could never have existed had it not been for his boldness, foresight and determination; and sailed on in *Hero of Malown* to Bencoolen, leaving behind him not only a respectful, if relieved, community of British people and at least one devoted Malay friend in the shape of Munshi Abdullah, but also, among his finest monuments, the beginnings of that splendid Institute that was to bear his name throughout the future years.

CHAPTER 6

A TIRESOME INCIDENT

That difficult year of 1823 was drawing to a close and Alexander would be glad indeed when Harrington returned.

Things were piling up on him. First of all there had been the double 'ejection', with the two new warehouses to erect, one after the other, with all the worry and expense that that had entailed. Then came the stabbing of Farquhar – and even worse the latter's complete removal from power – which had robbed him of a friendly old counsellor and had seen his replacement by a much more brilliant but cold and unapproachable Resident Crawfurd. Next he had suffered the dcparturc of Sir Stamford Raffles, under whose strong patronage he had already reached a somewhat precariously high position; and now finally occurred this maddening incident of John Sergi, which had suddenly assumed such unpleasant importance.

It had been appallingly hot in the stuffy little wooden courthouse; and just bad luck that on Guthrie's particular day to sit as Magistrate no less a defendant than the wretched young John Sergi should have appeared before him, on a charge of taking part in a drunken brawl. Alexander lashed out severely in rebuking his conduct – the more so as he knew the boy rather well (as who did not) – but his words had stung the sensitive pride of that handsome young Malacca-Portuguese to the quick.

Sergi had therefore immediately presented himself before the Resident and laid a complaint on oath that Guthrie had intentionally set his dogs upon him as he was passing Alexander's house.

This was bad enough, for Sandy's two fox terriers, both local 'pi-dogs', had certainly not made a good impression on John Sergi with their barking and licking all over the place – and of course they had jumped up at him in the way dogs do – but what made it all quite insufferable was that young

James Guthrie

Singapore Waterfront, 1848

Samuel Bonham, Crawfurd's new Assistant and Registrar, had there and then gratuitously stated publicly in open court that 'Mr Guthrie was in the habit of setting his dogs on everyone that passed his bungalow'!

This being altogether too much for Alexander's high and haughty temper, he had written immediately to the Resident demanding that Bonham prove his damaging statement. Bonham had then denied he had ever said such things in open court but only in private to the Resident as he was taking down Sergi's complaint. John Purvis, Guthrie's friend, had signed and sent to the Resident a statement declaring that Bonham *did* say the words in open court – and the whole ridiculous episode had boiled over in a bubbling crescendo of bad blood, spite, jealousy, frayed tempers and fatigue, that culminated in Sergi's dashing at Guthrie in the High Street and attempting by all manner of abuse to create an affray, which might – had Alexander not exercised almost superhuman restraint – have touched off a positive explosion.

* * *

What a relief at last to be able to take a glass of wine with portly, good-natured old Captain Harrington – sitting there in the cool of Guthrie's new house and discussing the future and all that had occurred.

He and Marianne were on their way back to Malacca, on a farewell visit to Mrs Harrington's relatives. The Captain's wife had remained there whilst they were about their 'China adventure'; and had preceded them to England, where they would all meet once more after Harrington had concluded his final item of business at the Cape.

The Captain had not been home since 1820, when he had stepped out high, wide and handsome, in his own typical fashion, with a rented house at Number 18 George Street, Hanover Square; his old Charlie Capon from the *Scaleby Castle* as his valet; and an excellent carriage and pair. Now he was longing once more for the fleshpots: and beginning to feel the weight of his years. He had decided to leave the 'China' side of his business to a friendly firm to supervise, and to join his Agents, Messrs William and James Burnie, in London. He hoped to arrange later with his son to carry on the business at Cape Town; and would now discuss with Alexander the future of the undertaking at Singapore.

This was showing signs of becoming a prosperous concern under the able guidance of young Guthrie. Its connection with the Cape Town business was now virtually non-existent; and it would clearly be wise – under continuing association with Burnie and Co of London – to launch it as a separate and independent entity. Harrington and Guthrie therefore together formally dissolved partnership by a circular letter dated 8th November 1823; and a short interim in the firm's history occurred, during which the day to day work proceeded apace whilst both counselled together as to whom they should invite to be Alexander's new partner.

Shortly after having said farewell to Colonel Farquhar and his family, who left Singapore aboard a small ketch for Malacca and Penang at the end of the year ('thousands following him to the sea shore', as Munshi Abdullah says, 'firing cannons, guns and crackers till all wept and he wept also'), they decided to invite a comparative newcomer named James Scott Clark to accept the vacant partnership.

Quiet and unobtrusive, Clark soon settled comfortably into a business association with Alexander, which he was to maintain with uninspired efficiency for the next ten years.

* * *

By yet another circular letter in mid-February 1824, the public were informed that the new house of Messrs Guthrie and Clark had come into being; and at last that complicated organism known as a 'business', with its strange dual 'inner' and 'outer' nature consisting both of the Man as well as the plant he inhabits and directs, had budded off from the stem and taken on its own life, from now on to weather the future storms unaided and as best it might.

The jovial Captain Harrington, after an uproarious dinner-party, was rowed aboard his favourite old *Fessel Kerrim* on the evening of 7th March 1824, bound for Malacca, and thence, with trans-shipment at Calcutta, for England, taking with him the dark-eyed Marianne, soon to be married, who will appear no more in this story.

BOOK TWO

STRUGGLE FOR LIFE

CHAPTER I

JAMES GUTHRIE

Twenty-two years later in 1846, young James Guthrie sat back and closed a pair of remarkably penetrating blue eyes; drinking in the clean west wind of early summer, already filled with the English scent of new-mown hay and of hawthorn.

The open-sided railway carriage rocked and swayed rhythmically forward, as the train meandered north from London through the pastoral countryside; lulling him to sleep as he overcame his apprehension at entrusting himself to this strange new contrivance which hissed abominably and spouted steam and smoke from every vent, smelling like some vast worldwide washing day and at times shrieking in such a crisis of hysteria that someone said they ought to 'hold her feet, slap her hands and bring her to'.

Home at last, on furlough. The joy of it – that very first leave now just unfolding before him. The excitement and wild delight could never again be captured in this world, however long he might live.

It had been seventeen years since he had seen such fields as these and had breathed in such cool and heartfilling balm. He had been a boy then; and if it had not been for uncle Sandy from Singapore sitting beside him in the stage coach, would that homesick young fifteen-year-old ever have torn himself away from Menmuir? He wondered, stroking a bristly, bright gold beard and smiling inwardly at the child he had been. Younger son of course – that had been the trouble. Mother's darling. He had always taken after that bright carrot-topped mother of his; and was very close to her. Elder brother Alec, who was to have had Burnside, had been a real Guthrie – in fact when uncle Sandy came back home from Singapore, that first time seventeen years ago, all the family had laughed to see them together; young Alec so handsome at seventeen, even though he had been born prematurely (or so they said) and 'old' Sandy, identically like him but for the bronze on his skin of four years at the Cape and eight on the equator at Singapore.

But the 'Grant' strain from James's mother's side was different. Tougher perhaps not so good-looking certainly, but with some down-to-earth quality of Eastern-Scottish solidity in it, that quenched and left no trace of the 'fey' Guthrie romanticism.

And then, in 1834, just the very year after Clark had left the firm to join Captain Stevens in business ('sailor Stevens' as he was called for having at one time commanded the *Elizabeth*, the first sea-going vessel ever built in Singapore) and whilst James was still feeling a little sad at having been the cause of his resignation (for obviously Alexander Guthrie would now keep the firm in the family) – just at that time, when there was in fact far too much to do and not enough people to do it, along had come the news of that tragic epidemic of smallpox that killed in one blow so many in the Glens, including his own father, David, and elder brother Alec too.

* * *

A changed world indeed it would be to which he was now returning, but returning, praise be, not a failure.

It had been a hard task right from the beginning and uncle Sandy had not hesitated to lay responsibility on his shoulders from the moment of their arrival in Singapore. Quite extraordinary how that town had grown incidentally. Why, when they had first landed that day in 1829 there had only been one European shop – George Armstrong's – at the end of Market Street down by the river, just next door to the Guthries' Boat Quay godown! And now, in 1846, just look at the place!

Uncle Alexander Guthrie had known how to train up his successor. Even aboard ship he had had him working on Marsden's Malay Grammar right through from eight bells of the morning watch till mid-day, the whole way out. And no sooner settled in at the house in the High Street and handed over to Hanyut, the major-domo, (to fall immediately under that fine man's influence as the object of his special care and affection) than 'up at gunfire' was the order of the day – 5 am, when the gun boomed out over the sea from the Battery, – to check incoming cargo with the tally-clerk down at the waterfront or break out stores from the warehouse.

And what a fuss there was – only about eighteen months after his arrival – when thieves had broken in through the 'atap' roof and stolen all those bales of cotton cloth from the godown. They never got the stuff back of course, but had decided to make it harder for thieves in future by opening up the land along the side of the small creek at the back and building a plank and round-timber bridge across it. That was the same rickety structure they called 'Guthrie's old wooden bridge', or the old 'wooden horror', and was now soon to be demolished to make way for a fine large iron affair.

The theft in '32 had really been a great trial. The East India Company's charter was to expire the following year, to everyone's delight (at any rate among the business community) and, after consulting the 'Grey' ministry at home, Lord William Cavendish-Bentinck the Governor-General of India had taken up the question of reorganising the Straits Settlements administration with Mr Ibbetson the Governor,* whose headquarters were at Penang. This had provided Alexander Guthrie and his friends with precisely the opportunity they wanted; and a spirited correspondence had broken out between them and Ibbetson, which was to lead, in 1835, to the Straits capital being shifted from Penang to the already much more important centre of Singapore.

Thus, at the very moment when uncle Sandy's knowledge and experience were most needed, he was tied down with letters and meetings which could not be delayed. The checking and re-checking of the entire stock in trade had fallen upon James Clark and himself – a backbreaking task, but one that did much to turn him into a businessman.

* * *

After that episode uncle Sandy had left practically all the warehouse work to 'Jimmy'; and later, after Clark had

* Mr Ibbetson had first come East in 1805, with Captain Harrington aboard *Ganges* in company with Raffles.

handed in his resignation and the firm was renamed 'Messrs Guthrie and Company' in 1833 (James being the 'Company' of course at nineteen, just think of that), Alexander Guthrie had introduced him to a mass of new duties.

First of all there was the nutmeg and the clove estate at the far end of Orchard Road to be supervised, where a mysterious disease was beginning to decimate the young plants. Next, endless minutes to be copied out for his uncle, who was Chairman of a Committee appointed by Mr Samuel Bonham, now the acting Governor, to propose a new Constitution for Sir Stamford Raffles's 'Institute', which had fallen on evil days and was much neglected – and of which uncle Sandy was also Trustee. ('Strange how uncle never seems to care much for Mr Bonham, by the way. Must be some old history there, I suppose'). Then came the merchants' petition to Bonham against the Government's whole principle in the matter of urban assessments and rural land taxation, which had been traditionally decided by the Governor 'ex cathedra', whereas Guthrie and his Committee of freelance friends fought a battle – in which in 1835 they prevailed – for the right of the citizens to a voice, by an advisory Committee of freely elected land-owning members, in these affairs. And finally, to cap it all, arose the great struggle in 1836 against the Indian Government's intention to clap port duties on ships calling at Singapore.

That really had been too much. Right from the very beginning, from the very time of Raffles himself, the whole prosperity of Singapore had hinged upon its unique offer to the traders of all nations to load or off-load cargoes of all descriptions to or from anywhere with no questions asked. Free port – really free port – status was the lifeblood of Singapore. And now this had been threatened on the specious plea that the town was rich enough to support itself and pay for its own defences, if normal and sensible port dues and import-export duties were levied. India had claimed that as Calcutta and Madras had already sent down thousands of long-term prisoners to Penang, Malacca and Singapore, all these could surely be employed as cheap, or unpaid, labour.

Did India not realise that prisoners must eat, must be housed, must be supported and kept unprofitably idle when they fall sick or grow old? Did India not know that it took three healthy but unwilling prison labourers to do the work of one free man? And had they not heard that the only decent people among the whole 'prisoner' population were the murderers – all of whom were immediately taken on by officers' wives as houseboys and children's attendants, because of their kindness and honesty?

James Guthrie was set the task of preparing a draft petition to the Supreme Government on the whole question of Singapore as a free port. The united roar of Singapore's leading private people (Johnston, Alexander Guthrie, Purvis, Spottiswoode, Syme, Maclaine, Boustead and even the quiet young Portuguese Dr Joze D'Almeida) was the startled, angry, outcry of a band of disturbed and dangerously frightened men. It shook the rafters of Governor-General Lord Auckland's office in Simla, where he was relaxing from Calcutta's heat, and even shook the austere fastnesses of Lord Melbourne's sanctum in London, where, as Prime Minister, the matter came before him.

The shortsighted proposal was withdrawn; but not before the alarming possible consequences of India's ignorance and lack of wisdom, as just revealed to them, had forced Singapore's merchants to a searching reappraisal of their position.

The Indian Government was not to be trusted. Singapore's prosperity – its very existence – was now seen to be at the whim of a far distant and almost totally indifferent Government; a mere pawn in a game of political expediency.

Not only was there this question of port duties, but one of the main reasons for Singapore's very founding – the expansion of Britain's commercial influence throughout the whole South-east Asian area, as pointed out by Raffles in his final dispatch to Crawfurd in 1823 – now seemed open to variation or abandonment, as the desires of a distant Governor-General, or the timidity of the local Governor, might dictate.

Raffles, dismayed at the Penang Government's standing aside whilst Siam ravaged Kedah in 1821, had recommended Crawfurd to make such arrangements for the security of Johore, at least, as might be prudent.

In Farquhar's time the Temenggong of Johore had begged for British protection against the Rajah Muda of Rhio, who was threatening his State at the instigation of the Dutch. A British flag had been sent to him as an assurance of Britain's interest – an action thoroughly in line with the Singapore Merchants' 'forward' policy. They saw trade in this – and rightly – together with the opening up and advancement of a sadly neglected country.

But on instructions from Calcutta which Crawfurd had not seen fit to combat, the British flag had been forcibly withdrawn from Johore (to the embittered disappointment of the Temenggong) and the merchants' hopes were dashed.

The port duties affair had merely been the final straw.

Uncle Alexander, realising the merchants' individual weakness in a battle of wits with the Government, had consulted A. L. Johnston and others, to the end that in 1837 there had come into being no less a powerful body to represent their united voices than the 'Singapore Chamber of Commerce'; a solid phalanx of the Settlement's merchant leaders which henceforth was to influence Britain's South-east Asian policy 'from behind the scene'.

And it was in that same year of 1837, after all the digging up of material and the preparation of memoranda in addition to a full day's work in the office for months at a stretch, that one night old Sandy had come to him and said, 'James, you are a good lad. From now on you shall be my partner.'

* * *

Happy days. James could not restrain a smile as he recollected his joy in a partnership at the age of twenty-three – a partnership in a firm that was not only now among the largest in Singapore, but one whose name was known – and whose voice had been heard – as far afield as in the Parliament of Britain.

One of the first things that the Chamber did was to confirm and define the 'rates of commission' chargeable by Singapore 'Agency Houses', which had been worked out and adopted at a general meeting called by Johnston and uncle Sandy in 1830 – a most important decision which had bound the business community closer together and prevented cut-throat competition between them.

James had put in a deal of work on that one; and it had become in his mind one of the landmarks of his early days as a partner. Its completion had coincided with the outbreak of the first Anglo-China Opium War, when trade boomed through Singapore and there was already enough lawlessness in the port without having the merchants at each other's throats.

But the essential aspect of being a partner was that you had to bear your full weight of responsibility. It was less than four years later that the entire burden of the firm fell for the first time upon his shoulders with the departure of the senior partner to Britain.

The need was for a suitable young man of good background to be chosen as the growing firm's assistant; and such persons were by no means easy to be found in the hurly-burly of a roaring seaport town such as Singapore. Alexander Guthrie could of course have made inquiries among the various business friends of his at home, but eleven years is a long time to remain in an equatorial land without rest; and uncle Sandy was off, leaving James on his own for at least twelve months.

William and James Burnie had been excellent London Agents, especially after Captain Harrington had joined them in 1824; but in 1828 Harrington had started up on his own at Number 76 Cornhill, London, taking Guthrie's business with him – and then almost immediately after that break with the Burnie firm, the old sailor, red faced, choleric, far too good a trencherman and game to the last, after a mountainous 'Malacca-curry' prepared as only his faithful Hileabucks knew how, had suddenly keeled over and died.

From that date Guthrie had employed no Agents in London; for which reason Alexander himself had occupied his holiday in Britain about this quest for an assistant.

Alexander returned to Singapore in 1844, having chosen a very presentable young man, a Mr John James Greenshields, aged then about nineteen, who was to join them the following year.

Greenshields arrived at Singapore in 1845 – a splendidly energetic, good-natured and intelligent fellow who settled down immediately to his duties; and whom James was thoroughly delighted to see. Now at last, with uncle Sandy back and a new assistant, the way was clear for his long-yearned-for leave.

* * *

Not a bad time though, being alone, for all that.

James let his mind dwell on the little Singapore Theatre

they had all combined to start and which was now going so well; the establishment of the Singapore Library (Founder member, $30/-); how he had agreed to donate to the funds for a Catholic School – why not? – he was no bigot; wondering how the Pauper Hospital he had helped to set up with Mr Tan Tock Seng was faring; and reminding himself of that hilarious St Andrew's Night Celebration and Ball at which he had been the 'steward' almost immediately before he had sailed – a very normal and decent young fellow dozing and smiling to himself as he jogged peacefully north in the soft sunshine of that summer long ago.

Suddenly he remembered the first wild race meeting they had organised in February '43; the 'Race Ball' in the new Singapore Assembly Rooms later that evening with all the fun and the sherry – which they supplied – followed by the stampeding race home at midnight in company with old Dr Moorhead, Bill Napier, Charles Spottiswoode, that crazy Shetlander Lieutenant Andrew Hoseason and Christopher Rideout Read's son (of A. L. Johnston's), the mad wild young Billy Read; and all the croppers they had come in Orchard Road! James burst out laughing; and awoke to find the grey eyes of a young lady in the carriage regarding him with quizzical amusement.

CHAPTER 2

THE SCOTTS OF BALWYLLO

On the 26th August 1846, James Guthrie married Suzanna Scott. He was thirty-two years old and she was twenty-one; small, as so many Scottish women are, with the high cheek-bones and their shadowed hollows that artists love.

It happened in this way. James had been staying at Brechin with his married sister Mary Stewart at the 'auld Neuk-House', as the Guthries' rambling town residence had been named for generations; and had driven down in the buggy one fine morning in July with his uncle Charles's son, as far as Arrat's Mill.

There his cousin had left him to fish – and thus he had spent the day, happily enough, on his own.

He was a sociable person; seventeen years is a long time; and he was lonely.

In the late evening light, before reeling in for the last time – for he had eaten no more than a bap with some ham in it the whole day through and he was hungry – he had struck into a big one just up-stream of the Bridge of Dun.

'Good', said a voice from the bridge, when he had at last angled his catch into the shallows and got it safely ashore, 'that must be the best part of twenty pounds'.

A tall figure came across in the dusk and introduced himself. 'Robert Scott.' Aged about nineteen. 'From the Mains of Balwyllo, Sir; just up the road; by the House of Dun.'

'Then you'll be the brother of Helen, as like as not; the one that married my cousin David Guthrie of Brechin?', inquired James.

The two kinsmen strolled together through the evening light to the greystone farmhouse of Balwyllo; through large barnyards and cowbyres; through a gateway in an old stone wall to a garden rich with tobacco plant, lavender and night-scented stock; to a warm welcome from Robert's elder brother James who now farmed Balwyllo and to the affectionate and stately presence of the boys' mother, widowed for the last three years and still in her white 'mutch-cap' and black weeds.

Two others emerged into the circle of lamplight as they stood together, relaxed and happy, whisky glass in hand – a bouncing fourteen-year-old young Tommy, Thomas or 'Tam', and one other, Suzanna, whose path, crossing his for the second time, was to consolidate and determine James's future and have consequences that would be vital to the progress of South-east Asia and to Britain's business in Singapore.

* * *

It need form no part of a chronicle such as this to record the courtship of a humdrum young Scotsman with a prosperous farmer's daughter a hundred and twenty years ago.

The marriage itself took placc bcfore Mr Mackie the Registrar in the Schoolhouse, as a result – widespread throughout the north at that period – of one of those deep clefts in religious conviction that have successively shaken the frame of Scotland since the ancient early-Christian Culdees first confronted the Augustine discipline of Rome. Ancestor James Guthrie the Martyr had died for the primitive faith in 1661, his children disinherited and his head stuck on a spike at the Nether-Bow in Edinburgh. And now James's cousin, the Reverend David Guthrie, soon in turn to be pilloried and banished to Loch Lee in the Highlands, was rousing the Glens with his impassioned sermons for a 'Free Presbyterian Church' of Scotland.

James Guthrie from Singapore, like any other Guthrie, would think shame to give countenance to cousin David's opposers by wedding within the precincts of a church.

James and Suzanna returned to Singapore, travelling through France and Italy to Brindisi, then across the sands of Suez from Alexandria and on to the lush and muddy warmth of mid-nineteenth century Singapore.

* * *

Alexander Guthrie, a grizzled, confident man of fifty by now, brown-skinned and with the hard visage and humorous twinkle of his race, not only met them with joy but had prepared for them a surprise.

The newly married couple were to have a house of their own – aptly named by uncle Sandy 'St James' – that he had quietly been having built for them on his land by Tanjong Pagar. They moved in at once and surveyed their new domain.

Singapore was now a place of real beauty with a fine residential area all along Kampong Glam. Large houses dotted the low hills to left and right of the 'Orchard Road'. Back from the shore had grown a splendid treeless 'Course' or esplanade, where the horses and buggies of the young men and the open, parasol-blossoming carriages-and-pair of the Tuan-besars'* languorous ladies moved in an elegant cavalcade in the golden dust of a sunny afternoon.

And such nice people too. Dear Colonel Butterworth, the Governor – what a dandy; and what a delicate social sense (from the ladies); what a crashing snob (from the men).

He lives up there in the big house on Fort Canning where the flagstaff is, facing the sea. (They flew different flags on it to notify the arrival of outgoing and homeward bound vessels at one time – till there was nearly a riot when they flew the yellow 'Q' and all thought there was fever in the town!)

Then uncle Alexander still lives in the High Street of course, and young Mr Greenshields shares house with him; and since his friend Mr A. L. Johnston left for home five years ago his 'Tanjong Tangkap' in Battery Road has been rebuilt and is now lived in by his former assistants Drysdale and Bain, as well as by young Billy Read, (the son of uncle's old companion Christopher Rideout Read), a real little devil whom we all love – mad keen on horses, splendid jockey, and nearly got himself killed the other day by poking a live tiger with a stick (he thought it was dead) in a tiger trap! They all have their new 'chummery' just next door to the Spottiswoodes.

In the High Street, by the Esplanade and quite close to uncle Sandy, is Mr Boustead on the one side; and Dr Martin (who has taken over the private practice from kind, fat old Dr Montgomerie the Resident Surgeon) on the other. Dr Montgomerie has now been transferred to Barrackpore.

* 'The Big-Lords' – Government Officials and leading merchants.

After Martin comes Mr Church the Resident Councillor, who used to be Governor during the time of Mr Bonham – until Calcutta found out that Bonham was senior and then they had to change places. Just like Bonham to complain; and it is a relief that he has gone on to this new 'Hong Kong' place as Governor. Clever fellow and excellent host, but fearfully sticky and pompous beneath his 'bonhomie'. And there was all that fuss and flutter too about his so-called 'Amah' Chee Hoon – damned pretty girl at one time by God; so there was no reason for him to assume such tremendous airs. Of course, there is no doubt about it that Church had resigned earlier on, so when he rejoined the Service he was put at the bottom of the promotion list; and there is a yarn too that when he went to see Sir Charles Metcalfe, the Acting Governor-General at Fort William, Calcutta, Church was far from communicative on the subject of his former resignation. But that sudden reversal of seniority in mid-career was most upsetting to us all out here and pretty bad form we thought. Church will never get anywhere now.

Well then, close to Mr Church comes the 'Raffles Institute', which is occupied by the Headmaster Mr Moor and his family, as well as the assistant master Mr Dickenson and Padre Milton the Chaplain. After them come Mr and Mrs George (Mrs George is one of old Colonel Farquhar's daughters) – and then the nice John Purvises who are uncle Sandy's very close friends and are soon going on retirement. Mr Napier the lawyer is believed to be taking over their house.

So many pleasant people live in Kampong Glam too – along the 'Beach Road' as they are now beginning to call it. Old Sailor Stevens has now dissolved partnership with Clark and they have both started up on their own. Miss Grant runs a little private Missionary School. The Carnies, the Kerrs, the Frasers, the McMickings of Syme and Company, the Whiteheads, the Bernards (of the Police. Mrs Bernard is another daughter of Colonel Farquhar) and old Dr D'Almeida and his family, who also have an orchard and a fishpond, are all in Beach Road. They all live in extremely fine houses in that area, each one in a large garden and most of them with their own billiard rooms, either indoors or in an annex.

Then there is Colonel Man the architect, in that handsome street named after his predecessor Mr Coleman, who died five years ago in 1841, which also serves the excellent new hotel of that French painter, Monsieur Dutronquoy.

Out in the country there is Dr Oxley, the new Resident Surgeon from Malacca, on a good rising piece of land; and the plantation of Mr Carnie, which he calls Cairn Hill, where he has built a charming house under two beautiful varingin trees planted by himself; then further out there is uncle Sandy's estate of course, while Mr Behn, Mr Meyer and Mr Schreiber of Behn Meyer and Company live close in at Mount Sophia.

Dr Alexander Martin has been living at his estate 'Annanbank' north of us in the River Valley Road, but is now returning to his house on the Esplanade, as he is very ill with an ague that seems to strike up from the ground on some parts of this island. People think it may be due to rotting vegetation, in places where they have been clearing the jungle, giving off some gas or miasma at night-time.

His partner Dr Little, who lives out at Tanglin at 'Bonniegrass House' near Adam Sykes of Robert Wise and Company, is carrying on the practice – and for that matter we are thinking of letting 'St James' and moving out to Tanglin ourselves, where it is said to be very cool and fresh . . .

* * *

Thus the chronicle sinks into the past and speaks in the 'present tense' of that time. It drifts back over the hundred and twenty years to a 'present' now far sunk below today's horizon; to a morning where the first glimmers of a rising sun, twelve decades set, strike shafts of gold through an early mist just a trifle colder than cool. Dew-laden grass and leaves, spangled with cobwebs that catch on our shoes and knees, give precisely the impression of frost as we stride out on that essential Singapore practice 'the morning walk' – a brisk turn of two or three miles through the bamboo-sided lanes to the Race Course and back, where the 'syces', who have been up since half-past-four, are exercising the horses.

Home by 7.30 for a bath in chill water from an earthenware jar, ladled over the head in a dark stone bathroom on the ground floor under the bungalow; a close shave from the itinerant Hindoo barber who comes daily for $1/- a month; coffee and fruit in sarong and baju; and an hour of letter writing to catch the homegoing mailship. Then dress in white nankeen trousers, thin black morning coat and silk cravat (if a male), or wide, flounced, silk costumes with low neck (for the ladies), preparatory to a simple breakfast, exactly at nine o'clock (watches and clocks are set by the distant rumble of the 5 am sixty-pounder gun from Fort Canning), of curry and rice, some fish and perhaps an egg or two; washed down with a glass or so of passable claret.

Then a kiss for Suzanna, into the smart little 'turn-out' and clatter-bang down over that badly built bridge into town, where horses and buggies parade round the Square for at least half an hour, exchanging light chatter and last night's jokes before settling down to the business of the day.

In the evening there is cricket on the Esplanade or 'fives' for the men (in an excellent new court by the Esplanade itself), at both of which Mr Greenshields is a great champion; while the ladies watch and gossip. Dinner is at 6.30 pm, with billiards or cards afterwards, usually 'vingt-et-un' or 'loo', unless it is a 'Band-night' of the Regiment or a dance is held either at the Assembly Rooms or a private house – or unless of course it is found more congenial just to sit on the long verandah in the deep purple dusk, smoking cheroots and watching the fireflies, till yawns and the call of a mosquito-curtained bed become irresistible.

* * *

But it will be observed that this story's heroes are now no longer dedicated and hardbitten pioneers. They would now seem to be most elegant and well favoured young merchant princes. What has happened over the years to produce this influx into Singapore of young Englishmen, recognisably similar to the insouciants, golfing, sports-car-owning young 'nuts' and business tycoons of our own early days out East?

The answer is, of course, a simple one. A long peace; an expanding Asian economy; great prosperity at home and in British possessions overseas; and – in Singapore at any rate (and from the aspect of the matter at issue quite the most important point of all) – no new and exciting outlet for a young man's abounding energies; no fresh challenge; no wild adventure into the unknown; no more 'worlds to conquer'.

From the north, where Malaya met Siam – from a frontier long since firmly defined by the Burney Treaty at the northern boundaries of Perak and Pahang – to Singapore itself, the mainland of the Malayan peninsula remained inaccessible to Western influence and virtually 'terra incognita'.*

Adventurous traders – Dutch, Spanish and British – were exploring new coastlines and extracting produce from new hinterlands throughout all South-east Asia. Hong Kong had been secured for Britain by the Treaty of Nanking in 1841. James Brooke was opening up Sarawak and had just been knighted and appointed as the first Governor of the Island of Labuan in addition. Everywhere the tide of progress was at flood – except in the three Settlements along the Malacca Straits.

Meanwhile, from every one of those three – from Penang Hill, from Malacca Fort, from Bukit Timah on Singapore Island – a gorgeous, jungle-covered, riverine mass of unexplored land, its far blue mountain ranges beckoning and luring their hearts out at dawn and dusk, remained temptingly close at hand yet maddeningly inaccessible.

The Indian Government, burdened with far too many territorial commitments already – none of which it ever wanted – remained inflexibly opposed to any interference whatsoever in affairs upon the Malayan Peninsula.

Mewed up on Singapore island – and admittedly making fortunes from the rapidly expanding volume of trade that continued to surge through the port in a golden flood – most merchants turned to sports and pastimes, to clubs and plays, to fine buildings and an elegant existence – to 'la dolce vita'.

* * *

Alexander Guthrie was deeply delighted with his nephew James and with his new niece-in-law Suzanna. A man who had had little contact with women, he became like a father to her and grew to love her as a favourite daughter.

Waiting only until the young couple had comfortably

* Except for Province Wellesley opposite Penang; the 'Dindings', a coastal strip of Perak acquired in 1826 in an effort to suppress piracy; and the small settlement of Malacca.

settled down, in the year 1847 Alexander decided to hand over the Singapore office entirely to James and to station himself in London, where he would have a better opportunity of promoting the interests of Singapore with the Home Government.

Delaying his departure long enough to attend the birth and baptism of James and Suzanna's first child Susan, he was off home in the autumn of that year to install himself in the Oriental Club, Hanover Square, till such time as he could move into his new home at Number 3 Tenterden Street.

For two years James continued busy with office work as well as with uncle Sandy's forty-five-acre nutmeg estate 'Everton' at Tanjong Pagar, which now had 2,250 trees in full bearing and was a very valuable property indeed; and with his other plantation 'Claymore' in Orchard Road – both of which were by this time not only good estates, but potentially gold mines for housing development.

Young Greenshields, now twenty-four, was a tower of strength – and in 1849 James made him his partner; in which same year James and Suzanna's second daughter, little Katherine, was born.

Things were going well. Suzanna had had a difficult time with Katherine, but had been pulled through by kind, capable Dr Little, now alone in his practice since Dr Martin had died; and toward the end of the year she was able very sweetly to declare open Guthrie and Company's attractive little iron bridge over the muddy 'Purvis' or 'Guthrie' creek, which had formerly been spanned by that rickety round-timber structure known as 'Guthrie's old Wooden Horror'.

In the following year a still further addition was made to James and Suzanna's family.

Katherine had been born in 1849, leaving Suzanna weak and ill; yet it was no more than thirteen months later, on the 19th of May 1850, that she once more hovered on the brink of death in bringing to birth her first son, whom the delighted parents christened Alexander.

All this while James was immensely occupied with a range of official duties – each one flattering, unavoidable and a tribute to his increasingly high position in the community. His blue eyes and ginger beard were seen everywhere. No function was complete in his absence; nor indeed could many seem to have been organised without him. After a busy day in the office, James's public work would begin; with committees and meetings on such matters as the St Andrew's Day celebration on the one side, to a dinner for Admiral Sir Henry Keppel, the sailor brother of Lord Albemarle, on the other. Keppel was off with HMS *Meander* to the Australian station; and at his farewell dinner a seat of honour needed to be reserved for Mr Ho Ah Kay, or 'Whampoa' as he was affectionately nicknamed (from such being his birthplace near Canton), who was one of the Admiral's closest friends. Hence James must call upon this famous Mr Ho – one of the very first among Singapore's 'Commission Agents' who had risen to be a millionaire – in his immense mansion out in the country by Katong, in order that the invitation might be suitably delivered.

Upon James's broad shoulders too fell the task of organising the public receptions for the visit to Singapore of Lord Dalhousie himself, the Governor-General of India. Dalhousie was a family connection of the Guthries, his grandfather, Fox-Maule of Brechin, being the man who had entered James's grand-uncle Thomas Guthrie into the East India Company's Marine Service all those years ago – that same Thomas by whom uncle Sandy had been introduced to Captain Harrington of the Cape, from which event the firm of Guthrie and Company had sprung.

Thus, day after day, James's busy hours were spent. With the best will in the world, Suzanna, sitting alone all day in the great house at 'Tanglin' with nothing to do – pale now, anaemic and longing for the clean air of her northern home – was lonely.

'If only I could see some of the family again', she had found herself sobbing to James one night, to her shame.

'No sooner said than done', good James had replied. 'We'll call out Tommy, your favourite young brother.'

So, though she knew it not, a new transfusion of strong Scottish blood was by her means brought into the body of the Guthrie firm – a refreshing draft of energy that would carry the business forward from strength to strength, branching out into untried and exciting developments until the turn of the century, when yet two further mutations, again emanating from that same cold northern land, would alter the whole texture of the growing plant and bring it to a remarkable flowering.

CHAPTER 3

THOMAS SCOTT

On the 7th of July 1851, nineteen-year-old Tom Scott landed in Singapore, after an almost interminable voyage of 143 days aboard an unsound, unweatherly old barque called *Coaxer*.

A tough, game and laughing youngster, with his modest height, good manners and thatch of brown hair, Tom filled his sister's heart with joy and the Guthries' Tanglin house with a fresh wind of happiness as he settled in and made himself at home.

Nothing was too much trouble for Thomas Scott. Learn Malay; clear up the accounts of the fancy dress ball they had held in March, four months before his arrival ($5/- family ticket; $2/- single) for which several people had still not stumped up. Work on the plans of the Sailors' Home, for funds for the erection of which that wretched dance had been held – arguing in committee about the site for it on uncle Sandy's land in Tanjong Pagar (and with the architect, Colonel Man, on details of the design). Join the Volunteers with John Greenshields (you ought to see them in their scarlet tunics with green facings, white trousers and peaked shakoes!) Even join Bousteads' instead of Guthries' for a short while so as to gain outside experience and 'be on his own' (this was James's idea – and a good one). And finally never miss taking sister Sue 'out of herself' and into the fresh air in the open carriage each morning or afternoon for long friendly rambles; reminiscent, with their jokes and fun – sometimes too reminiscent for poor Suzanna – of happy childhood days by faraway Montrose. If only she could be well and strong again; had not this awful fever every now and then; and did not feel so weak and pale.

But, in the end, dear Tom could always make her laugh by going back to his 'old hobby-horse'.

'Why the devil', he would exclaim, banging a fist on his knees, 'why the devil have you gone on so long out here without having a quayside? Landing from the sampan that first time, I was mud from head to foot – and look at the way they handle cargo up and down that filthy beach! It's laughable; and disgraceful. If Government won't do anything, as cousin James says, then why can we not do something ourselves? Uncle Sandy has all the land in the world down there at Tanjong Pagar. If he gave me leave I would have a shot at drawing designs and getting a quayside of some sort built there myself!'

But of more immediate importance was the fact that Suzanna would not – just could not – get well.

And she was going to have another baby.

* * *

It was about this time that James Guthrie began to be beset by an entirely new public danger, to add to this domestic worry.

Mention has already been made of the Singapore merchants' resentment at the nonchalant attitude of the Indian Government toward their affairs. India had obstructed their expansion into the Malay states. It had attempted to abolish free port status. It had insisted upon Singapore maintaining and paying for a very large and unnecessary military garrison, whereas what was needed was adequate maritime defence, not troops. And its continuing policy, to which great objections were raised, was to dump Indian convicts upon the unfortunate residents of the Straits Settlements.

On top of all this, as though that were not enough, a new ingredient was soon to be poured into the already bubbling mixture which would cause it to froth over in a ferment of bewilderment and indignation.

The cause of the trouble was the currency used in the Far East – the Mexican, or 'Spanish', dollar.*

This 'dollar' had been the coin of commerce throughout the Archipelago for hundreds of years before Britain obtained any footing in it; and it therefore became the circulating medium in the British Settlements as soon as they were established.

* Minted in Mexico and exported as bullion ('pieces of eight') to China and East Asia – where it had been used for centuries.

But these 'Settlements' were part of the East India Company's territories. By an Indian Act of 1835, legal tender throughout the Company's holdings was declared to be the newly minted coin known as the 'rupee'; and this therefore became legal tender in Singapore from that date, in common with the 'Spanish dollar', at the exchange rate of 220 rupees to 100 dollars. So far so good; and no harm done. The dollar in fact fully retained its position and the rupee was scarcely ever seen, except in payment of Government employees' salaries.

No official copper coinage existed for fractions of a dollar; and this had resulted in the manufacture and circulation of a wide variety of copper tokens, or 'duits' as they were called, turned out by private individuals and of varying inferior value. A further Indian Act of 1844 had in fact introduced a copper coinage for fractions of a 'rupee', but although these were legal currency in Singapore they made no impact in a land where the *dollar* was virtually the sole medium of exchange; and the curious little home-made 'duits' continued to circulate as before.

In 1847, among the very last things that Alexander Guthrie had achieved through the Singapore Chamber of Commerce before leaving the East for London, had been to prevail upon the Indian Government to accept a state of affairs which they must see was unavoidable; and to coin for the Straits Settlements a sufficiency of copper cents, half cents and quarter cents of the Spanish dollar. These new copper coins therefore quickly superseded the former 'duits', drove them entirely out of the market and became the only copper currency of the Straits Settlements.

In that year of 1847 therefore, the situation was that the Company's silver rupee was a legal coin in the Straits – but it was hardly ever used. The dollar was the only silver coin current in the Straits; and it was also a legal coin. The Company's cent, half and quarter cent of the dollar were the only copper forms of currency.

No one was dissatisfied with this state of things. It worked well; and the commerce of the Settlement was thriving on it. The only improvement desired was that the Honourable Company should coin a dollar of its own, with half and quarter dollars, thus doing away with some slight inconvenience caused by the lack of silver of a smaller denomination. But no one for a moment wished to overcome these trifling inadequacies by making use of any part of the 'rupee' currency. Such a suggestion, if ever made in Singapore, would have been looked upon with horror as a certain ruination to the smooth running of business, as a direct invocation of the Devil and a gratuitous burning down of the pigsty to roast the pork.

However, notwithstanding these well known and frequently expressed opinions of the inhabitants of Singapore, news arrived in 1853 that the Indian Government – carried away by what mania for regularity or windy afflatus of bureaucracy no man from that day to this can tell – was proposing to introduce a Bill (and in 1854 did introduce a Bill) to make the Company's own copper fractions of the rupee, known as the 'pice', 'double pice', 'half pice' and 'pie', legal tender in the Straits Settlements, equally with the cent, half cent and quarter cent of the Spanish dollar. Each of these two copper currencies was to become legal tender, not only for fractions of its own representative in silver, but also for fractions of the other silver coin. In other words, cents were to remain legal tender for fractions of a dollar and were to become legal tender also for fractions of a rupee; whilst pice, double pice, half pice and pie, besides becoming legal tender for fractions of a rupee, were now to become also legal tender for fractions of a dollar!

God help us – it was enough to make a man's head reel! And reel the merchants did – though admittedly with helpless, incredulous laughter.

Imagine the chaos, the pandemonium, in the markets, when a voluble and polyglot mob of Chinese, Hindoos and Malays, all yelling and gesticulating in their own languages over their purchases, strove to equate cents, half cents and quarter cents with pice, double pice, half pice and pies in the ratio of 100 to 220! The thing was utter and complete lunacy. It must be stopped before irreparable damage was done.

The Singapore Chamber of Commerce met in outraged conclave and staged a public meeting of protest, while the *Singapore Free Press* flamed '. . . It behoves the community of this place, as well as the two other Straits Settlements, to lose no time in offering their determined opposition to the progress of these mischievous and most ill-judged measures, both in principle and detail, and the doing so will also prevent an argument which would otherwise certainly be brought up, when the future and still more decisive steps are to be taken, that they had tacitly acquiesced in the change. A Public Meeting has been called for this day to consider the subject, and we sincerely hope that it may result in unanimous and firm representations against such causeless and wanton tampering with the lifeblood of our commerce – the circulating medium.'

Following the public meeting a petition was drawn up to be forwarded to the Legislative Council in India; and a letter was sent with it to the Governor, Mr Blundell,* acting for Colonel Butterworth, who presumably added such comment to it before forwarding as accorded with his position, state of health and prospects of promotion.

James Guthrie, on the other hand, wrote an immediate letter to his uncle Sandy; and another, 'confidential and most urgent' to his friend Admiral Keppel in Australia.

Neither recipient was slow in acting. Keppel wrote at once to his brother Lord Albemarle; and Alexander Guthrie in London hurried round to old Surgeon John Crawfurd, the veteran Resident of Singapore, with an urgent invitation to accompany him – together with Nichol, Fraser, Gilman and Paterson, all 'old Singaporeans' – to the office of the President of the Board of Control; an invitation which the former accepted there and then 'con amore'.

The President – that high dignitary of the British Government set as a watchdog over the affairs of India – was by no means unimpressed; and, to compress a tale of eighteen months into one of assimilable length, James Guthrie in Singapore was elected Chairman of a further public meeting, at which a long list of resolutions was passed for inclusion in a petition to be addressed to both Houses of Parliament.

So it came about that Admiral Keppel's brother, Lord Albemarle, had in due time the pleasure of introducing the following notice to the House of Lords: 'The Earl of Albemarle to present a Petition from the European, Chinese and other Asiatic merchants of Singapore, remonstrating against the introduction by the Government of India of a novel and highly inconvenient currency instead of a long-established, convenient and satisfactory one; thereby throwing confusion into the Commerce of that and the associated British settlements in the Straits of Malacca.'

* Great great grandfather of Sir Eric Griffith-Jones, chairman of The Guthrie Corporation Limited since its formation in 1965.

The Earl of Albemarle gave an admirable explanation of the views of Singapore's merchants, with the result that the Bill did not pass and the dollar currency continued to be the legal tender of the Straits, as it is to this day. The mercantile community had won their point – and one vital to the interests of Singapore.

* * *

But the foregoing, for ease of explanation, has run forward to the year 1857.

Pausing merely to note how great a hand the firm of Guthrie and Company are now beginning to play in the history of Singapore, steps must at this stage be retraced to a sad day in 1853 when poor weak Suzanna was brought to bed with the birth of yet a fourth child.

It need not delay us long. Suzanna and her baby died.

* * *

As intense activity is the surest antidote to grief, it is perhaps not surprising that James was able to take so great a part in the dispute over the Straits currency.

It is however astonishing to find how much other work he was doing at the same time.

In addition to his full occupation as senior partner of a large business undertaking (assisted only by his junior partner John Greenshields and young Thomas Scott) he managed to induce the local Government to construct a carriage road down to his uncle Sandy's property at Tanjong Pagar – for which he not only gave up the necessary land free of acquisition costs but persuaded his neighbour Mr Cursetzee Formmurzee to do likewise – a much more difficult task!

He also found time to cause his uncle Alexander to engage a London policeman, a Mr George Wahab, as the first Deputy Superintendent of Police for Singapore.

He was able to write to his cousin the Reverend David Guthrie, LLD, (reinstated in favour after his successful 'battle of the Glens' and subsequent banishment to Loch Lee and now busy founding the 'Ragged Schools' of Scotland for which his name is famous) for a suitable Minister for the new Presbyterian Church at Singapore, in response to which there arrived a certain Reverend Mr Fraser.

Thereafter – as a splendid survival of the old 'Guthrie' spirit – he decided to establish, at his own expense both for capital cost as well as for subsequent maintenance, a school for no less than forty Malay boys at Tanjong Pagar.

Finally – and in the midst of all this toil and sadness it seems incredible how he contrived to do it – he insisted on John Greenshields taking his furlough in Britain at exactly the appointed time. James Guthrie was sick at heart; he was longing for Scotland; but Greenshields's first ten-year period of service was at an end and off he must go.

Suzanna's embalmed body had been sent forward to London, where uncle Alexander had purchased a catacomb at Kensal Green Cemetery immediately he had received the sad news; and now James must merely await the return of Greenshields before he too turned his face towards home.

It throws an interesting sidelight upon the friendly and intimate nature of the firm – in common no doubt with many other 'family' businesses at that time – to discover that John Greenshields's first act on reaching Britain was to proceed to Scotland, visit the home of his senior partner in Brechin and pay a call upon Suzanna's and young Thomas Scott's mother at the farm of Balwyllo.

Matters thereafter pursued a predestined course; and it need surprise no one to learn that on the 18th July of that same year 1855 John James Greenshields married no less a person than Margaret, the eighteen-year-old sister of Thomas Scott.

As has happened so often in Scotland, both before and since, the holdings of an ancient inland family were being absorbed by well-to-do coastal burghers – in this case the prosperous merchant and farming Montrose family of 'Baltic traders' and city Burgesses known as the Scotts.

In 1856, just as soon as Greenshields and Margaret had returned to Singapore, a much saddened James Guthrie, the light gone from his life and his old zest and courage well-nigh eclipsed, with his two motherless girls and a five-year-old son, said goodbye to them all and took a P & O steamer for home, to join his uncle Alexander in London.

The following year, at the age of twenty-five, Thomas Scott became a partner.

The Guthries, after one more successful effort shortly to be retailed, are to recede now from the chronicle; the new, 'Scott' graft of so much importance to it – and which to human eyes seems to have been introduced fortuitously and as a mere sideline to the Guthrie history – will now soon, and for a long period, take the forefront of the field.

CHAPTER 4

THE DEAD HAND

In the matter of currency the merchants of Singapore had scored a resounding victory; but the whole event had left in their mouths a sour after-taste of distrust and suspicion of every action of the Indian Government. True, they had been given an honest, if unimaginative, administration; but one so dependent upon Calcutta that, even in such a small matter as the control of public vehicles, no redress of grievances could be obtained after a correspondence that had dragged on over a period of twenty years.

Nor was it only these pinpricks – for there were larger considerations at issue than lack of imagination and scandalous delay. First of all there was the Civil Service itself, upon which the local administration depended. As may be supposed, few officers serving in Bengal, with all the opportunities for promotion in that large State, would be willing to volunteer for rustication in a distant and minor outpost – and one in which the chief appointments usually went to elderly military, not civilian, personnel. Hence the 'Indian Civilians' who were drafted to the Straits Settlements were not of high calibre – and these, too, generally made a point of returning to Calcutta or Madras as quickly as they could; and so did not consider it worth their while to learn the local languages. As Lord Canning, the new Governor-General of India, was to recognise, the system was 'a positive evil'; and he did not hesitate to doubt whether officers transferred from India under such a plan would ever be suitable for the Straits.

Secondly there were the long-standing grievances over the Settlements' use as a dumping ground for Indian convicts; the expense Singapore was put to in maintaining an unnecessary military garrison with an outrageous proportion of field officers; and the total lack of a Council of any kind to represent the views of the population.

Finally (and in the eyes of the farsighted the most serious

The Padang in Singapore, 1851

Singapore from Mount Wallich, 1856

grievance of all) was the fact that the Indian Government and its officers had altogether neglected to cultivate good relations with the neighbouring Native States.

Whilst India's lack of interest in the Straits Settlements is easy to understand – being unpopular with its officers, far from Calcutta, and redundant as far as India was concerned, since that Government had lost the monopoly of the trade with China – a digression is necessary here to underline the justice of the merchants' dissatisfaction.

A glance at Singapore's financial returns for 1856 shows that the revenue of the Settlements had risen to the very satisfactory figure of £192,000; whilst the civil expenditure had, alas, closely followed its upward curve to the tune of £114,932, with – and here was the rub – the sum of no less than £81,073 to be met for military charges in addition!

Moreover, and this is where the settlers on the small island of Singapore had indeed good reason to complain, of the total Revenue shown above, two thirds were derived from 'excise farms' auctioned by Government for various periods of time to local 'entrepreneurs' for the monopoly of selling opium, spirits etc; £26,000 from stamp duties; and only £6,705 from lands and forests.

Whilst the Dutch and French were penetrating further and further into neighbouring countries of the Far East and denying trade to the British in the process, Singapore (which could and should serve the hinterland of the Malay peninsula as it had so far served the trade of China, Siam, the Archipelago and until recently Cochin China) was compelled to remain inactive, deriving a mere pittance from land, the development of which on the adjacent mainland would have been by far its greatest asset. Frustrated in its efforts to make reasonable trade agreements with the Sultans on the peninsula, whose exactions were always supported against the merchants by the Calcutta authorities, the Singapore Merchants were subjected to every form of slight and obstruction that the disapprobation, indolence or indifference of India could devise.

It was against this background, therefore, that the merchants may be seen chafing at their bonds and awaiting their opportunity.

* * *

In the year 1857 there broke out the Indian Mutiny. By good fortune the detachment of Sepoys stationed in Singapore, comprising a company of Native Artillery and two regiments of Sepoys, had remained staunch (possibly because a large proportion were from Madras Presidency, where their brothers-in-arms had resisted all efforts to subvert them). But it had been a nerve-racking experience, more especially as a convoy of British troops on its way to China and watering in Singapore – upon whom all had been relying for aid in case of need – had been hastily diverted back to Calcutta; providing an advertisement of the gravity of the crisis in India as well as an unexampled opportunity for the Sepoys to revolt.

Quick and effective staff work on the part of Thomas Dunman, the newly appointed Commissioner of Police, had succeeded in averting the only attempt made by the Singapore Sepoys to rise in mutiny; and one which, had it not been for him, might well have led to the shambles of a general massacre.

Singapore was saved, in fact, by the infectious friendliness of one simple, good-natured man. Thomas Dunman had been an assistant with the Singapore firm of Martin Dyce and Company until his persistent camaraderie with the local people (somewhat unusual in those days) had persuaded Samuel Bonham, and later Colonel Butterworth, to try him out as a Police Magistrate in 1843. Thereafter he had soon been offered, and in 1845 accepted, the full time post of Superintendent of Police, Singapore.

In this position he had endeared himself to his subordinates, many of them Indian Muslims, by his personal coaching of them to pass their examinations for promotion. This disinterested kindness resulted twelve years later, at the outbreak of the Mutiny, in his having a troop of friends under his new command as Police Commissioner more loyal to him than to the most intimate ties of their own kith and kin.

One of these – a member of the Sepoys' secret councils – had at the risk of his life disclosed to Dunman the plot of a certain Subbadar Gurmakh Singh to butcher the entire European community whilst they were in church the next Sunday morning; and this would no doubt have been attempted (at this distance of time it would seem with much chance of success) had Dunman not swooped upon the entire party like a hawk and delivered them all over to their own officers for court martial.

But now the Mutiny was over; and the Europeans in Calcutta, horrified at the brutality and bloodshed they had seen, and dismayed that the Indian Government could so completely have been caught unawares, were agitating at home for the Government of India to be placed directly under the Crown.

This was Singapore's chance. Mr Joachim D'Almeida, the Sheriff (Dr Joze D'Almeida's son), called an immediate public meeting of the European inhabitants at the newly built 'News Room' on 15th September 1857; and a unanimous decision was made to join in the movement originated by the inhabitants of Calcutta in their petition dated 3rd August, requesting both Houses of Parliament to present an address to the Crown 'beseeching Her Majesty to place the whole of British India under the sole government of the Imperial Parliament'.

To this, J. J. Greenshields for Guthrie and Company added the wise resolution 'that the Petition to Parliament set forth the grievances under which the *Straits Settlements* had laboured during the government of the *East India Company* and prayed to be placed directly under the Crown, with a *Separate Government*, and *not* as at present under a delegated authority in India'.

Acting on the farsighted suggestion of Greenshields therefore, a *separate* Petition was thereupon addressed to both Houses of Parliament by the European inhabitants of Singapore and was very numerously signed.

* * *

When these notices were presented to the Houses of Parliament in March 1858 there ensued a discussion worthy of the magic pen of Sir A. P. Herbert – and one which lacked only his presence to render the Honourable Members' cogitations immortal.

In the House of Commons Lord Bury, Albemarle's eldest son and Admiral Sir Henry Keppel's nephew, led off to a fine start with an amusing outline of Singapore's progress; and of the Indian Government's blundering inefficiency in the matter of the Straits Settlements.

Mr Bailey, Secretary to the Board of Control of the East India Company (one can see him uneasily fingering his collar with embarrassment as he replied), was free to confess that the subject had not sufficiently occupied the attention of the Government. The fact was that they did not consider it necessary. 'At least' (he adds hurriedly), 'not yet, at a time when the whole Government of India is about to be discussed – er – to deal with questions of detail respecting what must – at present at all events – be considered a portion of the Indian Empire. And then again, it would be necessary, in taking this subject into consideration, to communicate with the Governor-General . . .' (He was clearly getting out of his depth.)

But, said he, rallying, though he was not sure whether India would not be quite glad to get rid of the place, now that they had the Andaman Islands for their convicts, he should point out that if the Straits did become a Colonial possession, Britain would need to defray the total military expenditure amounting to about £300,000 a year (poor man, he had fallen into the fatal trap of guessing), which the Colonists could not afford as they could only now barely manage to meet their own Civil Expenses. And then again, he could not altogether admit the justice of the complaints in the Petition, especially about the Port Duties and the Currency; because both these grievances had been redressed; nor about the expenses on the military garrison either, as these were *not* paid by the Colonists. (He was wrong). And as for the convicts, well this had started when the Settlement was very small and he understood they had been of much benefit at one time. However, perhaps this was a complaint that did require some consideration and – well – there you are . . . Or words to that effect.

At this stage the petitioners were fortunate in the presence in the House of a Member who knew what he was talking about – a certain Mr Horsman, proprietor of the Province Wellesley sugar properties of Caledonia, Golden Grove, Jawee, Kreean, Valdor and Victoria.

'From all I can hear', he said, 'Singapore is an outstanding example of utter lack of sympathy with the problems of the inhabitants, which is by no means creditable to the Legislature. What has Singapore got to do with India?' he asked. 'Why should that Colony be governed by India? India might just as well claim to govern Ceylon or Hong Kong. Singapore is inhabited by Chinese, about whom India knows nothing. In spite of the grievances quoted in the Petition, which are perfectly valid ones, the commerce of Singapore has increased by seventy-five per cent during the last six years. The petition before you is one well worthy of the consideration of the Government and I trust it will receive at their hands that degree of attention to which it is entitled.'

Honourable Members were now, however, to be edified by a peroration from Sir J. Elphinstone, Member for Portsmouth, which it is a delight to have rescued, as a gem of purest ray serene, from its century of dusty obscurity.

Of course he knew Singapore very well, declaimed the oracle of Portsmouth, he had called in there twenty-seven years before. Singapore, he explained, whilst originally needing very few troops to defend it from the excellent prisoners, who had kindly been sent there by India to undertake all the public works of the place, had now become most lawless and hence required many – this being due to its having become the resort of the most ferocious and savage races of the Eastern world, to wit the Bugis, and Dyaks, and the Syaks from Sumatra; added to which a heavy influx of Chinese males without women had resulted in the creation of a race, of mixed local and Chinese descent, known as the 'Klings',* a most disorderly people. It was in fact because of them, and not the harmless convicts, that it had been necessary so heavily to increase the military strength of the Straits Settlements. He was inclined to agree with the Secretary to the Board of Control that it would certainly prove a great burden to Britain to take upon itself the charge of maintaining peace among that mixed and lawless population.

There was however one insuperable obstacle to the colonisation of the island of Singapore, and that was the immense number of tigers that swam over from Johore, from which State Singapore was separated by no more than a small stream. Scarcely a day passed without some native being carried off bodily by those animals . . .

The reader will be able to stand just so much of this, but no more. Suffice it – to reduce this sorry farce to some sort of order – to mention that the London *Times* took the part of the Singapore petitioners and that the London *Examiner* of 24th April 1858 praised Lord Bury and Horsman for their

* 'Kling', in fact, was the European rendering of the word 'Kalinga', the name of the highly respectable Hindu community of Singapore – many of whom originally came from the 'Telingga' or 'Telugu' districts of that part of India known as Andhra-Desh.

matter and lucidity, which had been answered by Mr Bailey 'in an oration which had neither of these qualities', whilst making delightfully merry over Elphinstone's Dyaks, Syaks, Klings and tigers!

In regard to the last, a question was, as a matter of fact, referred in time to Colonel Orfeur Cavanagh, the new Governor of the Straits Settlements from 1859; and that bluff old peg-top of a soldier (he had had a leg blown off in India) astonished Whitehall by replying that on investigation he was satisfied it was a gross exaggeration; and that no more than two hundred persons were destroyed on Singapore island by tigers every year!

Allowing for the fact that the menace of tigers on Singapore island was very real indeed, what he had not realised, of course, (what perhaps can only be understood in retrospect), was that a situation had arisen whereby there were in fact three separate ruling bodies on that Island – the Government, the Chamber of Commerce, and the Chinese Secret Societies. It was the internal intrigues and rough justice of the last named, not the tigers, that must surely have largely contributed to this appalling death roll.

* * *

It had become fairly clear by that year of 1858 that the Home Government wanted to take over the affairs of the Straits Settlements. Lord Canning finally tipped the scale in favour of transfer to the Colonial Office by a remarkably able Minute written in November 1859, in which he touched on the increasing revenues of Singapore, the general absence of objections to the proposal and the character (so different from that of the inhabitants of India) of the Chinese.

A Bill for severance of the Straits Settlements from India had in fact been promulgated earlier that year. Though Mr Blundell, late Governor of the Straits, had mirrored the Indian Government's traditional attitude by raising strong objections to the proposal, not only such statesmen as Lord Canning but now even Mr Gregson, Chairman of the East India Company Association (who might well have been excused a certain bias) were proving themselves warmly in favour of the 'Transfer'.

At this juncture it merely remained for a final leverage to be applied before the mass weight of growing opinion in its favour rolled forward and resolved such subsidiary questions as military expenditure; Singapore's ability to meet these from its own exchequer; and whether or not the Straits Government should pay for the extensive fortifications now in process of construction, as these had been designed for Imperial, not local, interests.

An insight is afforded into the importance of the Singapore Chamber of Commerce – and of the 'Guthrie-Greenshields' close-knit 'Cabinet' within it – by finding that on the 16th June 1860 it was none other than Alexander Guthrie and his nephew James who supplied exactly that very impetus.

Recruiting to their aid Mr Gregson, together with Mr Surgeon John Crawfurd, the former Resident of Singapore, the four of them called on the Duke of Newcastle, the Secretary of State, who received their suggestions very favourably and became their powerful supporter.

Matters from then on, though attenuating themselves over the next seven years to an exasperating degree, moved forward to a certain end. Greenshields in Singapore kept up the pressure of his representations for accelerated action; repeated meetings of the Chamber of Commerce were held; further petitions and letters in answer to Parliamentary inquiries were expedited to London till it became a matter of wonder what, if anything, the ostensible Government of Singapore was doing other than act as postman. During these critical years the course of events may be observed with an interest at times not untinged with amazement.

Mr Gladstone, the Prime Minister, had committed himself to a heavy programme of military fortifications for Singapore. Crawfurd and the Guthries had persuaded the Duke of Newcastle that these were a useless waste of money. Gladstone therefore delayed bringing the matter of Transfer forward before Parliament adjourned in August 1861, in order to save himself a possible defeat in the House.

In 1862, by a strange act of folly, the Indian Government had once again attempted to impose port duties upon Singapore – a most powerful stick thrust into the hands of Greenshields and the Chamber of Commerce with which to belabour their backs, as they did – resulting in a further highly satisfactory visit of the Guthries, together this time with Boustead, Fraser, Nichol and Richardson (all important

Singapore personalities) as well as old Surgeon John Crawfurd, to the Secretary of State, whose 'courtesy', to quote the *Singapore Free Press*, 'offered a strong contrast to the demeanour of his colleague the Secretary of State for India'.

Finally the India Office demanded, as a condition of transfer, that the Straits should take upon itself the whole of the accumulated local debt since 1821, on the ground that the Indian Government had consented to forgo any claims of late years in respect of Public Works.

This last demand – the final throw of a now defeated Indian administration – was refused by the Chancellor of the Exchequer as 'out of all reason'; as payment of interest alone would absorb the total surplus revenue shown in the estimates of the Straits.

An important letter to Sir Frederick Rogers, Under-Secretary of State, dated 1st February 1865 and signed by Crawfurd, Alexander Guthrie, James Guthrie as well as by Boustead, Read, Little and some others, cleared the ground by showing how even a seventy-five per cent increase in revenue over the last six years had been unable to keep pace with the Singapore Government's ever mounting and top-heavy expenditure on military commitments and senior personnel. The letter showed how unnecessary both were and how easily the defence of Singapore could be maintained by efficient naval coverage and a small military detachment reinforced by local European Volunteers.

As a result of this, a further meeting occurred between the Guthries, Crawfurd and Gregson on the one side, and Cardwell for the Colonial Office on the other, at which 'they were as courteously received as they had been by the Duke of Newcastle, which is saying a great deal'. By 1865 the Treasury, the War Office, the India Office and the Colonial Office were at last agreed upon the desirability of the Straits Settlements' transfer to the Crown.

* * *

Alexander Guthrie's work was done. That great man – the founder of, by now, one of the only two original Singapore firms (Johnston's and his own) to have survived the stormy years – could at last look confidently ahead to the culmination of his life's most remarkable endeavour; the achievement for which his name will for ever be held in affectionate and honoured memory – the removal of the Straits Settlements from the dead hand of India to those of the Crown Government. This, and only this, would make it possible for commerce to enter the closed doors of the Peninsula and so bring in its train new trade to Singapore, prosperity to Malaya and a new life and a new hope to the Native States' troubled and unhappy population.

A lonely man – for since the death of his niece-in-law, Suzanna, he had retired very much into himself and seemed to see little in the future but his one remaining task – racked with bouts of fever and crippled by backache from the enlarged spleen (the 'ague-cake') that comes of much malaria – Alexander had battled through the bitter winter of 1864 at his house, Number 8 Upper Wimpole Street, where he had been living for the last few years.

Early the next year he was able to hear, with exhausted relief, that a Bill for the Transfer of the Straits Settlements was to be introduced to Parliament; and with the tired satisfaction of a man who has fought the good fight – and won – on the 12th of March 1865 Alexander Guthrie died.

As Alexander had foreseen, the Bill, first read unopposed in the House on 13th June 1866, became on the 10th August of that year an Act of Parliament 'to provide for the government of the Straits Settlements' – chapter 115 of 29 and 30 Victoria.

By an Order in Council dated 28th December 1866, the 1st of April 1867 was ordered for the Act to come into operation; and by Letters Patent dated Westminster, 4th February 1867 the necessary authority was given constituting the new Government of the Straits.

CHAPTER 5

BRANCHES OF COMMERCE

Let us now make our way along Collyer Quay one fine morning, en route for Messrs Guthrie and Company's office . . . stepping over muddy puddles and jostled, among the heavy wooden-wheeled bullock-carts, by yelling Indian and Chinese coolies bearing bales.

It is October in the year 1867 – six months after the 'Transfer'.

The harbour is jammed. Far off the astonishing sight of more than one hundred square-rigged vessels at anchor fills the horizon. Cargo is being off-loaded into a mass of strange box-like 'twakows' – craft with enormous eyes in the bow that hold upwards of twenty-five tons each and are manipulated by one large oar astern. These are at present surrounding each foreign-going ship like ants attacking a grasshopper.

Closer in there is a positive fleet – they must be at least fifty strong – of high-pooped schooners from Macassar, with their slender tripod masts, whose beautiful and appropriate name is the 'prahu pelari', meaning 'runners', from their great weatherliness and speed. They always come at this time of the year and leave in November with the change of monsoon.

Nearer again – with bow lines out and sterns almost touching the quay – are two very different types of craft; one being white-painted and giving precisely the impression of an elongated egg floating in the water, from their possession of beautifully curved and white-painted roofs that exactly reproduce the hull shape in reverse – with the addition of two forward-sloping stumps sticking up that surely cannot be masts. The other type are astonishingly low, lean, vessels about sixty foot long overall, painted black – double enders, with crotches for six oars a side, spaces for a further sixteen paddlers and one rather ineffectual-looking mast, stepped well forward.

The egg-like boats have sailed all the way from far-off Bali; and when, on these small stumps, the Balinese crews set their twin high-peaked lateen-sails of ochre or of blue, they are the very butterflies of the sea.

The others are the 'pukats', so called; twenty-tonners with a crew of twenty-nine, that work the Straits of Malacca on both sides (and up the east coast too from April to October when the wind is in the south-west) dodging in and out for cargo and hoping they have speed enough to beat the pirates. They are owned and run by the Chinese; and each one has a clerk or cashkeeper who often ends up as a ship-owner himself – if he can live that long.

And everywhere, under the racing monsoon cloudlets, the choppy blue-and-green waters of the harbour are dotted with small craft of all descriptions – scotchies, koleks, sampans – under oar and under sail, heeling over, shouting to each other, sending up showers of spray, with creaking blocks and drumming halyards, coming and going between the neighbouring mainland and islands and the great mart of Singapore; the whole, in the bright light and clean wind of morning, creating an unforgettable scene of active life and happy industry.

In all these – and in the great junks from China which come down on the first of the north-east monsoon just before Christmas, and the 'country-brigs' that do not arrive till March, after the December opium-sales in Calcutta – we see the justice of Robertson's words in his *History of India*, when he said: 'In the history of past times the exploits of conquerors who have desolated the earth, and the freaks of tyrants who have rendered nations unhappy, are recorded with minute and often disgusting accuracy, while the discovery of useful arts and the progress of the most beneficial branches of commerce are passed over in silence, and suffered to sink into oblivion.'

* * *

Messrs Guthrie and Company's head office on Collyer Quay* is a fine building, of two storeys with a central tower, the office being on the first floor and the warehouses below. Mr

* See Appendix B.

James Watson is in charge of the godowns; James Guthrie being in London and Tom Scott busy with his 'Tanjong Pagar Dock Company'. John James Greenshields is upstairs, just back this year from leave.

Watson leads the way into a dark and aromatic cave, vast in the half-light and stacked from floor to roof with grey and indistinguishable shapes. Here is the domain of young Gan Eng Seng from Malacca, the storekeeper (though only aged twenty-two) whose long pigtail and bright eyes seem more those of a handsome girl than a young man, as he smilingly glides through the dim vaults. 'This is the export side', Mr Watson says, 'the stuff we send out rather than what we get in.

'Of course', he adds, 'they are both the same really. There is nothing here of Singapore's own. We are what they call an entrepôt.'

* *

But what an entrepôt! 'Basically', he explains, 'and this is where people often make a mistake, our main trade is with South-east Asia. Of course it all started years ago with the very fine idea of selling our British manufactures and our woollen and cotton piece goods to China, for which they would exchange their teas. But nothing of that sort ever happened. The Chinese regarded everything that we made as completely comic; and when it came to cloth they would much rather wear their own fine silk. We tempted them with opium for some years, and they did bring us some few teas in exchange, but that is all over now. The opium goes straight from Calcutta to Hong Kong without stopping here; and the teas straight from China to London in those racing tea clippers. Just as well it does, because the English taste in tea has entirely changed, as you know. People like fresh tea nowadays – the first picking of the year's crop – and if we had to store it here in Singapore between the monsoons we would never make a sale. Nobody would ever buy it.

'Mind you, tea does come down to Singapore from China all right – but it is not for us. It is black tea for the local Chinese, and they like it very much. Very expensive, and it comes by junk.

'And don't run away with the idea that we don't sell lots of opium too – because we do – but not to China. You see, it has all worked out quite differently from the way they expected, as I shall show you by and by.'

* *

'Around Christmas and the New Year the junks come. There are hundreds of them – and the whole town goes mad. The first one in is the signal for a public Chinese holiday; and everyone who can walk gets down to the harbour and hires a sampan out to the fleet, which becomes a sort of floating market. They rig thatched roofs all over the decks and sell everything they have brought, straight over the side from on board.

'What do they sell apart from black tea? First of all (for ballast really, though they have a great sale) they bring a surprising amount of pottery and earthenware, flooring tiles and carved coping stones. You would never think that, would you? And then straw, which seems extraordinary, for thatching the local Chinese "chukias" – though of course it *is* difficult to buy straw here when you come to think of it.

'But that is just the bread and butter. The real fun begins when it comes to selling what we call their "China goods" – paper umbrellas, dried fruit, weird confectionery, medicines of all sorts, silk shoes, mushrooms, Chinese tobacco, joss sticks and gold lace. You never saw such a muddle in all your life.

'And in return for all that they take back Straits produce – which is where we come in.'

* *

'Straits produce? Well, it is almost anything really, that we get from this part of the world. For instance, it includes spices of all sorts, such as pepper, cloves, nutmeg and mace (which is only the thin red tegument surrounding the nut inside of a nutmeg), together with every sort of rich-smelling aromatic substance like camphor, sandalwood, vanilla, cinnamon and benzoin, as well as the heavily scented distilled oils of patchouli, vetivert and ylang-ylang, all from leaves, flowers or roots of shrubs and trees. And then of course eatable things they are mad on, – seaslugs, birdsnests, sharks-fins, seaweed – to say nothing of the ingredients for medicines guaranteed to make you 'very strong', like 'dragon's-blood' and rhinoceros-horns. Also, they usually take quite a load of tin and antimony, with coffee, beeswax, ebony, tortoiseshell, ivory, rattans, amber, gold dust and a parcel of seed-pearls. What you might call a general cargo.

'We have got it all here in the godown – except for the pearls and the gold dust. They are in the strongroom upstairs.

'But as I say, the Chinese market is not really our main interest at all nowadays. We do still ship a little opium by junk up to China at times, but it is all very tricky and contraband – and we have a considerable trade that way in British cotton piece goods (though not by junk). But most of the cotton trade with China is now direct from Liverpool, and the opium goes, of course, straight from Calcutta to the hulks off Hong Kong at the island of Lintin. Neither calls at Singapore.'

* *

'But you would like to see what we have in the godown.

'To begin with I must explain that, except for what comes to us direct from England, Calcutta or Labuan, we buy everything *from* the local Chinese merchants and we sell everything *to* the local Chinese merchants. That is the way to be happy and to live long in the land. People have tried it other ways, but I don't know where they are buried.

'I mentioned Labuan on purpose, because that is where we are now getting quite a supply of coal, which we store in the docks at Tanjong Pagar for the steamships and is therefore not exported.

'All the rest comes in at one door and goes out at the other, leaving a shaving of profit, needless to add, in the hands of our excellent establishment; for it is in that manner that the commerce of the world is performed.

'Now all that bulk in the other godown that you passed as you came in is made up of iron-copper-and-lead-pipes and bars from Britain, as well as cotton piece goods and woollens in bales, manufactured articles such as agricultural implements, wheels, pumps and what would you, together with a certain amount of arms and ammunition in wooden crates – all from Britain of course.

'At the far end there is a store of Punjab wheat in bags, a few tons of gunny sacks, a large consignment of Indian cotton piece goods and about sixty chests of Malwa opium – all these having come down to us from Calcutta, mostly by small "country" barques and brigs.

'But you would be surprised where all the stuff in this godown comes from, and where it goes to.'

* *

'Take coffee for instance. Up till about ten years ago the great majority of that came from Bali and Lombok. But they did not grow it there – not most of it, anyway. Oh no. Java coffee was a Dutch monopoly till 1857, and always had been. So Bali and Lombok became the great smuggling centres for coffee from Java. The trade was run by Chinese living in Java, with junks sailing to the north coast of both Bali and Lombok islands, from where it was brought here by Bugis traders or Balinese. On Lombok there was a Mr King who ran the whole business, with his assistants, Bird and Lange. He made a vast fortune.

'After a bit, Lange – an enormous Dane – moved over to Bali and started up on his own. I don't know what happened to Bird. Lange became a millionaire. He married a Hokkien ward of the Rajah of his locality – a place called Badong – and one of their daughters married Abu Bakar, the Maharajah of Johore; and is now the Maharanee.

'King had two sailing vessels of his own, and twice a year he used to bring us a great deal of rice, tobacco, coconut oil, tallow and sarongs as well as coffee, in return for which we used to load him up with opium, Chinese coins (that is odd, isn't it?) and British manufactured goods – most of which would find its way from Lombok to Java in the end, by Chinese junk.

'Did you know, incidentally, that long before Singapore was founded Bali and Lombok, as well as Java itself, were the main centres for manufactured goods of all sorts from Britain trickling their way into – of all places – Japan? Raffles mentions it in one of his letters. This Eastern trade is very old.

'However, to go on with the story, old man King moved from Lombok to Koti in Borneo some years ago, and we get no more coffee from Lombok now. My boss Mr Guthrie in London and his friends forced Parliament to put pressure on the Dutch and the trade is now open. We get it cheaper straight from Java nowadays.'

* *

'But the whole trade is shifting and altering the whole time.

'The junk trade, especially with China, is being taken over more and more by square-rigged vessels; and for the last fifteen years – since they passed a thing called Act XXX in 1852 – more and more of these are being run and owned by our local Chinese merchants, who have now full privilege as British citizens. We like that, because it has been a great help to the "China" side of the business.

'Modern vessels can beat up to windward against the north-east monsoon in winter time, thus greatly increasing our trade with China, as Magniacs's little Baltimore-built opium schooner *Dhaulle* did for the first time in 1827 – immediately followed, of course, by many other vessels in all branches of trade – and this meant a great improvement in our sale of tin, cotton and Straits produce to Canton.

'Our Chinese merchants here – the Towkays – know the mainland Chinese market, which we could never do, and they now have all the trade at their finger tips. This suits us splendidly, as we are the collecting agents for all they want. Another thing is that since they began to take shares in sea-going vessels based on Singapore or Calcutta, the Chinese Towkays are at last beginning to appreciate the advantages of insuring their goods in transit, which no junk skipper would ever think of doing. Mr Greenshields will tell you more about that when you go upstairs.

'There have been other changes too, both in what we buy and sell and in where we buy and sell it. Putting it simply, Singapore first thought it would sell British cotton and Indian opium to China; and send home teas in exchange.

'Well, it didn't; in spite of giving the barque *Houghton* a seven gun salute when she brought in the first cargo of Chinese teas in 1834.

'So Singapore turned to the South-east Asian market, as Raffles always said it should; and that meant a head-on collision with the Dutch.

'It has been a running battle all these years; and if Raffles had not chosen the best site in Asia when he did – and made it a free port – I don't know where we would have been.

'In a furious effort to copy our success, the Dutch made Rhio, just opposite, a free port in 1829; Pontianak, Sambas and Succadana, all in Borneo, free ports in 1834 and 1835; Macassar in the Celebes a free port in 1847; the islands of

John James Greenshields

Cairn Hill House

Menado and Kema free ports in 1848; and Amboyna, Banda and Ternate free ports just fourteen years ago in 1853.

'But it didn't matter. We have the best geographical position and they cannot beat us at our game.

'Macassar was rather a scare, as it is right on the alternative route from Britain and India to China via the Sunda Strait – which is why our Mr Guthrie and his friends were so wild about India trying to levy port duties just at that time – but we got through all right, although Macassar did affect us to some extent.

'Then along came Labuan in 1842 – a British possession granted, but right on our main Singapore-China trade routes and a good deal closer to China. There was a fuss about that, but neither old Mr Guthrie nor our young Mr James Guthrie seemed to worry their heads about it for some reason – and it worked out just as they thought. Labuan is one of our best feeder ports in Borneo now, just like Penang is, up the Straits here.'

* *

'Labuan – and the whole west Borneo coast with Kuching in Sarawak as its centre – is being a great help in fact.

'In the very early days, shortly after we first opened in Singapore, Chinese junks used to come in from Brunei and Sarawak with cargoes of rattans, pepper, camphor, beeswax, birdsnests and mother of pearl – in fact some very precious loads which included pearls, gold dust and even diamonds. But the strangest cargo they often brought you'll never guess – Chinese women, enticed or kidnapped from their homes, to be sold at fantastic prices to the girl-hungry population of Singapore's Chinese. There is a story to be told, if you like!

'In return we used to send opium, arms and ammunition, rice from Siam, Sumatra or Bali (which Borneo was always short of), some Indian brassware, British household utensils and a fair quantity of cotton piece goods, mostly coloured shirting, of which they seemed to prefer grey.

'And then, in the early thirties, they discovered a rich ore deposit of antimony in Borneo. That started the trouble – and bloodshed over antimony broke out in Sarawak much the same as the fighting going on just now in Perak and Selangor over the tin.

'James Brooke went there, as you will remember, took the

side of the Chief at Kuching, and became the Rajah of Sarawak himself; since when our trade with Borneo has not been half as much in Straits produce (or even Chinese girls!) as it has in antimony ore, which goes home to Europe as ballast in the barques and other large vessels.

'Two other quite new trades have started up in Borneo also, since Rajah Brooke took over. One is pearl sago, which is coming on very well – in fact it is the only place we get it from except Sumatra – all of which goes either to Europe or America; and the other is guttapercha.'

* *

'This guttapercha is most interesting stuff. Take a look at it. Black slabs. It is almost as hard as wood when cold, but you only have to warm it and it becomes all soft and you can mould it into any shape you want.

'We always sent a certain amount of this home – mostly for the handles of surgeons' knives and other medical appliances – but the recent demand has been astonishing. This is due to all these new submarine telegraph cables they are laying down everywhere. The stuff is impervious to water and an excellent insulating material for electricity, apparently.

'Peninsular Guttapercha is one of the Maharajah of Johore's monopolies, and much of it comes by sampan from Johore Lama and other ports around the Johore coast. Then again we have always imported as much of it as we used to need from Siak in Sumatra by the "pukats" – but from now on this new supply from Borneo, which is increasing all the time, is proving itself a godsend.

'We may well need all the guttapercha we can lay our hands on before we are much older.

'This other queer-looking grey substance comes sometimes from Borneo , as well as from Sumatra – but the greater part of it from the Native States throughout the Malayan Peninsula. Caoutchouc or "jelutong" it is called. Unlike guttapercha, it stays soft all the time. These new telegraph cables are causing a tremendous demand for this also, and one only wishes one could get up into those countries and organise the collection. There appears to be masses of it, but the aboriginees who tap it from the jungle trees only bring it down to the river mouths when they need a little tobacco and salt.'

* *

'All this middle section of the godown is taken up with imports from the Native States on the Peninsula – and this is one of the chief parts of the job and is growing every year. Apart from caoutchouc we get rattans of poor quality in large quantities; a good deal of black pepper (mostly from Penang, which is included in the same section) and, most important of all, a great deal of gold dust from Pahang up the east coast – also quite our largest supply of tin. For this we exchange opium, piece goods, salt-fish, and salt; for Penang, British manufactured goods; and of course lots of beer, wines and spirits.'

* *

'But here we are in the final section, which is also of the greatest importance. This is the Siamese division, which, for us, also includes Cambodia. It used to include Cochin China as well – until the French moved in seven years ago, since when that aspect of our import trade has finished.

'Siam has always given us a very large block of business – even during the "bad" years between 1824 and 1855 when rice was forbidden to be exported from Bangkok, and teak too after 1841. The old King of Siam and his family were traders on their own behalf; and kept the commercial strings very much in their own hands as an imperial preserve – but, even so, you would be surprised what a quantity of goods came through, due to difficulties of control and administrative connivance.

'After the old King died in 1855 everything became much easier – and all has gone perfectly smoothly with Siam and ourselves since Sir John Bowring came out and arranged the Siamese treaty with the new King Mongkut in the same year.

'The whole run of trade with Siam is changing too. For the last six years much of the cargo between Bangkok and Singapore has been taken by the two Siamese steamers *Chow Phya* and *Alligator*. I often think that if it goes on like this we will soon find ourselves cut out and all the trade going direct from Siam to Britain and Europe by steamer.

'That is an alarming thought, because we have always bought more sugar from Siam than anywhere else – and all that sugar now goes straight home to Britain from here in big ships. From Siam we also get coconut oil and salt in large quantities; a vast supply of rice, in spite of the prohibition; iron pans, earthenware, hog's lard, elephant tusks, gamboge and sapanwood for Europe; teak for Britain and sticklac for China.

'In exchange for that we send Siam cotton goods, opium of course (though it is against the Siamese law), tea, sago, paper, glassware, Straits produce, arms and ammunition, iron and steel, a great deal of copper sheathing for their sea-going vessels, and British manufactures of all descriptions.

'Then we get a queer mixture from Cambodia; much the same as Siam but in different proportions, with the addition of horns, dried meat and buffalo hides, together with that aromatic gum known as benzoin that used to be called frankincense. They export chick-peas too, funnily enough; and cargoes of large box-like nuts called cardamoms, as well as a very hard timber that goes by the name of "eaglewood". They seem to want mostly opium and cotton goods, but we send them a fair cargo of steel, gambier and agricultural implements as well.'

* *

'So there you are – and now you see how some of us live.

'In general you might say that we import practically nothing from China, but that with them we do about a third of all our export business.

'The other two thirds of our total commerce – import and export – is with the Native States on the peninsula first of all, then with Siam, and after that Sumatra, while all the rest may be blocked together under the general name of the "Bugis Trade", which – important as it is – probably comes fourth in the list.

'But I must not keep you, as Mr Greenshields will be waiting for you upstairs.'

CHAPTER 6

THE CONTROL ROOM

A trifle dazed by all this, it is a relief to accept Mr Greenshields's kind offer of coffee and a Manila cheroot in his large open office upstairs; to stretch the legs and to relax in a deep leather armchair under the cool and alternating breeze of a punkah.

The room is very large and high, with a clear draught of fresh air blowing in from the windows facing the sea right through to the other end of the long hall, where other windows open onto the main business centre of the town known as Commercial Square. This upstairs room is a cavernous space occupying all the area of the godowns below it. Here Chinese merchants may wander in between the busy clerks at their desks and sit themselves comfortably down to sip tea and discuss business with one or other of the European 'Tuans', whose large desks and attendant chairs for guests loom up invitingly here and there beneath the rows of punkahs, like islands amidst the round black hats and pigtailed heads of the Chinese staff.

* *

'So', says Mr Greenshields, 'you have now glanced at what may be described as the "pots and pans" side of the business; the "bread and butter" of our firm, as I dare say young James Watson may have called it, as he often does. Well, it is good bread and butter, and in its way quite interesting. An excellent job for a young man – not too exacting, and dealing with tangible material things rather than imponderable schemes and ideas. I often think the happiest days of my business life were spent in that old godown'. He mused; a large, greying, sensitive man with a kind mouth.

'But first you must meet our staff. My senior partner, Mr James Guthrie, is in London; and then Thomas Scott is busy today with the Tanjong Pagar Dock affairs. James Watson, our other partner, you have already met. Here is Arthur Douglas Forbes, our senior assistant, who joined us last year, wasn't it, Arthur? And this is our second assistant, Rowland Montague Salmonds, who is much younger but has been with us since about 1863.

'Then we have our Chief Clerk, Mr Khoo Tian Bee, who took over from our old Mr Laow Chang Wat about seven years ago, when he went on retirement; and this is young Mr Wee Lim Guan; and then the messenger-boy, Simon Aroozoo. And there we are.'

* *

'I am sorry you could not have met young John Guthrie – a charming boy, but very unstable. He was Mr Alexander Guthrie's – well . . . I don't know. We never knew very much about the old man's private life you know. But one of the last things he did eighteen months ago, just before he died, was to send out and make sure that we took young John into the firm. I don't believe anybody before had had the least idea. He did not seem to us at all a marrying type of man, or to have had many dealings with women. But it would be just before he left Singapore for good – when his nephew James was away on leave – and he was lonely no doubt. One cannot tell. Poor John only stayed with us a year and left us to go to sea last autumn in 1866, when I was at home on leave. We have quite lost track of him now.

'However, to go on about the firm. We have never been merely an import-export establishment, and nothing else, as you know. Right from the beginning the old man, Mr Alexander Guthrie, had his fingers in all sorts of other pies – and that has gone on ever since.

'First of all there is the Everton estate down at Tanjong Pagar, half of which is now a built-up area and bringing us in a tidy sum in rentals; and we keep selling little bits too on Government requisitions for road access and one thing and the other. The same applies more or less in regard to our property up Orchard Road, except that it is still largely agricultural and producing extremely profitable nutmegs.

'Then during the early years, when the money first began to come in, Alexander Guthrie saw no sense in letting it lie idle, so he took to financing other people's ventures, first of all in the China trade and later in all manner of construction and housebuilding works here in Singapore.

'It was a good endeavour – though risky – and an honest one; and there are more sawmills and factories and brick-works in this town built with old Guthrie's money than you would know about.'

* *

'As time went on and godown trade increased, Alexander found – and James after him – that every sort of sea-trader, Bugis, Balinese, Pukat or local sampan, would demand spot cash for his goods from the Chinese middleman, but required extended credit from him when it came to selling Singapore exports up the Malay peninsula or among the islands. "No give, then all right – no trade."

'But often enough the Chinese merchant had insufficient ready cash to pay for goods supplied to him from our godown – or said so at any rate – so we and all the other Agency Houses were pushed into the position of giving the Chinese merchant long credit too or going without business.

'There was a danger in this, which was offset as far as possible by charging the Chinese a handsome rate of interest.

'Fingers were burnt many times – especially after the Government passed that absurd Insolvency Law in 1848, against which both Alexander and James Guthrie fought so hard, as it meant that the defaulter could just peacefully slip off to China instead of being dealt with by our own methods – but on the whole the interest rate levied on the Chinese merchant for long credit on imported goods created a steady additional income to build up the firm.'

* *

'Looking through our records I find that, quite apart from buying and selling, this Company made a steady and handsome profit up till 1833 on the pure transshipment business – in other words, holding goods when they were off-loaded from the East Indiamen until they could be reloaded into private vessels and vice versa; a fair percentage of the goods in this case being owned by East India Company officials . . . "Opium to China and raw-silk home" was their great trade in those days, and it seems we in Singapore used to charge one per cent of gross value for mere trans-shipment alone, with warehouse charges in addition. All that stopped of course when the East India Company's charter ran out in 1833 – and it is just as well it did as events proved. These extra costs were causing our China trade to be undercut by the Americans.

'And I remember hearing that shortly before I arrived out East we had made a tremendous killing during the Chinese War in 1842, when the bottom dropped out of opium prices and junk-loads came down for safe keeping in Singapore. I expect we traded in the islands for years on that opium!'

* * *

'But a company cannot exist just on occasional windfalls. Other than pure trading, our steadiest lines have always been banking and insurance.

'We have been agents for the London banking firm of Coutts ever since 1830; and when I came out here as an assistant in 1845 we were already agents for one insurance company – the Commercial Insurance Office, of Calcutta – and young Thomas Kerr used to run it. It did quite well.

'Then in '53 we took on the agency for the London Fire Assurance Company and the Triton Insurance Company, which were better; and in '61 we added to those the London and Provincial Marine Insurance Company, which is very profitable indeed, especially as the Chinese are at last beginning to insure their sea-borne cargoes – and we ended up with a full-house by becoming representatives for Drummonds Bank as well as Coutts. And that is how we stand just now.

'It was lucky we took on the Marine and Provincial Insurance people when we did, as a matter of fact; as they stood us in good stead two years later when the Confederates' *Alabama* called in here on 21st December 1863. I went aboard her on the 23rd, at Captain Semmes's invitation when she was alongside the wharves in the New Harbour; and thought her a fine vessel indeed. She was built for the Confederate States by Lairds' of Birkenhead – and would do fourteen knots under power, well armed too – six 32 pounder broadside guns with smooth bores and a big 100 pounder rifled gun on a pivot up forward; a Blakely, I think. She had another large gun aft as well – a smooth bore 86 pounder.

'Captain Semmes was a funny little weazened fellow you would take for a Georgia cotton planter rather than a sailor; but he did us plenty of damage all the same.

'We had consigned a considerable cargo for the Union aboard the British-registered barque *Martaban*, and a little in the Union ships *Sonora* and *Highlander* too – and within a week of leaving here *Alabama* had sunk the lot. As I say, it was lucky for us that our cargo was well insured.'

* *

'But to continue. Finally (and quite recently) we have been indulging in heavy speculations with a variety of Chiefs and Rajahs in the Native States, who are in a terrible state of confusion, as you know. For the last seven years we have been lucky to have the professional advice in these matters of Mr James Guthrie's nephew, Mr James Guthrie Davidson, who is a lawyer out here, with an intimate knowledge of native affairs. But it is a tricky game – and we are only in it because we have to be. If we don't – and if we now move into the Malay States as a result of the new Transfer to the Crown, as we devoutly hope – we would find ourselves completely defeated by our competitors, in having failed to make friends and prepare the ground.

'So that is the general state of affairs; to which I might add two rather disturbing features.

'The first is that the trade depression in Europe and Britain has had a disastrous effect on Singapore over the last three years, to the extent that quite a number of businesses failed last year and there was a rush on all the banks, several of which collapsed in London and India as a result.

'And the second is that we are now pressed in on all sides by the most vigorous competition, especially from the Germans, who have managed to get hold of not less than a quarter of all Singapore's foreign trade.

'There were six Agency Houses including Guthries' when we arrived here in 1821 – and now there are sixty! It is absolutely necessary for us to find a new outlet soon, or we will be starving each other to death!'

* *

'When all the chips are down you may say we have two strings to our bow – the mere trading; and our various other non-trading business activities. In the latter I suppose I should also include a great deal of work we do as Agents for landed property on the island, and as General Trustees.

'At present the trading side is perhaps the slightly more profitable, but not significantly so; and one may well foresee a time when our non-trading activities may take the lead.

'By the same token, whether we succeed in getting our feet into the Peninsula or not, you may be fairly sure that we will manage to survive somehow.

'Thus you now have some idea how it comes about that our partners dare look forward to rather pleasant houses in Britain on their retirement, where they may see their children grow up in some comfort, while the old people nurse their enlarged livers and spleens for their few remaining years!

'We work hard enough for those few last years, heaven knows; and as Britain is a nation of traders, I hope we may be remembered as people who have helped our own country as well as ourselves.

'If we can bring law and order to the Native States in addition, then indeed I shall feel that we have set South-east Asia on its feet and have nothing to be ashamed of.

'There is a new Club just opened out in the country at a place called Tung-Lien, meaning in Chinese, 'Eastern Wood'; and I had hoped you would take luncheon with me there. But it is a long drive in the buggy on this hot day, so come with me to the Singapore Club.'

BOOK THREE

BREAKTHROUGH

CHAPTER I

APRIL FOOLS' DAY 1867

At mid-day on the 1st of April 1867, Colonel Harry St George Ord, CB, of the Royal Engineers, mounted the dais in the new Town Hall of Singapore as the first Colonial Governor of the Straits Settlements.

His Official Reception had been joyfully prepared by a thoroughly well disposed community.

It would be tempting to pause here and rejoice in the booming guns and fluttering bunting; and to mingle for a while with the happy crowds of all races, who stood so patiently for hours to await the coming of that wonderful being, the first of such species they had ever seen, the Queen's Governor.

At the forefront of the leading residents waiting to welcome that great man stood Thomas Scott, now the senior 'Singapore' partner of Guthries', with his tall hat removed and in his dark frock-coat, taking his honourable place among the four first non-official members of the new Legislative Council. He had been made a member of 'the Government of the Straits Settlements', in fitting recognition of the immense work the two Guthries, Greenshields and himself had shouldered over the years to bring this memorable day about.

But to dally here would lead this story through such a tangle of ill-feeling between Ord and the merchant community of Singapore, that it is painful to look back upon it even today.

Dismay had broken out from the first moment of Ord's arrival, when he unsmilingly ignored the greetings of his welcoming Councillors and the curtsies of their ladies. This was the first painful shock of unmerited rebuke, one that drew strength from every crushing word and hurtful attitude of his from that time forth; and which only ended six and a half years later with his unlamented departure in the autumn of 1873.

Sir Harry Ord, as he shortly became, was a man of most

unfortunate temperament; tyrannical, overbearing, quarrelsome and tactless, with an enormous opinion of his own importance. He lacked independence of mind and was totally reliant for his livelihood upon the good esteem of the Colonial Office.

Yet in his defence some few words must be said. First and foremost, the various Secretaries of State during his period as Governor – the Duke of Buckingham and Chandos, the Earl of Granville, and finally the Earl of Kimberley – had all firmly expressed the policy of the Colonial Office that there must be 'no intervention in the Native States'.

Secondly, in spite of this, he did at times visit the various Rulers and attempt somewhat feebly to intervene on one side or other in their endless disputes, though on these occasions, 'while sacrificing the impartiality which might have allowed him to arbitrate, he lacked the force to make his intervention a success'.

Thirdly, having found the Straits Settlements in a sorry financial position in 1867, he left it in a very prosperous condition indeed in 1873.

And finally, the merchant community hoped for too much altogether from the new administration. Their disappointment over the years almost certainly lacked full justification, though it was very understandable.

True though these mitigating facts are, it must nevertheless be admitted that Sir Harry Ord's term as Governor was an unhappy failure. It was doubly unfortunate, too, that this should be the first instalment of Colonial administration to be experienced by Singapore.

It is, therefore, a pleasure to move away from that ill-starred April fools' day to an afternoon six and a half years later, at the end of October 1873, when an outcome of these tribulations was already in sight, and when the good ship *Donnai* of the Messageries Maritimes was about to bear away the late Governor Harry Ord to spheres in which the citizens of Singapore need no longer trouble him, nor he them.

* * *

The month of October 1873 marked both the end and the beginning of two distinct periods in the chronicle of Guthries'.

It was at this point that death claimed one of the great architects of the firm, who had done so much for it, as well as for Singapore, in time past. He was one whose personal history has so far had little mention in this story – John James Greenshields, who died alone like some sick animal in its lair, in circumstances which will be touched upon in their place.

Greenshields is one of the six great men who stand out in this history – Alexander Guthrie, James Guthrie, John Greenshields, Thomas Scott and two more yet to be encountered. Of them all, it was the brilliant but truncated career of Greenshields that alone would seem to have fallen short of its deserved fulfilment.

It was in that same year of 1873 too, that the Straits Settlements Government was to be found in one of its recurrent conditions of crisis.

The animosity between Sir Harry Ord and the Legislative Council had reached bursting point; and the non-officials had resigned en bloc in a concerted act of protest which was to be the final episode of Ord's unhappy term as Governor.

The longed-for breakthrough of the Straits administration onto the mainland of Malaya – the much delayed assistance to commercial interests and the creation of business links between the Singapore 'Agency Houses' and the Native States, which had been one of the main reasons for the Transfer in the first place – was brought a long stride nearer by the action of Thomas Scott and his fellow members in resigning from the Council. It put the final seal of dissatisfaction upon Ord's regime and ensured that his departure on leave would this time be final.

Their resignation was brought on by what Scott described as 'political rough riding' on Ord's part over a question in which it would not have hurt him to give way – an amendment to legal procedure by the abolition of the Grand Jury, which might well have been left for the passage of time to achieve without heart-burning. Ord, however, the touchy autocrat, chafing under any form of control by Council and with an almost pathological contempt for the 'box-wallahs' of commerce, was deaf to reason and dashed what remained of his reputation to destruction. But that was merely the final incident in a long and bitter quarrel – the spark that detonated the explosion.

The underlying causes were graver and more deep rooted. Not only did Colonel Ord seem to dislike the entire European business community of Singapore, but he seems also to have done all he could to damage their activities and hamper their progress.

This attitude had already caused a division of opinion among the businessmen of Singapore. All were unanimous in opposing the Governor's efforts to institute port duties – heresy according to the merchants and an insult to the memory of Raffles. All objected to his attempts to override the voice of his Legislative Council, for which he had even drawn down upon himself the distant thunder of the Home authorities. And all combined to denounce Sir Harry's extravagant expenditure on a vast Government House for himself and a new steam yacht.

But in 1870, when matters came to their first intense crunch shortly before the Governor returned to Britain on his first and only furlough – and when, at a public meeting called by the dashing Billy Read, of A. L. Johnston, a petition to the Secretary of State was proposed underlining Ord's total *unsuitability* – the more level-headed and forbearing members, including Thomas Scott, refused to have anything to do with it; and they remained of that view in a praiseworthy effort to settle matters domestically until the final collision in 1873.

This division of opinion among the businessmen of Singapore was to be reflected in the emergence of two separate commercial groups, with differing political affiliations, when it came to that vital matter of entry into the Malay States.

* * *

Nevertheless – whatever the provocation may have been – it is safe to say that on Ord's final departure in 1873, Thomas Scott and his group had no part in such letters to the papers as: 'The wives of some officials are said not to disdain diamond rings offered by enlightened Malay Rajahs. One hears of slabs of tin and elephants' tusks being judiciously presented by Native Chiefs with an eye to maintaining cordial relations with what are called "The Authorities"; and when Oriental generosity had become torpid it has been stimulated into action by timely reminders.'

They would have deplored – even though there may have

been substance in it – such an open letter as appeared in the *Singapore Daily Times* in regard to the departing Governor Ord and his Clerk of Councils Mr Plow as: 'Are shares likely to go up in the various mining companies of Singapore when such a valuable sample of "ore" left the Colony yesterday? It was thought a large portion of it was gold and diamonds. The ore must have been highly magnetised to draw with it an agricultural implement famed for its crushing and turning up qualities!'

Something indeed must have been very wrong with the morale of the Colony when the *Singapore Daily Times*, in its leading article on Monday 3rd November 1873, could say: 'Governor Ord has left us, and his departure is felt to be a relief to the Colony. Few indeed are the friends he has left behind him – and those few can hardly be called sincere ones . . . every misadventure and collision can be traced to the disposition first displayed and pertinaciously persisted in; personal aggrandisement at any sacrifice, and political rough riding were his ambition and delight . . .'; or when a poem was published in the same newspaper 'To Sir Harry St George Ord, CB' beginning with the words 'Unhappy Governor!' and concluding with the lines

> And now you leave us – would you have us mourn?
> Should we, to keep you, some bad reason find?
> Can we forget you've treated us with scorn?
> Or to your faults remain forever blind?
> Misguided man! You've courted your own fate!
> We offered you our love. You chose our hate!

Fundamentally, Ord's great failure, so far as the Singapore merchants were concerned, was that, under him, his administration remained at best indifferent (and at worst openly antagonistic) to their entry into any sort of trade on the Malayan Peninsula.

'If merchants', stated an official utterance from the Government in the time of Ord, 'knowing the risks they run, choose to hazard their lives and properties for the sake of the large profits which accompany successful trading, they must not expect the British Government to be answerable if their speculation proves unsuccessful'.

That official statement shows the Governor's attitude to the merchants, whilst making it clear that he knew the affairs on the Peninsula to be in a dangerous mess.

The position in all the Malay States, from north to south, was in fact desperate; and any prudent Governor would have been well advised to take a serious interest in it for the safety of his own territories.

Inland, from Siam to the Straits of Johore, bloodshed and terror were widespread, in a disordered tangle of jungly and ill-defined States, where 'All classes and nationalities are in arms, fighting for different causes or different leaders. Neither life nor property have any safeguard, except the owners' strength and will to defend them. Robbery, or murder, or any other crime meets with neither inquiry nor punishment. Peace and order will not be restored by any voice from *inside* the disturbed regions, and the wisest counsels, unsupported by *power* to enforce them, will be given in vain.'

In order to make it possible to achieve the restoration of peace in the Malay Peninsula, a very important move had reluctantly been made in London no more than fourteen months after Sir Harry Ord's arrival in Singapore. This was inspired by no less a person than the firm's senior partner, Mr James Guthrie, in mid-1868 – by which time news of the Governor's disturbing conduct had begun to reach him from Greenshields and Scott in a growing crescendo.

* * *

From the very first meeting of the Singapore Legislative Council onwards, it had become clear that Ord was one of those who seek advice from all, but take from none.

No detail of administration was too small for him to bedevil it with a volume of new Standing Orders and inapplicable instructions. No question before the Council was too petty for him to deliver ex-parte judgement upon before members had had an opportunity to express their opinions. Nothing seemed to please him more than to pick upon one of the previous grievances of the Singapore community which had resulted in the Transfer – such as the desire, for instance, to be responsible for the Settlements' legislation – to appear to agree with that grievance – and then to proceed to answer it in such a sickening overflow of excess as to bewilder the proposers and render the motion a savage mockery.

As the *Singapore Daily Times* was to remark, in referring to this point: 'We doubt whether, if the citizens had had any idea of the *avalanche* of ordinances which has descended upon their unfortunate heads during the last six years, they would have been quite so keen for the Transfer – at least ... without some guarantee that their wishes would not be quite ignored ...'

In this situation, James Guthrie had once more called upon his old companion in battle, the ancient Surgeon John Crawfurd, first Resident of Singapore; and together they soon co-opted the support of that same Mr Horsman, MP who had proved such a valuable ally in the Parliamentary debates leading to the Transfer. The result was that, after several meetings in the London houses of one or other of these notable personalities, a body was brought into being named the 'Straits Settlements Association' to take such action as might seem best. Greatly as it must have gone against the grain to set up an organisation so suspicious of the Governor's intentions, the need was pressing and, as always, men were not lacking when it came to the vital hour.

Surgeon John Crawfurd was unanimously elected President of the new Association, Mr Horsman, MP, Vice-President; and as additional Vice-Presidents, James Guthrie was appointed the London representative for Singapore and Greenshields the spokesman of the Association in Singapore itself.

The final stage was reached on the 26th of September 1873, when, by the new submarine cable to the Far East, which had been at last completed after many difficulties in 1871, the following telegram reached the London office of the Straits Settlements Association: 'Notwithstanding unanimous protests of non-officials on 9th September and strongest opinion of public meeting on 15th against abolition Grand Jury under new Criminal Procedure Act of 9th September, Governor precipitately enforcing Act, for Sessions 10th October. Ignoring appeal Home. Great discontent. Ask Secretary of State suspend action pending reference Home.'

The Chairman of the Straits Settlements Association sent this immediately to Lord Kimberley, Secretary of State for the Colonies, with the words 'I have no doubt that in view of the strong expression of opinion against the measures in question, Your Lordship will do what is in your power to meet the wishes of the Singapore community on the subject.'

On the 1st of October a further cable reached the London office: 'Unofficials except Whampoa at Council last Monday unanimously resigned, consequent on Governor's arbitrary conduct re Grand Jury.'

This too was forwarded by the Chairman to Lord Kimberley in a note of the same date, saying 'I am sorry not to be in a position to give any additional information on this question for Your Lordship's guidance, but the conclusion is forced upon me that there must be something beyond and behind the mere abolition of the Grand Jury to create the very strong feeling under which it is abundantly evident these messages have been despatched; the more, from the fact that the resignation of non-official members of Council must include gentlemen who have been steady supporters of Governor Ord during the whole tenure of office. The circumstances may present difficulties to immediate solution; but I would fain hope that a course may be open to Your Lordship to prevent the prolongation in the Settlement of the grave position which is now submitted to your Lordship's consideration.'

Sir Harry Ord's term of office as Governor of the Straits Settlements was over.

* * *

The stage was now at last set, six and a half years after the Transfer from the Indian Government, for Britain to move forward into the Peninsula of Malaya. Though this was first and foremost a measure of self-interest, it was additionally necessary, being the only means of affording security of life and property to thousands of helpless people in urgent need of protection.

Before tracing the course of Britain's entry into the Native States, a point of some interest should be mentioned. This concerns the ethics of the British Empire's colonial expansion during the nineteenth century, upon which there are two divergent views.

One body of opinion holds that immediately before every case in which Britain advanced into a fresh field of colonial riches, some quite accidental event occurred which positively forced that country, against its will, to absorb yet a further burdensome but ultimately most profitable responsibility. The other is persuaded that the whole thing was a deep-laid plot, engineered with diabolical cunning by a witches' coven of nineteenth century boffins, huddled by candlelight with maps and plans over a Downing Street dining table.

Both views are, of course, quite false. The truth is that Britain's increasing dominion over the dark places of the earth during the last century was spurred neither by idealism, of which it is only capable by fits and starts (and then almost always at the wrong time and place) nor by subtle and well planned cunning, which is, and always has been, utterly beyond it.

The initial impetus will generally be found to have stemmed purely and simply from the efforts of dogged British businessmen – frequently dour and bearded Scotsmen with faces like Aberdeen terriers – who have seen an opportunity to sell or buy something and have then proceeded unemotionally to complete and fulfil the contract. If there is a lot of shelling going on, if the village is on fire, law and order abandoned or a despot on the rampage, 'Well, that is just a pity; and we shall have to add a wee bit to the cost c.i.f. to cover the overheads.'

To take the case in point, it has been aptly remarked that before the 'Transfer' and subsequent intervention, 'Malaya, as we know it, did not exist. It remained for the British to invent it.' To this it may justly be added that whilst the 'invention' was inspired and brought about in the first place by British businessmen in the interests of commerce, the country of Malaya, 'as we know it', was designed and built by generations of devoted British administrators, who willingly gave their whole active lives to its construction, for little reward other than the satisfaction of work well done; and who were imbued from the first days of their service with the orders of Queen Victoria to Disraeli 'to bring on the peoples of these countries to the stage where they can govern themselves'.

* * *

Before the Government took action in 1874, the various 'Native States', as they were then called, largely consisted of dispersed village communities that were either the remnants of the ancient incursions of Javanese or Sumatrans into a virtually empty land, or much more recent arrivals of Bugis traders deprived of their maritime carrying trade in the eighteenth century by the arrival of the Dutch.

When Stamford Raffles founded Singapore, the northern States of Kedah, Kelantan and Trengganu were tributaries of Siam (and remained so until the twentieth century).

Perak, the western central portion of the peninsula, comprised a string of villages beside the river of that name. It had been inhabited for many centuries by a sparse but indigenous Malay population.

Johore claimed all the rest except for the small triangle of Malacca, which had been populated by a Malay race from Palembang in Sumatra, who had built a stronghold on the island of Tumasik (Singapore) in the ninth century, but had been overrun by the Javanese in the fourteenth century, compelling them to flee to a river mouth where they had built the stockaded village of Malacca, eventually captured from them by the Portuguese in 1511.

But Johore, as such, was in fact unopened jungle except for a small southern portion opposite Singapore. Bugis and Sumatran traders had therefore made themselves at home about the year 1700 in and behind the five estuaries along its north-western seaboard between Malacca and Perak, now known as Selangor. Most of its east coast up to Siamese Trengganu had been claimed, as from much the same date, by a Chief at the mouth of a river flowing into the China Sea which drained a large ill-defined area known as Pahang.

At the time of Raffles, the Chiefs and their many sons and relatives lived well in their large palm-thatched houses on stilts. Their lives were usually short but eventful, controlling bands of servants; taxing river traffic; intriguing, laughing, playing games of chance and romancing; fighting with the adjoining Chief, or amongst themselves on the least provocation.

Their people – the 'Ryot' – exercised their simple and admirable philosophy of keeping themselves alive with as little trouble as possible. They grew a little fruit and caught fish, whilst their womenfolk planted rice. The growing strength of their Islamic faith, steadily overcoming their primitive animism, shielded them from the worst horrors of ever present sorcery and witchcraft.

Travel, except for short distances up and down the river, was unthinkable for the Ryot due to the expense of boatmen and supplies, the usual enmity of neighbours, the permission first to be had from the Chief (unobtainable except for important reasons of State), and the dark wall of surrounding, tiger-haunted jungle.

Each village, therefore, lived in a separate world of its own, hemmed in by the dangers of nature and by the animosity of neighbouring hamlets. Each villager also was perpetually bound from birth to death to serve one or other of the Chief's family by payment of goods in kind and service in war. Large numbers were bound by stricter laws of servitude, of which there were two kinds – one being the servitude imposed upon all who were not of the Islamic faith (captured jungle tribesmen, imported negroes etc) and the other being a device known as 'debt slavery', whereby they were made the chattels of the Chief or his relations in recompense for debts they or their ancestors had incurred. Both these forms of servitude were hereditary; and the life of any one of them could be forfeited without reason at the whim of an unjust master.

In spite of this – and no doubt also because in their scattered rice-fields they could often long evade their Chief's spasmodic and unpredictable authority – they remained on the whole a forbearing, kindly and philosophical folk. For so men must live – and so men had from time immemorial.

From high to low their outstanding characteristics were personal pride, self-respect, a realisation of their dignity as human beings; a genuine courtesy without trace of subservience; physical courage; and an acute and sardonic sense of humour. They were fatalists with little intellectual enthusiasm; a people who could be led to do anything but could never be driven.

These attributes resulted in a tendency to say what was pleasing rather than unpleasant. They would tell their interrogator what they imagined he wanted to hear. To do otherwise would cause him pain and would therefore be rude. It would thus lower them in his estimation, which would be a situation not to be endured.

To their friends they were loyal to the death – whilst they remained their friends. But as their allegiance was given without any regard to the rights or wrongs of a particular cause – which were abstractions as vague as truth – they frequently found their friendship betrayed or their dignity impugned by some real or supposed slight, which would lead at once to an embittered enmity.

In addition to their undoubted vanity and bravado they were a race of much dignity of feature, particularly when old; and when young, with their large eyes and cherubic countenances, were often of great physical charm.

The Malay and Bugis races of the peninsula were, in short, an almost ideally preserved mediaeval people, whose personal standards and way of life were probably far in advance of anything the West could show at a similar stage of development. They were undoubtedly cleaner, kinder, quicker and certainly better looking.

Chinese prospectors and tin miners had worked in the forests in small numbers for many hundreds of years, and were no strangers. Most of the tin, however, was mined by the Malays, who brought it to the estuaries for collection by the Portuguese and later by the Dutch – over 340 tons weight of it being annually exported to Europe from Malacca by the middle of the seventeenth century. The Malays had little contact with the Chinese, and still less with the Dutch or Portuguese.

Things went on as they always had. Then suddenly the West was upon them. First Penang and then Singapore, to both of which the Chinese swarmed.

Finally, in 1848, a large deposit of alluvial tin was found in the Perak Districts of Larut and Matang. Two warring armies of Chinese miners poured in to exploit these riches. Pandora's box was opened.

When the following pages tell of the events that thereafter overtook the Native States from north to south and from east to west – the intrigue and avarice, the weakness and falsehood, the disorder and bloodshed – the British people would be wrong to preen themselves upon any pretended superiority. They should remember what their ancestors underwent at the same stage in their country's evolution. They should above all read the history of the Highland clans of Scotland, which the Malays in many ways resemble.

A country's development is similar to the growth to maturity of a human being, with the childish sicknesses it must suffer; the growing pains; the difficulty of learning; the rebellion of spirit before it submits itself to the hard yoke of discipline. Two thousand years have gone by since Europe was first colonised and underwent the awakening rod of

Rome – and the Romans were, after all, a people of similar 'Caucasian' stock to those they conquered and colonised.

In a twentieth of that time – one hundred years only – a totally alien modern world with all its virtues and vices, its unsolved problems and its immense panorama of the future, had fallen upon the Malay race like a crushing cataract.

There is no time in this fast moving world to shield the less advanced races till they can grow naturally. This is the way development has to happen. The muddled, mediaeval childhood is over and the results will in time be good. But it was a harsh awakening.

CHAPTER 2

WATSON AND GLASS

Up to 1873 it is still possible to list the total range of Guthries' senior personnel. But already, amongst those whose names appear in the firm's records, are some whose history has faded to shadow as unrevealing as an ancient photograph.

These lived; they left their distant homes to seek adventure, riches or fame in the mellow sunlight and green heat of a dangerous, fever-ridden, equatorial land.

Freed in the evenings from their labours in offices cooled by the slowly moving punkahs of those days, or from dark godowns reeking of cordage, cloth and aromatic oils, they filled their lives as full as men do now with laughter and love; with greed; with sports and fun; with hopes and ambitions and folly and friendship.

Their movements, no less than those of men today, made an impress on the world around them – yet in so short a time as the span of one life, in that fast growing, fast dying, fast forgetting land, the small mark they made upon matter or humanity has been washed away as by a tropic storm of rain. Their story has become smothered in the all-pervading jungle lushness of the East. It is not even known where they were buried.

Take James Watson, for instance. His figure emerges in the yellowed pages of a copy of the *Singapore Directory* for 1863 as 'Partner of Messrs Guthrie and Company'; living, as it states, at 'Tanjong Paggar' Road, a highly respectable area. Working back through mounds of old paper, it is satisfactory to find his name ten years before that time (in 1853, the same year that poor Suzanna Guthrie died) coupled with young Thomas Scott, then aged twenty-one, in the team of the first full eleven-a-side game of cricket ever played in Singapore. He, too, must have been young then, perhaps no older than Scott, with the future unrolling endlessly before him in eternal sunshine, as it seems to do when we are young.

And then another glimpse of him is caught as a man of consequence in Singapore and a Justice of the Peace, attending a public meeting at the Town Hall convened to discuss the financial implications of the forthcoming Transfer – a meeting at which he and his partner Tom Scott are momentarily seen together with one James Guthrie Davidson, of whom there will be further mention later. After that – nothing. The next surviving *Directory*, dated 1873, makes no mention of his name. What happened? Was he married? Did he have children? Did he die in the meantime? One does not know.

The white ants and the worms have digested his history. The graveyards have been built over by new concrete offices; and if any records of his life survived the years, they were burnt and scattered and blew aimlessly away down the dim streets emptied under a rain of modern bombs.

One Louis John Robertson Glass is an almost identical case. Beyond a drawing of a handsome young man with a heavy moustache, record of his treasurership of the Fives Club, of his accepting a partnership in the firm of Guthrie and Company on 7th August 1874, and the birth of his daughter Dorothy Elspeth in 1887, the chase peters out in 1905 in a somewhat acrimonious mention of his name in connection with £500 sterling accepted by him 'in full satisfaction'.

But history must be confined to the great figures; leaving the lives of others to be guessed.

* * *

James Guthrie had withdrawn, as has been told, from the active scene of Singapore in 1856, when he bade farewell to Singapore on the quayside at the P & O Company's wharf in the new harbour, on the day that much saddened man left for home with his two small daughters and son.

But time heals wounds – or at any rate accommodates men to them – and in the busy life with his uncle in London he was once more soon able to face the world and even to make repeated trips back and forth to the East on one important affair or another.

Though he fades into the background of this history, it should not be forgotten that until the end of the century, either in the London office or in his large private home at Tunbridge Wells, he remained a power for good, an elder statesman in far eastern commerce and the 'éminence grise' behind many of the Company's decisions.

Also, in the fullness of time, he married again – this time a Mrs Sophia Cumming James (née Fraser), a widow, who took his children into her warm care – she had none of her own – and survived James Guthrie's death in 1900 by many years.

* * *

Next in chronological order stands John James Greenshields, who first arrived in Singapore by sailing ship as an energetic man of twenty in 1845.

John James Greenshields had the world at his feet as a young man. Of brilliant mentality, tall, handsome and universally popular, there would seem to have been every reason why he should succeed to the highest position in the firm and none why he should not.

A partnership in the large Agency House of Guthrie and Company at the age of twenty-four – three and a half years after his arrival out East – would seem a very fine beginning, as indeed it was; and, from then on, the course of his public life and of his work to enhance the great name of his firm should have assured his place, at least as senior partner in Singapore (and no doubt other well deserved honours too) as the years rolled by.

He flourished in his private, as well as his public, life. His name appeared regularly in the local press, as an Elder of the Presbyterian Church of St Andrew in Singapore and an office bearer in the Masonic Lodge. He is remembered as having performed an important masonic ceremony at the official laying of the foundation stone of the famous Horsburgh Lighthouse off the eastern entrance of the Singapore Strait; an event which took place in 1849, the same year in which he became a partner of Guthrie and Company.

He married Margaret, the sister of Thomas Scott and sister-in-law of James Guthrie, at home on leave in Scotland in 1855, and was a member of the Grand Jury of Singapore in 1856, in which year his first child, a daughter, was born.

His was a life, in short, filled with committee work and

meetings on every aspect of the government of the Settlement. Apart from his business undertakings, he busied himself with questions ranging from the freedom of the Press, the convicts, the currency and the law to such details as the conduct of the public library, the Raffles Institute and the fives courts – a busy and fulfilling life in office as well as out; whilst the children of his successful marriage came into the world in steady and pleasing succession.

The first daughter was born in 1856, as already mentioned, a son in 1858 whilst he was busy fighting the Indian authorities in the matter of their use of Singapore as a dump for convicts, a daughter in 1859 when he was leading the Currency Commission and a son in 1861, one year after he was first elevated to the high official post of Foreman of the Court of Criminal Sessions.

Then a blow; grave – not so mortal as to spell certain disaster to a man of Greenshields's philosophy and courage – but perhaps the turning point of his luck. It was the first sign of ebb in the tide of his fortune.

It happened in 1863; he and his family were home in England on leave, staying at their house at Number 15 Canning Street, Liverpool. Margaret was having yet another baby. Their friends out East had hardly had time to rejoice at the news in the *Singapore Free Press* of the 1st February 1864 that she had had a daughter on the 12th of December, when their happiness was dashed by reading in the edition of 14th February that Mrs Greenshields had died on December the 24th.

In that same year, 1864, John Greenshields returned to his work in Singapore. He would appear to have borne his loss well and to be engaged once more in his successful and rewarding career.

He became interested in the new Singapore Gas Company, which began its services to the public in mid-year, and attended a dinner given by 'Whampoa' (the well known 'Towkay' Ho Ah Kay) in his palatial mansion, to show off his fine gas-lit chandeliers, while passers-by gingerly touched the lamp-posts at the gateway and marvelled that they could give so bright a flame 'yet were not hot'. He assisted in forming the Singapore Railway Company; accepted a directorship in the Eastern Telegraph Company; and became a Vice-President of the Straits Settlements Association, as already mentioned. Outwardly it would seem that by 1870 he had recovered his spirits; and that nothing could now go wrong with such a life.

Suddenly he left Guthries' and that beautiful great house on Cairn Hill, with its pillared portico and shady varingin trees, that James Guthrie had bought for him from old Mr Cairnie several years before.

He lodged now at some obscure address in a downtown area known as Edinburgh Road, and hired a godown in the name of 'Greenshields, Ledward and Co' and advertising himself as the agent for the Lancashire Insurance Company.

What had happened? Evidently nothing discreditable, for in 1870 his name was included for the first time as a member of the Singapore Legislative Council. But the sands in John Greenshields's hourglass were running low. All that remains of his life is soon told. In 1873 he appears in the passenger list of the P & O steamer *Travancore* bound for Venice – and a record in Somerset House dated 29th October of that year simply states: 'John James Greenshields, male, aged 48, merchant, died of hepatitis, (chronic), cardiac disease, (mitral), exhaustion, at 42 Sefton Terrace, Princess Road, Liverpool.' A certain Mary Appleyard appears to have been present at his death; and that is all.

The firm of Guthries' was very much a family concern; and this history will have gone far astray in its delineation of that firm's central core if it does not show how close-knit that family connection at all times was.

Greenshields, granted a Scot though born and bred in Liverpool, was nevertheless a stranger; he did not belong to the family.

Greenshields was seven years older than Thomas Scott, six years senior to him in joining the firm, eight years senior in becoming a partner and fourteen years before him in marrying and settling down. John Greenshields's marriage, moreover, to Margaret Scott, James Guthrie's own sister-in-law and Tom Scott's sister, might be thought to have been a sufficiently strong tie to bring him into the family.

Nevertheless, in the year 1867 it was Thomas Scott, not Greenshields, who was chosen as a member of the Legislative Council. By that time it was very definitely the former, not Greenshields, who was the senior partner.

In considering why this should have been so, the jaunty character of little Tom Scott, his personal charm, to say nothing of his independence of mind and action, should not

James Watson

Louis J. R. Glass

Alexander Johnston

Thomas Scott

be overlooked. But the fact remains that, in the last resort, it was surely James Guthrie's recollection of Thomas Scott's kindness to Suzanna and her fondness of 'her favourite brother'; the memory of his wife in every word he uttered and in his every gesture, from the moment he had first cast eyes upon that mop-headed youngster at Balwyllo all those years ago, that assured Tom a permanent place in the inner circle of James Guthrie's affections – and equally made it a foregone conclusion that in time he would inherit the leading position in the firm.

Greenshields swallowed this bitter pill, with some distress it may be supposed, more especially as the first ascendancy of Scott to a leading position over him began shortly after Margaret Greenshields died, when he was struggling against depression, certainly not at his best in spite of his many activities, and in no mood to recapture his command by an immediate assumption of authority.

The end came in 1870. Greenshields, bearing the brunt of the work and responsibility, writing late at night at home, when a lonely man often takes just that one more whisky than he should, suddenly received news of the impending arrival of yet another family connection which would remove the firm still further from his grasp. Alexander Guthrie, James Guthrie's only son, now aged twenty, was on his way out East to join the Company and would be arriving by the next steamer.

That was it. He resigned; and like so many others, before and since, tried to start again – a dangerous experiment for an unwell and prematurely ageing man.

Such then, is the history of Greenshields – to which might be added the ironical footnote that if he had possessed prophetic powers, or had had sufficient health and determination to stick it out, he would have had his wish in the end.

Thomas Scott, too, spent an increasing amount of time in England, prior to his becoming a London partner as from 1875, so Greenshields would have had it all his own way in Singapore. But he did not.

Young Alexander Guthrie had done well at Cambridge but seems to have been a trifle lost among his business compatriots in Singapore. He presents a vision of a rather lonely young man, given to solitary walks and bathes – an element of not unattractive 'unclubability' which culminated eight years later in a bathing tragedy, resulting in his sickness and death.

* * *

The story now, therefore, turns once more to that cheerful character, Thomas Scott. In spite of his later ascendancy over Greenshields, he must take his place after him in this chronicle, as the fourth of the six great figures with which it deals.

Much of his early history has already been told.

To pick up the threads of his personal life, he is discovered in 1860, strolling the decks of a P & O paddle-boat, as she heels to the south-east monsoon under the press of canvas normal to a steam-assisted brig; booming along northward up the Malacca Strait on the first leg of her voyage home, with wet decks shining in the sun and lee paddle-box awash.

Tom is off home on his first leave after nine years in Singapore; goodbyes said to old John Greenshields, who took time from his work on the Court of Criminal Sessions to see him off – aged twenty-eight, and the junior partner of the firm of Guthries' for the last three years.

Among the first class passengers is a charming family – the McNairs – consisting of a young Captain John Frederick Adolphus McNair of the Royal Madras Engineers, qualified geologist and surveyor, with brevet rank of Major in virtue of his post of Adjutant of Artillery, Singapore; together with his attractive wife Sarah and three small children.

The story of Scott can scarcely be told without dwelling at some length on the McNairs.

Adolphus McNair was a 'winner' – and he was one of those rare souls who, though attracted by women and attractive to them, remained universally popular with men. A sort of D'Artagnan; dark-haired, handsome and brilliantly alive – his friendly smile softening the endless jokes and lightning repartee that were his delight – he endeared himself to all wherever he might be; including, when he had been little more than a boy – a mere Ensign in the Indian Army just out from home – no less than one John Payne, a merchant of Madras, and his French wife née Desgranges. At an absurdly young age he had succeeded in carrying off their beautiful daughter Sarah – and here the McNairs were, after two years in Malacca on transfer from India and four years in Labuan and Singapore, on their way home on furlough, with their nine-year-old Elizabeth and little Grace and Arthur.

Elizabeth, as one might well imagine with such parents, was not only a positive picture, but was capable of setting her cap, in the innocently wicked way some girl children do, in no mean measure at the good-hearted affectionate Tom Scott – and in the sight of them both careering round the deck at hide-and-seek like two children, or taking turns in the swing rigged by the bo'sun, the mind's eye already glimpses the first outline of the thing – that very excellent thing – that was in all due time to come into both their lives.

The McNairs passed most of their leave in London, where Adolphus, with his usual enthusiasm, was throwing himself into learning the technique of that wonderful new art, photography; at which, incidentally, he later became so great an amateur that on return to Singapore he was inundated by demands from the leading families – to which he always good-naturedly acceded – for 'portraits'.

Whether Tom Scott joined them in London is not known; but it is evident that a fast friendship was formed aboard ship on that happy homeward voyage that was to stand the test of time, and to culminate nine years later, in 1869, in Tom's marrying the seventeen-year-old beauty Elizabeth McNair.

To complete the pleasant tale of Tom Scott's domestic history – which was in fact one of almost unclouded sunshine until sickness dimmed it a trifle late in life – it should be added that he had a son, Robert Frederick McNair, born the year after his marriage, a daughter Lilian born one year thereafter and a third child, Amy, born in 1873.

Three years before Scott died in 1902 at the age of seventy-one, an honoured and much loved father and husband, in his fine house of Auchenreoch near Edzell in Scotland, his son Robert married Alice Nystrom of Sweden, to found the family of McNair Scott.

CHAPTER 3

THE SECRET SOCIETIES

Just as it would be impossible to tell the story of Guthries' without sketching in the historical background, so is it equally necessary to illuminate that back-drop in the light of its own true, if often harsh, colours.

It seems strange today to realise that less than a hundred years ago the inhabitants of the Straits Settlements were not only faced by those great killers, malaria, dysentery and cholera, one or more of which they were certain to suffer from sooner or later, but also that they (the Chinese particularly) were beset by the very real danger of death at the hands of murderous gangs of Chinese 'secret society' members on land; and that all sections of the population sailed in constant preparedness against Malay, Illanun or Bugis pirates when at sea.

It is by touching on these two great hazards to life and property – piracy and the 'societies' – that two of this history's main characters are now set into their surroundings.

* * *

John Greenshields was a friend and admirer of that admirable person Thomas Dunman, ten years his senior and already translated from his office desk in Messrs Martin Dyce and Company to that of Superintendent of Police and Magistrate two years before Greenshields's arrival in Singapore.

As time went on and the voice of Greenshields in public meetings and the Chamber of Commerce became heard in the land with ever increasing force and frequency, it was of the Chinese 'secret societies' in their midst – together with the pressing need to strengthen Dunman's Police Force and so bring these associations to heel – that he often spoke with the greatest eloquence and urgency.

The 'Tien-Ti-Hui', or, as it is named in English, the 'Triad Society', is of ancient origin. Of its peaceful existence as a secret guild or cult in China from the earliest ages there is little doubt; but it rose to great prominence as the 'Hung League' in the seventeenth century, as a political and subversive weapon – a 'fifth column', in support of the surviving 'Ming' heir to the Dragon Throne in deadly antagonism to the usurping 'Manchu' dynasty of the Chings, who had seized the reins of government in Peking in 1644.

From that time on it ceased, in China, to be a mere guild or benevolent association and became an underground fighting army.

Chinese immigrants brought the Triad cult with them to Singapore. There, in the absence of any political reason for its activities, it soon became an organisation in the first place for the support and assistance of the Chinese community as a whole against all comers, right or wrong; and secondly as a most powerful force to stir up intrigues and the warlike spirit of the Chinese tribes and sub-clans one against the other. It was in that respect that the Triad cult's presence in the Straits Settlements became chiefly objectionable.

Virtually from the moment of its arrival in Singapore the Tien-Ti-Hui had broken down into separate 'Hoeys' or secret societies, representing the four main tribes of immigrant Chinese – the Amoy (or Hokkien), the Kheh, the Teochu and the Macao (or Cantonese) – and these Hoeys reflected the animosities of the clans; murdering each other's members; holding trials in secret cabal at night; inflicting punishments on backsliders or on those of opposing Hoeys caught extorting protection money from shopkeepers within their own territory; and holding the Chinese population in subjection from their strongholds in the nearby jungle.

In 1831 there was known to be an armed force of over one thousand of these part time desperadoes within three miles of the centre of Singapore; and it seems to have been beyond the combined power of the police and the military to suppress them.

By 1841 their membership had grown to more than six thousand, with midnight meetings brazenly held under protection of their own armed guards in a temple no further away than the outskirts of Kampong Glam, which was already part of Singapore town itself. By now they had organised themselves into a central council of four officers, each representing one of the Hoeys. 'The refuse of the population of China', as they were at that time described, they issued orders and carried out grim sentences; burning off victims' fingers or hands whilst still alive; garrotting; breaking the necks of offenders and disembowelling the more serious cases, the latter to suffer the additional affliction of five deep claw-like incisions in the back (which may later have lead Governor Cavenagh to believe that the numerous corpses discovered in the jungle had been killed by tigers).

In 1849 the *Singapore Free Press* reported that the police were 'unable to compose the differences existing between the Chinese Societies in Singapore', and praised a brave Chinese merchant, Mr Cheah Eu Chin (ancestor of many leading Malayan Chinese families today) who had had the courage to try to settle their arguments by arbitration – for which fine though unavailing deed he was made a Justice of the Peace.

By 1850 there were not less than twenty thousand Triad members in the island of Singapore alone; and in 1851 matters had reached such a pass that the police station of Bukit Timah, seven miles from the centre of the town, was attacked and overrun. Warrants of arrest were issued, and the unfortunate man charged with the duty of serving these on the offenders. a Mr Henry Kraal, commander of the small gunboat *Charlotte* in the Johore Strait, was attacked by a troop of 500 armed Chinese (though with a large military escort himself). A smart action was fought in which the military forces were compelled to beat a hasty retreat with loss of life, and the pursuers did not break off the engagement till Kraal and his men had been chased ignominiously into the built-up areas of Singapore.

General alarm and fury knew no bounds. A public meeting was held to force this 'most dangerous combination against the security and peace of Singapore' to the attention of Government, pointing out that the whole interior of the island was in a most disturbed state. Greenshields made it clear that the spear-head of the attack was launched against the Christians among the Chinese community, whose growing number was already weakening the power of the societies.

At last Government acted; and the somewhat ineffectual Governor Blundell found himself compelled to take notice of it all and strengthen the police force.

* *

A division of opinion about how the problem should be tackled began. It was to smoulder miserably on; was to place Dunman and Greenshields in opposing camps and was to find no solution for the next twenty years.

The bone of contention was whether punitive police action, however firm, was the real answer to the problem, or whether there was not some more effective means of inducing the majority of the island's population to obey the law of the land.

Greenshields was convinced that mere force would get them nowhere. However, it was not till twenty years later, in 1870, that this view was to find expression in the appointment of a Mr Walter Pickering, first as Court Interpreter and later as 'Protector of Chinese'. Pickering was to make an immense impact upon the history of Malaya. He was one of that country's chief administrative architects; and the man who ultimately devised the machinery for winning the Chinese to the side of law rather than of hounding them to desperation by punitive action.

But twenty years before that – in 1851 – Greenshields's opinion was, inevitably, brushed aside as the murmuring of a dreamer.

* *

A grave situation was now developing on the mainland. In 1848 a minor Chief of the State of Perak, one Tungku Sulong, known to history as 'Long bin Jaffar', had discovered large deposits of tin on his lands in Larut and Matang.

Bands of Chinese from Penang, belonging to the two antagonistic Triad Society Hoeys of the Hokkien and the Kheh tribes, had dashed ashore and inland to exploit these riches; and warfare had broken out between them which resulted in 1854 in rioting in Penang, Malacca and Singapore and from north to south of the whole country. The bloodshed was considerable and the Government was unable to quell the disturbance.

This state of affairs continued unabated – and without British intervention – for a whole fourteen years until 1869, when even more serious Chinese rioting occurred. During this same period the scene becomes yet further confused and darkened by the outbreak of a quarrel among Malays of the State of Perak over the succession to their Sultanate.

Allying themselves with one or other of the Malay factions,

the two belligerent Chinese parties plunged heavily into the political, as well as the commercial, mêlée. As early as 1864 this situation had caused the *Straits Times* of June of that year to remark: 'We trust that the complication of affairs in Perak will lead the Rajah to appeal to our Government for assistance; we could scarcely interfere without. There is not the slightest doubt that the natives would hail our arrival with pleasure. For several years a civil war has devastated the Kingdom and, since the rule of the present sovereign has been established, his efforts to restore order have been fruitless. Would not this be a favourable opportunity for us to offer to purchase the country? It would be a valuable acquisition for the Settlement, and we fancy the Royal family of Perak would be delighted to get rid of it at any price.'

But this was mere wishful thinking. With the 'Transfer' from India in the offing, the uproar in the Malay States certainly provided the Guthries and John Greenshields with much ammunition in their demand for haste, but could scarcely result in the dramatic solution suggested by the Press. Three years were still to go by before that great event took place – the Transfer – with the miserable initial outcome already described.

Held in chains by Sir Harry Ord from 1867, the business community of the Straits were compelled to stand by inactive, passively watching the conflagration on the mainland spread from end to end of the peninsula.

A triangular war was now also raging in Selangor, in which certain Singapore merchants had become involved.

These merchants had 'leased the Tax-farm' (i.e., contracted to collect the taxes for a fixed annual sum paid in advance) from Abdullah, the Rajah of Klang; and this dignitary had been attacked and beaten by his rival, one Rajah Mahdi. Before long the latter had in turn been forced to retreat and had taken the Fort of Kuala Selangor, from which stronghold he was committing acts of piracy upon shipping in the Straits of Malacca.

Rajah Mahdi's allies, the 'Kah-Yeng-Chew' clan of Hokkien tin miners of Kanching in northern Selangor, were carrying on a bloodthirsty warfare against the supporters of the Rajah Abdullah of Klang. These latter were the 'Fei-Chew' Kheh miners of the rich and recently opened tin mining village of Kuala Lumpur.

Clever old Abdul Samad, the Sultan of Selangor, had

retired gracefully to Jugra in the southern part of his State, being powerless to intervene and seeing no solution other than to 'let the young men fight it out'. He tended, however, to favour the cause of the Rajah of Klang, who was now being helped by his English-educated son-in-law Tungku Kudin, with troops from Kedah.

Strong arguments for intervention were therefore on the side of Greenshields and the non-officials in the Singapore Legislative Council. These were, first and foremost, piracy on the part of Rajah Mahdi; secondly the legitimacy of Rajah Abdullah and Tungku Kudin's cause, as it was favoured by the Sultan; and thirdly the heavy loss incurred by the unfortunate businessmen who had leased the Tax-farm, and were being prevented by these troubles from recouping their losses.

A fourth argument, unexpressed but certainly in the minds of the non-officials, must surely have been the channel for trade that would open before them if the Straits Settlement Government took the side of Tungku Kudin and the Rajah of Klang with the approval of the Sultan. Four years earlier, the ten thousand miners of Kuala Lumpur, (only nine years after that tin-field had first been discovered) had been sending down river five times as much tin as had come from the whole of Selangor in years gone by. A right to open trade relations with this rich and powerful mining community might certainly be expected if immediate steps were taken to defeat the Rajah Mahdi and restore order.

* *

In 1871 an event of the greatest assistance to the non-officials occurred in the departure on leave of Sir Harry Ord. His temporary replacement was Colonel A. E. H. Anson, the Lieutenant-Governor, from Penang.

The 'Administrator', to give this officer his official title, was a man of very different character from Ord – an active and sympathetic person with much knowledge of affairs on the peninsula and a firm believer in the desirability of 'frequent communication between the Government and the Native States'.

Learning of Rajah Mahdi's piracy, he immediately dispatched Captain Bradberry with the 400-ton *Pluto*, together with Commander Robinson of the small seven-gun steam vessel *Rinaldo*, up the coast to reduce the Kuala Selangor Fort – a departure which marks the first act of armed intervention on the part of Britain in affairs of the 'Native States'.

After a spirited action by shore parties lasting some days the fort was taken with little loss of life.

The Colonial Secretary, J. W. W. Birch, called on the Sultan in HMS *Teazer* – forcing her up river to the very walls of the old man's stockade at Ulu Langat. Firm, even if wrong, decisions were made, upon the well proven rule that any clear-cut action is better than none. Tungku Kudin, apparently still the Sultan's choice, was appointed under him as the 'viceroy', or 'responsible officer' of the Selangor Government. Singapore stocks, already vested in large sums in mining ventures in Selangor, boomed, and the voice of Britain was immediately treated with greatly increased respect throughout the length of the Malacca Strait.

But Ord returned in early 1872 and undid all.

Birch had been peremptory; *Teazer* should never have been sent; the Sultan's agreement to accept Tungku Kudin as 'viceroy' had been forced upon him; the merchants had hoodwinked Anson into action that would bring profit to them and expenditure to the British taxpayer.

Through Ord's failure to recognise that when strong action has once been taken it must be supported and maintained, *Rinaldo's* and *Pluto's* work was rendered worse than useless through lack of 'follow through'.

* *

In December 1871, Greenshields and his followers in the Legislative Council had obtained Ord's approval to appoint a member of that rare (at that time almost unheard-of) species, the 'Chinese-speaking European', as interpreter to the Singapore Court.

Walter Pickering, aged thirty-one, had begun his career as an apprentice in the Merchant Service. He was a newcomer to Singapore. On leaving the sea, however, he had joined the Chinese Customs Service and had served both on the China Coast as well as Formosa, where he had acquired an excellent knowledge of Cantonese and other Chinese tongues.

Being a man of intelligence whose mind ranged far beyond his day to day duties, he soon saw that what was needed in the matter of the secret societies, which occupied so much of the time of the Court, was not 'laissez-faire' until their members did something wrong and then punish them, but a means of bringing them into the favourable, rather than the punitive, aspect of the Government's administration.

He was Greenshields all over again, but twenty years later. By now, too, the world had moved on somewhat; and the Government – certain sections of it at least – was less disinclined to listen.

'Register every Hoey, with the names of each one's office-bearers', was his constant slogan. 'Take an interest in their affairs. Give them every proper assistance in your power. Offer to arbitrate in all cases of dispute. Promise effective police protection in support of decisions made by such arbitration, and make sure that such protection is given. Lastly never – but never – disclose the name of any informer to anyone; however criminal his record may be.'

So – first in a little shophouse and later in a modest office in Havelock Road, Singapore – began a function of Government that was soon to be known throughout the Settlements as the 'Chinese Protectorate' in English; and 'Peh-Kih-Ling' (a corruption of 'Pickering') in Chinese.

So, too, began a certain proneness to schizophrenia in the Government's way of thinking – a tendency on the part of the soldier and policeman to take an opposite view to that of the administrator and the Protector of Chinese.

This may be seen growing through the years from the first skirmish between Dunman and Pickering over that same question of the identity of 'the informer' – Pickering refusing to disclose the man's name and asserting hotly that to do so would be a breach of faith on the part of the administration, and one which could only result in the stoppage in future of all such sources of valuable information.

This led the irate Mr Dunman to demand to be informed how the devil, in that case, he could be expected to enforce law and order, now that a Government department had been created for the special purpose of shielding and defending criminals. Pickering was supported by Greenshields; and Dunman departed in a huff to send in his papers and resign from Government service.

Over the years Dunman's successors laid their own traps for evil-doers without Pickering's assistance or even knowledge – and in dismay the situation developed to the point, in

1887, where astute police work led to the arrest of one of Pickering's trusted informers – who wrongly believed the latter to have betrayed him – and who thereupon dashed into Pickering's office and hurled an axe at his head.

Pickering slowly recovered; but during the awkward period between 1885 and 1890, when Clementi-Smith, Weld and Dickson were playing musical chairs with the office of Governor, the first succeeded in forcing a new law through for the total suppression of all 'Secret Societies' despite the opposition of Mr Dunlop, who had succeeded Dunman as Superintendent of Police.

Pickering, still a sick man, threw in his hand and departed from the East. But his work lived.

The Protectorate – later named the Department of Chinese Affairs – consolidated its position, however, and grew to be a mainspring of Government in ruling the immigrant Chinese.

CHAPTER 4

PIRACY

Pirates have already been mentioned several times; and the subject must now be touched on in some detail.

Robert Louis Stevenson, Gilbert and Sullivan, and Richard Hughes in his charming fantasy *High Wind in Jamaica*, have together conspired to soften the character of the nineteenth century pirate and to gild his activities with romance.

But there is little romance in the cutting of throats or the murder of children; and no attraction at all in drowning in agony with hands tied behind the back.

A later and more realistic age sees the pirates for what they were – foul and merciless gangs of sub-human sharks; for whom mere hanging was far too good.

Hordes of these criminals – Malays, Illanuns and Bugis, the two latter from Borneo and the Sulu Sea – had pillaged the Eastern seas and terrorised coastal populations for hundreds of years.

Their practice was to range the seas in large numbers. Two fleets of over forty vessels each had assembled at Prai in 1792 to attack Penang, and smaller though still impressive numbers of these vermin continued to range off all the coasts of the Malay States throughout the nineteenth century. Their hunting grounds, of which Singapore was one of the chief pivots, were the main routes of commerce, which were yearly becoming more and more populous.

No fish were too small to swim into their net; and, though they had acquired a wholesome respect for the foreign or ocean-going trader, who was armed and would sell his life dearly, they still made a point of attacking these too whenever a good chance offered. Their tactics were sometimes to dispatch a captured trading vessel to intercept the oncoming merchantman as a 'Trojan Horse', to beg for stores and sneak a salting of pirates aboard before the main force attacked; sometimes to make a massive assault at midnight in a dead calm; and at times to lie hidden behind a headland near one of the principal fairways and fall upon the approaching ship in a headlong charge as she was going about or otherwise heavily encumbered, with all the watch busy at the braces.

Thereafter it was sack, steal, burn and kill without mercy and without regard to age or sex.

Year after year the miserable reports came in; ships were looted or burnt to the water's edge; cargoes were lost; bodies of friends and their families floated ashore.

By 1850 the Chinese had joined in the game. Pirates' stores, guns and ammunition were being openly traded in 'Kampong Glam' on Singapore waterfront. A junk was set upon and sacked leaving the very harbour, with the loss of forty-three out of the total of forty-nine lives. Severed heads were frequently to be encountered floating in the harbour, and passengers were robbed and killed in sampans when calling upon friends in the roads of Singapore.

* *

Yet all the time the answer was there; ready, waiting and growing in the ingenuity and scientific advance of Western man.

That answer was, of course, steam power. A vessel no longer dependent on wind could out-manoeuvre these pests, could dog them relentlessly till their rowers dropped from their thwarts with exhaustion; could lay a direct course to the centre of trouble and blot the pirates out by gunfire and musket before they could make safely back to their lairs.

Steam was no novelty in Singapore. No more than seven years after its founding, in 1826, the Dutch steamer *Van der Capellan* had called in on her way to Batavia. Lord Bentinck, when he visited the place in 1829, had come in a steamship. Eighteen steamers had passed through to take part in the China War in 1840; and by 1845 regular steam communication had been set up with Bengal and Batavia; also in the same year the large steam vessel *Lady Mary Wood* arrived in the Roads to open the P & O Company's first Far Eastern service from Egypt – and bringing mails, carried overland from Alexandria, forty-one days out from London.

Then why did effective action by steamships on the pirate menace hang fire for so long?

The answer to that query is provided by the total absence in Singapore till late in the 1860s of any port facilities suitable for the use and repair of steamers.

Thomas Scott, as we already know, had turned his mind to this problem from the first moment of his arrival in Singapore in 1851.

Others – and before him – had done the same. As early as 1834 a Mr Montgomery had applied for a plot of land on the island of Blakang Mati 'for a Dock'; and in the same year Mr Lorraine for Messrs Douglas Mackenzie and Company had also applied for land near the town for a similar purpose.

But nothing had been done in either case. And the reason is not far to seek.

No sailing ship skipper in his senses would poke his nose into either hole at any price. A lee shore. In the one case an impossible entrance with the wind blowing right into the mouth of it, and then all rocks and no room to turn round once you did get in; and in the other a muddy bottom – bad holding-ground for his anchors – with a breaking sea and a nasty cross-tide. No thank you. He would rather wait till he had reached Whampoa, Batavia, Fremantle or wherever he was going, where he could have his ship hove down comfortably and employ excellent carpenters and shipwrights for his repairs to spars and rigging.

Indeed it was not until 1848 that Captain Keppel, visiting Singapore in his new command *Meander* after serving many years in those waters in his beautiful corvette *Dido*, remarked in his diary: 'Pulling about in my gig among the numerous prettily wooded islands on the westward entrance to Singapore river, I was astonished to find deep water close to the shore, with a safe passage through for vessels larger than the *Meander*. *Now that steam is likely to come into use*, this ready-made harbour as a depot for coals would be invaluable . . .' And later, in 1849, we find him writing: 'Having reported to the Admiralty over twelve months ago the natural advantages of the inner harbour at Singapore as a *coaling station*, and no notice having been taken of my letter, I have now sent a similar statement, with survey, to the Secretary of the P & O Company.'

The mystery is explained. In the sailing ship era the construction of quaysides and dock facilities would not pay. The sailing vessel could not use them.

Steamships on the other hand, regardless of fair breeze or

foul, could creep up into any little nook or cranny such as the enclosed waters by Tanjong Pagar. Their paddle-boxes prevented their being hove down on the beach for cleaning and repair to their bottoms; and therefore dock facilities of all sorts, including a graving dock, were essential.

But until the '60s there were insufficient steamships in the area to warrant, from a business point of view, such a dock's construction.

* *

So it came about that whereas the P & O Company, now in regular service to the Far East, quickly accepted Captain Keppel's advice in 1849 and had built themselves a fine wharf 1,200 feet long, with warehouses and coaling sheds – all strictly for their own use – by the middle-fifties no public quayside or graving dock was worth building, from a commercial point of view, till the use of steam became more general.

For that reason – and because the Admiralty had so far constructed no naval dock of their own in spite of Keppel's advice – the whole duty of suppressing piracy by means of steam vessels had been confined for years to the use of one small paddle-wheel brig. The resources of Singapore Port, for bunkering and repairs, could not support more.

Even as it was, the impact made on the pirates by that one small vessel, *Diana*, under command of Captain Samuel Congalton, had been impressive. Forward-looking members of the community such as James Guthrie and Greenshields were already urging the immediate strengthening of this new and effective arm by the provision of improved port facilities.

In 1846 *Diana* was replaced by the larger and more modern *Hooghly*; but by 1850 she was already proving too slow for the pirates, who had also been improving their technique; and one anti-piracy steamship was obviously absurdly inadequate for the guarding of two thousand miles of coastline.

Something had to be done – and the man with the determination to break this vicious circle would win the gratitude of all the Straits Settlement.

* *

Tanjong Pagar Dock

Tanjong Pagar Dock

Two men, later to become great rivals, share the credit for overcoming this impasse – the first, William Cloughton, for making the first move; and the second, Thomas Scott, for his courageous carrying through of a vast new scheme to its successful conclusion.

Captain Cloughton was a character, if ever such a being existed on the face of this earth. A Yorkshireman born in Hull; thick-set, squat, dark and foul-mouthed; he had come ashore in Singapore in 1854 at the age of forty-three, having served for years in the Apcar Company's barques trading opium to China.

Passing frequently through Singapore, he had soon realised that with all these new-fangled floating kettles about, it must soon develop into an ideal place for a graving dock, of which he knew they seemed almost always to be in need. He had therefore let his sailor's eye rove the shoreline in search of a likely spot.

Up the 'New Harbour', as it was called – up the long arm of the sea west of Tanjong Pagar and close to the P & O Company's wharf under construction – he found just what he wanted.

He bought the land and settled in.

Daily he was to be seen in his pyjamas – he never wore anything else – with a pith hat on his head and his shirt tail hanging out behind. He would stroll the dockside, with an attendant beside him bearing a cup of tea; the dregs of which he was quite liable to fling in the said servant's face with a bang on the head accompanied by a flood of abuse, if it was not 'up to cocker'. Or he would sit at his ease, if the day was fine, going up to town in his old-fashioned sort of Victoria with a great high leather front, pulled by a pair of red and white piebalds. One syce would stand behind, fanning him with a fly whisk; whilst the diminutive driver cowered on his perch up in front, keeping well out of reach of cuffs and blows in case his steersmanship was not to his master's liking.

The old rascal Cloughton – with many a curse and many a kick at the ample stern of his black factotum 'Babu' from Africa, who had sailed with him for years – finished his work at last; and in 1859 opened his wonderful dry dock, which was immediately christened 'Cloughton's Mud-Hole'.

He had made enemies of course – notably with an ill-financed establishment known as the Patent Slip and Dock

Company that had begun building next door to him about the same time as himself. The two of them were, however, mutually at daggers drawn both with Mr Tivendale, who had set up a small shipyard at Sandy Point near the town, as well as with the Admiralty, who had at last (and most unwisely) selected part of the nearby small island of Pulau Brani as the site for a naval dockyard, in the full scour of the tide. The joy of the angels at the repentant sinner was as naught compared with Cloughton's jubilation when the famous transport *Himalaya* lying alongside the naval dock carried away her forward hawsers, springs and mooring lines and was nearly lost.

* *

Into this tangled skein is now introduced the cool and practical personality of Thomas Scott, who had quietly been awaiting the right moment to intervene.

That time had now come. The long distance from the town to the P & O Wharves, the Patent Slip and Dock Company's project, and to Cloughton's Mud-Hole was obvious to everyone; whereas Messrs Guthries' own land at Tanjong Pagar, with its great ledge of rock and sand running out into the sea at the very eastern end of the New Harbour – facing the port and roadstead of Singapore itself – would be the ideal site for wharves and a graving dock, now that steam was everywhere in the ascendant. It would be an easy matter moreover to lay a railway line from the dockside to the main business area in the town centre itself.

Thomas Scott first consulted Colonel Collyer, the Settlement Engineer. He then called together his business colleagues at meeting after meeting for the next three years; and finally – after news had reached Singapore that serious work on the Suez Canal was at last being undertaken – he convened a formal meeting in 1863 of all those interested in the business of shipping and formed a Committee, of which he was appointed secretary. This Committee consolidated itself into the first working directorate of a body soon to be named the Tanjong Pagar Dock Company; and the actual dock construction then soon began.

To recount that concern's growth; its difficulties painfully overcome – the washing away of the labour of two whole years when its retaining wall gave way in a great storm in

1865; the trouble that both Scott and Greenshields had in finding the finance to double its modest capital of $125,000 in 1866 in order to carry on the work; the great fire of 1877 that burned for a fortnight, destroying every building together with 42 out of 48 thousand tons of precious coal – would not be to the purpose of this history.

Let it merely be said that in time the Tanjong Pagar Dock Company bought out the Patent Slip and Dock Company (later renamed the New Harbour Company) and opened two dry docks, then the largest in the East, in 1868 and 1879. At the opening of the first of these, the Company suffered from what was tactfully described as 'competition' from Mr Cloughton, who in his fury advertised his future willingness 'to slip ships free of charge!' Tanjong Pagar even bought out that intransigent old tiger himself in the end; and finally, with Scott as its perennial guardian angel and frequent Chairman, the Tanjong Pagar Dock grew to such size as the greatest port in the eastern hemisphere, that in 1905, for political and strategic reasons, it was compulsorily acquired by the British Government.

A sum of twenty-eight million dollars was paid for it, with allowances for reinvestment on the part of the shareholders.

Guthries' and the other firms who had taken a share of the risk at its beginnings found themselves with over a hundred dollars in hand for every one they had staked.

More important still, the facilities afforded by the Tanjong Pagar Dock attracted so great a concourse of shipping as to alter the entire future of Malaya; and made Singapore the headquarters of the offensive against piracy which drove them from the Eastern seas.

Piracy, as a menace, was over by 1875.

* * *

Captain John Anderson, like many a sailor of his day, had led a tough and adventurous life. Born in Greenock in 1793, he had run away to sea at fourteen; could spit to windward at twenty (which means he had been three times round the Horn); jumped ship in Archangel; been washed overboard; twice shanghai-ed by the pressgang and once escaped by stowing away in a pork barrel. The usual sort of history in short, to be recounted, with variations, by the majority of those whose trade was the sea in those days.

His first adventure into matrimony had been an unhappy one – and then, when he became skipper of a steamer running between Glasgow and Belfast belonging to John Burns (afterwards founder of the Cunard Line) and when his two grown-up daughters had positively begged him to marry Janet Halley of their own age – a fellow school teacher friend of their's, the daughter of a shopkeeper in Glasgow (and granddaughter of the discoverer of the comet) – he had at first demurred because of the immense disparity in age, but had finally taken the plunge in 1848.

It was the best thing he ever did.

In 1855 – the year of the Ballarat goldrush – Captain John Anderson, then over sixty years old and owner of the little paddle-steamer *Shandon*, made his way under sail, with his paddle-wheels stowed below, all the long voyage out to Melbourne, where freight and passenger rates were said to be at a premium. He left his young wife Janet at home in Rothesay with the four children, Florence, Maggie, John and Minnie.

John Anderson's bold gamble did not prove the path to fortune he had hoped. Running his steamer between Geelong, Melbourne and up the Murray River was an unrewarding task, what with shortage of labour, exorbitant wage rates and all hands regularly deserting for the gold-fields.

He struggled on however, and in 1856 was joined by Janet and the children, who came out in that year with a Scottish maid in a clipper from the Clyde, settling down at Geelong in a small wooden house in a street appropriately named 'Singapore Terrace'. (The cottages there had been pre-fabricated in Singapore, where both wood and labour were cheap, and had been re-assembled in Australia – an isolated little fact which throws an interesting light upon the growing diversity of trade from that place even in those early days.)

And it was to no other than Singapore that in 1860 Captain Anderson, realising that the chancy game he had been so bravely playing in Australia was over, loaded *Shandon* with stores and water, took aboard Janet and the children, including little baby James, who had been born in Melbourne, and laid course.

They made it – which was a minor miracle – in spite of seas infested with Malay and Chinese pirates, and in defiance of all reasonable prognostications that they had insufficient fuel for more than half the voyage. Burning driftwood and mangrove collected from desert islands; drinking rain water – and finally stripping the bulwarks and paddle-boxes to feed the boiler fire; they limped in at last to Singapore.

Here *Shandon* made two successful trading trips up to Malacca, Penang and back with general cargo, whilst the clever Janet installed herself with the children in modest lodgings ashore and immediately found excellent employment as mistress of the Raffles Girls' School.

But, alas, misfortune still dogged the Captain's footsteps. On the 15th of November that year, on what was to be his third trip north with many passengers and a full general cargo, *Shandon* was rounding the new Raffles Light in the dead calm of a tropic afternoon when disaster struck. Misjudging the strength of a spring tide at mid-ebb, an easy thing to do in those unpredictable waters, Anderson crashed *Shandon* full tilt across the bows of a large British barque, *Sree Rajah Rajahshwire*, bound for Bombay and at anchor waiting for a breeze. Smash went the jib-boom, bringing the fore-topmast with it; and down went the funnel, and overboard.

Shandon was towed in by HMS *Victoria*, the local gunboat, that evening with all the passengers. Captain Anderson was ruined and his sea-going days at an end.

The old vessel was put up for auction and knocked down on 24th February 1861 to a Chinese merchant, who repaired her and used her for many years on the China trade; whilst the Captain found a shore billet as Assistant Harbour Master, which post he held until his death at the age of eighty-two in 1875.

With this last glimpse of a nineteenth century sailor's life – but keeping a watchful eye nevertheless on his young son John, now going to school at Raffles Institute – let us return to where Ord left off.

CHAPTER 5

SIR ANDREW CLARKE

Sir Andrew Clarke, KCMG, the new Governor as from 4th November 1873, was a very different man from the unfortunate first choice of the Secretary of State.

Confident, brilliant in his métier of 'fortifications', imaginative, breezy and completely at ease, he made friends with everyone at once. He knew exactly what he wanted to do and proceeded without delay to do it.

It was no time at all before he had held a friendly party at Government House, to which the leaders of all racial sections of Singapore's population were invited, and had persuaded all the non-officials (including Thomas Scott) to rejoin the Legislative Council.

Also, he had come out from home with completely different Letters of Instruction, following a change in the British Government's policy.

Outstandingly the most important new duty with which Sir Andrew Clarke was charged was to 'ascertain the condition of affairs in each State and to report whether there are any steps which can be taken to promote the restoration of peace and order and to secure protection to trade and commerce with the native territories'.

The equally important obverse of this coin was the command 'to consider whether it would be advisable to appoint a British officer to reside in any of the States . . . such appointment only to be made with the full consent of the Native Government'.

What a change! Somebody must have been busy in London with a vengeance; though perhaps it would be invidious to point too clearly to the Straits Settlements Association.

As events will show, even these wide and progressive instructions were carried out by Sir Andrew Clarke with a majestic liberality of interpretation. As he himself remarked in his old age, the condition of affairs did not permit him to 'ascertain and report', so he decided to 'act, and report afterwards'. If they did not like it, he would have the satisfaction of having done his best, and would be perfectly prepared to retire into private life. He did not depend on a pittance from the Colonial Office.

It did not take Sir Andrew long to observe two things that no one else seemed to have noticed. The first was that all previous meddlings in native affairs had been meaningless, because they had entirely overlooked the heart of the problem. They had been aimed towards composing differences between the Malay Chiefs.

But what made the Malay Chiefs have differences?

Money of course; tin; the tin-fields; the Chinese – whose internal struggles for wealth had excited the avarice of the Rajahs and brought the whole peace of the country tumbling down about their ears. Hitherto the Chinese, in almost all negotiations, had been virtually ignored.* But until their quarrels throughout the land had been settled there would be no peace for anyone. Merely talking to the Malay Sultans would do no good. They were entangled in the Chinese struggle for riches more deeply than anyone.

The second point, interconnected with this, was that the Chinese battle for the tin-fields on the mainland had now split the body of Singapore's leading merchants into two separate – at times opposing – camps.

Sir Andrew would therefore need first of all to adopt an entirely fresh standpoint in considering the problems on the mainland; and secondly he would need to assess the arguments of all his Legislative Council and 'business' advisers with a wary eye.

His action in the first matter will soon be seen, but the second point needs some explanation.

* *

Although events were soon to make Perak the cockpit of Malaya's destiny, Selangor was the State where the merchants' division into two parties had first occurred.

* Eighteen months after Walter Pickering's arrival, Sir Harry Ord had at last permitted him to make a first (though unsuccessful) attempt to settle the dispute between the Penang Hokkiens and the Khehs over the Larut and Matang Tin-fields.

Both the competing bodies of Singapore's merchants wanted peace in Selangor, for reasons of trade as well as in order to recoup the sums of money already advanced to one or other of the two warring clans of tin-miners.

But some had backed the 'Fei-Chews' and others the 'Kah-Yeng-Chews'; the merchants' attitude therefore depended on which side they had supported.

Notable on one side was the inevitable and recurrent Billy Read of A. L. Johnston, who had gone into partnership with one Tan Kim Cheng (son of the famous Tan Tock Seng who had founded the hospital); and who were together involved in the unfortunate matter of leasing the Selangor Tax-farm. Tan Kim Cheng was leader of the Hokkiens in Singapore and in favour of the Kah-Yeng-Chews and the Rajah Mahdi.

In agreement with those two was Mr Lipscombe of Boustead and Company; Sir Peter Benson Maxwell the Chief Justice (an enemy of Ord on a personal matter of precedence, who believed Ord was favouring the Fei-Chew party); and a Mr William Braddell, who, in addition to being the Attorney-General, had a handsome private practice as legal adviser to the Maharajah of Johore. The latter's State seemed more and more to be becoming infiltrated by the Fei-Chews, to which he strongly objected.

Upon the opposing, or Fei-Chew, side there emerge James Guthrie (in London), Thomas Scott, Dr Little, thirty-three Malacca merchants headed by one Teo Siong Chwee, 'Whampoa' and, last but not least, a most important figure, whose history must now be told, as it is intimately connected with the course of the Guthrie story.

This man was that same James Guthrie Davidson whose name has already been casually mentioned twice; a lawyer – a 'writer to the Signet', as they say in Scotland – from Edinburgh; his mother being no less than a sister of Guthrie and Company's senior partner, the redoubtable James Guthrie.

With that family connection it was not unnatural that at the age of twenty-three he should have decided to make his livelihood in the East – a step which he took in the year 1861, when on uncle James's advice he joined the office of Mr R. C. Woods, a lawyer of Singapore and editor of the *Straits Times*.

By that year 1861 the Fei-Chews had already been mining tin near Kuala Lumpur for five years with the assistance of Messrs Guthrie and Company. In their hope to obtain a footing in this profitable mining industry, Guthries' had advanced Yap Ah Loy, the clan leader, considerable sums of money to get them started.

Serious trouble had soon broken out between this clan and their rivals the Kah-Yeng-Chews, as has been mentioned; and Tungku Kudin, soon to be 'Viceroy' of Selangor, had taken the Fei-Chews' part.

As may well be imagined, Guthrie and Company, as potential mining suppliers, were therefore much to the fore in supporting the Tungku, to the extent not only of financial aid but, as and when the need arose, by the supply to him of brass cannon and other such somewhat unconventional items of mining equipment.

James Guthrie Davidson soon became Tungku Kudin's own legal adviser; and sometimes visited Yap Ah Loy in Kuala Lumpur on affairs of the firm's loans.

Shortly before Sir Harry Ord's final departure in 1873 Tungku Kudin's prospects had so improved that he was able to give his financiers, represented by Davidson, some security for the advances they had made him.

This took the form of a concession dated 8th March 1873, granted on extremely favourable terms, by which large tin-mining rights in Selangor were granted to Guthrie and Company for ten years, with royalties payable of only five per cent on the gross produce and $3/- per 460 lb 'bahara' of tin exported, as against ten per cent, which was the usual royalty. The legality of this concession, having been made by Tungku Kudin as 'Viceroy' and not the Sultan, was of course questioned by the opposition party headed by Maxwell and Braddell; but whilst this was going on Guthries' transferred the concession to a new group they had now formed, called the Selangor Tin Mining Company, with a nominal capital of $10,000/-; and successfully combated the opposition's arguments.

Thus by 1873 Guthries' would seem already in a fair way to have established a toe-hold at least in Selangor.

* *

Two hundred miles north, in the State of Perak, there had been nothing but trouble ever since 1848, when tin had been discovered; and when old Sultan Ali died in 1871 things had gone from bad to worse.

By 1873, Yusof, the heir presumptive and a man of great force of character, had made himself totally unacceptable to all the Chiefs by his uncompromising belligerency and bluntness.

Ismail, a puppet, was on the throne; and one Ngah Ibrahim, the rich Chief of Larut (the Sultan's 'Mantri' or Chief Minister) was supporting him till the time might become ripe to usurp the throne himself.

To add to the confusion, one Tungku Abdullah, a man of indeterminate character with a more doubtful claim for consideration, had already mortgaged, in advance, half the revenues of the State to Bousteads' Tan Kim Cheng, the Hokkien leader, in exchange for help in achieving what he hoped would be his birthright.

Ngah Ibrahim, the Chief of Larut, was the Kheh candidate, but all of them, Kheh or Hokkien, were busily intriguing to bring over the Malay nobles to one or other side.

* * *

Sir Andrew decided, first, to tackle the heart of the problem – the Chinese Hoeys; and, secondly, to favour no faction whatever, Chinese or otherwise.

He therefore dispatched Pickering to Penang to get to the bottom of this Chinese business; and called for representatives of all parties, Chinese and Malay, to meet him aboard *Pluto* at the island of Pangkor on 14th January 1874, with his Colonial Secretary Mr J. W. W. Birch, Colonel McNair and several others.

Pickering went to Penang and collected Chan Ah Yam, the Hokkien leader. Frank Swettenham, aged twenty-four (later to become the first Resident General, then High Commissioner, of the Federated Malay States) met Chung Ah Kwee, the leader of the Khehs, and took him to Pangkor. He then accompanied Commander Patterson of HMS *Avon* to the headquarters of Sultan Ismail, who agreed to attend the meeting, but finally turned back for home within a mile of his destination, on being assured that Ngah Ibrahim, his 'Mantri', was present, accompanied by no less than Mr R. C. Woods, his legal adviser. (Mr R. C. Woods was Guthrie Davidson's partner).

Chan Ah Yam (the Chinese Hokkien representative) came down from Penang with Pickering; Abdullah made a somewhat furtive appearance; and a session began which was to result in the signing of an understanding between Perak and the Straits Government on behalf of Britain, known thereafter as the 'Pangkor Engagement'.

By this 'Engagement' not only was a permanent peace established between the two Chinese antagonists, but also arrangements were agreed for a British Resident and his assistants to reside in Perak to advise the State Government on all matters *other than Malay custom and religion.*

Much trouble and heart-burning were later to arise from all this on the Malay side, caused not only by the inadequate translation of the 'Engagement' into Malay, but also from the fact that the Malays regarded almost every activity of the State Government either as 'customary' or 'religious'. However, Sir Andrew was lucky enough to leave these scenes before the mounting flood of difficulties and angers could sweep away his reputation, as they might well have done.

Through Sir Andrew's opportune efforts and forthrightness, rather than any farsighted statesmanship, his name undoubtedly stands beside Francis Light of Penang and Thomas Raffles of Singapore as one of the great figures in the making of Malaya.

More relevant, however, to the course of this story is the fact that when, a few months later, the Sultan of Selangor also agreed to accept an adviser, the British Resident who was appointed was no other than Mr James Guthrie Davidson.

In his letter to the Straits Government accepting that appointment he stated that his financial transactions with Tungku Kudin were at an end and that 'I have arranged to transfer my claim against the Selangor Government for money advanced and services rendered . . . to Messrs Guthrie and Company, merchants . . . to receive the interest and dividends in their own name'.

CHAPTER 6

HEAD OVER HEELS INTO NATIVE AFFAIRS

Now would seem to be the firm's chance – but James Guthrie and Scott were cautious. They had had dealings with the Native States for many years and were in no hurry. Trading, in the normal sense of buying and selling, had always been through the Chinese intermediaries, but, when it came to the issue of loans, much finance had passed direct from the firm's coffers into the hands of one or other of the large up-country businessmen, either against produce to be collected, or by way of loan at a good rate of interest. These dealings were widespread from Siamese Trengganu far up the east coast, on the one hand, to Seremban in Sungei Ujong on the other, where dwelt their clients Sheikh Abdul Rahman and Mr P. M. S. P. K. Karruppan Chetty.*

Much money had gone out, too, on financing Tungku Kudin of Selangor; and although he had now provided them with shares in this large tin concession in Selangor through James Guthrie Davidson, it would be wise to sell these at the best price obtainable to the newly formed Selangor Tin Mining Company and get rid of them as soon as possible. The situation was still too unstable.

* Chettys and Chettiars are hereditary South Indian financiers. They are both of the Vaishia caste (i.e. the third grade in the Hindu caste system of Brahmin, Kshettriar, Vaishia, Sudra), the Chetty sub-caste being worshippers of Vishnu and the Chettiars of Siva. The Chetty sub-caste is exclusively from the border country of Chittor and environs between the Tamil and Telugu countries of Madras State, whilst the Chettiars come from the Nattakotai and Pudukotai areas in the Ramnad district of the same. The Chetty sub-caste are large financiers concerned with banking, insurance and commercial underwriting, whereas the Chettiars are occupied mostly with loans of any amount, however small, to all comers; none of whom may ever, according to their doctrine, be refused. (Interest rates vary with the risk of course!). The initials – never less than three and more often four or five – represent, from left to right, the names of the great grandfather, the grandfather and the father of the Chetty; the fourth (and often fifth) being the name of the village from which the Chetty comes. In the present case the full elucidation of the name is Pallaniappan Mutthiah Sithambaram Karruppan Chetty of the village of Peria Koil.

The $10,000/- advance to Yap Ah Loy of Kuala Lumpur at fifteen per cent was not looking any too good either. He was being honest enough within the limits of that advance, certainly; but since Davidson had now ceased advising the Government of Selangor and been made Resident of Perak, his successor at the former place, this Mr Frank Swettenham who seemed to be making such stir up there, had begun to offer Government loans to tin-miners at ten per cent; and the majority of Ah Loy's business was therefore no longer being done through Guthries' at all. He was sending down masses of tin to all sorts of people; and only putting enough into Guthries' godown to cover his interest rate.

This was annoying, but one could do nothing about it. The wise course would be to wait for a while, watch developments and not get one's fingers burnt.

And there was much to watch. British intervention in the affairs of the Native States had been highly necessary from every point of view, but had resulted in a sea of troubles. Sir Andrew Clarke, having taken the decisive step, had handed over his command after eighteen months to Sir William Jervois, who was several years his senior in the Royal Engineers and who seemed anxious to outshine his junior predecessor by an even more vigorous forward policy.

Sir Andrew Clarke had left him with an extremely awkward problem in Perak by having bluntly suggested to the assembled Chiefs at Pangkor – to Guthrie and Company's annoyance – that they elect the wretched Abdullah as their Sultan; a proposition which the unhappy gathering of bewildered Malay elders had found impossible to decline, especially in the very presence of Abdullah himself, without exhibiting a discourtesy totally foreign to their good breeding. Ismail the puppet had failed to attend the meeting; and Yusof, the unpopular next-of-kin, had not even been mentioned. It was obvious what this powerful English Tuan expected of them.

Ignorant of Malay mentality and unaware of Malay custom, Sir Andrew honestly considered that all had gone off splendidly – little knowing how deep was the resentment behind those polite and impassive faces; or how powerless Abdullah would be without his royal regalia, which incidentally he never obtained.

The Colonial Secretary, James Wheeler Woodford Birch, a forty-nine year old administrator from Ceylon who had first come to Singapore with Sir Harry Ord and had thrust his gunboat *Teazer* under the nose of old Sultan Abdul Samad of Selangor at Langat in 1873, was Clarke's somewhat curious choice as Resident of Perak; and one which he only came to 'after prolonged consideration'. This was an odd and revealing statement, to say the least of it, particularly as the position of Resident was considerably junior to that of Birch's substantive post of Colonial Secretary.

A brave, well intentioned and kindly man, as anxious to shine as any schoolboy, but with no mature perception and a tremendous stickler for the letter of the law, Birch was soon at loggerheads with everybody.

The new Sultan, Abdullah, had achieved what he wanted and could now afford to spurn him and his 'advice'! As he was the Sultan's man, the mass of Chiefs opposing Abdullah were necessarily Birch's natural enemies. The riverine headmen flouted his instructions and continued to exact their traditional 'tax' from river traffic. Every land owner was astonished at his extraordinary theories – which he actually had the temerity to try to enforce – regarding emancipation from slavery.

Birch – who would rather die than be proved a failure in this new, though junior, post – wrote encouraging but sadly inaccurate reports on the general state of affairs to the Governor, relying for his personal safety on the various Chiefs' antagonistic aims and lack of unity. He was, alas, blind to the fact that in regard to one matter they were by no means disunited – and that was in their opposition and hostility to him.

It only remained for the new Governor, Sir William Jervois, to take a further plunge 'head over heels into Native affairs', as it was described at the time, for the fat to fall into the fire.

'Poke not the bees' nest', as the Malays say.

Among the first things Jervois did upon his arrival was to empower Birch with full authority as 'Commissioner' to supersede the Malay administration and himself conduct the total course of Government 'in the name of the Sultan'. This was poking it indeed.

In shocking similarity to the sacrifice offered in ancient days at the spring planting or at the blessing of a foundation stone, the new country of Malaya was to receive its baptism of blood.

Birch, the second – a possibly willing and certainly a self-appointed – victim, was stabbed to death with a spear thrust through the palm-thatched wall of his floating bath-house and his body thrown into the Perak river, immediately following the death of the first sacrifice, his poor interpreter, Enche Mat Arshad, who was killed with a kris whilst endeavouring to post up notices of the Governor's new instruction creating Birch the 'Commissioner'.

From that first outbreak at the little village of Pasir Salak on the Perak riverside, the conflagration had spread like wildfire and burst into flames as far south as the State of Sungei Ujong. The whole tragic affair cost much treasure and a deal of good Malay and British blood before it was brought under control, in a series of actions which in the end 'did more', to quote Sir Frank Swettenham's laconic summing up, 'in six months, to bring order and good government to Malaya, than could have been achieved by twenty years of peaceful persuasion'.

* * *

Indeed this was no time for a prudent firm to embark on fresh adventures on the mainland. There was no lack of business to be done in Singapore.

James Guthrie had remained at home for some years, and at the end of 1873 Thomas Scott had joined him there for the purpose of setting up a registered office for the firm in London, which had now become virtually a branch of the Singapore establishment known as 'Scott and Company', of Number 8 Idol Lane, Great Tower Street. Next door at Number 9 Idol Lane was the office of Messrs Chalmers, Guthrie and Company; whose chairman was later Walter Murray Guthrie (James Guthrie's cousin), son of James Alexander Guthrie of Craigie, a Director of the Bank of England. Guthries' were not without friends in the City!

Louis John Robertson Glass was the senior 'Singapore' partner in early 1876, with young Alexander Guthrie as his junior and no less than five British assistants. Among these – signing 'per pro' and on the point of replacing a Mr William McKerrow who was just leaving – was an extremely tall young fellow of blond pugnacious countenance, aged twenty-four, named John Anderson; in whom there is no difficulty in recognising that boisterous Raffles schoolboy who had sailed up from Australia with his old father Captain Anderson in *Shandon* all those years ago. His two pairs of trousers, one blue and one red, (named 'Alma' and 'Balaclava'), that were the joy of his scampish childhood, had long been replaced by the immaculate 'sponge-bag' of a young man about town. But beneath the adult mask there was no mistaking the plucky spirit of the boy who had caught a burglar single-handed in his father's house in Beach Road at the age of sixteen; who gave up school to join the Government and later the firm of Bousteads' as a clerk when his father grew too old to go on working; and who had struggled on to support the family after his sister Florence married Alexander Johnston* of the same firm. After the old Captain died, Thomas Scott offered him an excellent opportunity in Guthries' early in 1876. His widowed mother, retired at last from her endless battle to make ends meet, lived with him in some comfort in Thomson Road, before organising and becoming proprietress of The Young Ladies' Seminary, at Barganny Lodge in Oxley Road.

Ten years previously, in 1867, poor old Greenshields had mentioned the three insurance companies and the two banks for which Guthries' were Agents, and had touched upon the general extent of the firm's activities – which then seemed pretty numerous.

Since then business had expanded beyond all recognition. Not only had three new insurance companies, a coaling station and a New York bank been added to the agency list, but no less than four steamship companies – Eastern and Australian Mail Steamship Company; Castle Line; Hargreaves, Fergusson and Jackson; and the New York, London and China Steamship Company.

With Thomas Scott's lifelong interest in docks and shipping, it is easy to guess who had been the inspiration behind this remarkable marine proliferation.

Guthrie and Company had by now extended their trade as far as the Berau river on the north-east coast of Borneo, where the adventurous William Lingard,† captain and owner of the

* Alexander Johnston was in Bousteads' when John Anderson joined that firm in 1871. Johnston subsequently married Anderson's sister Florence, left Bousteads' and joined Guthries' in 1875. Thomas Scott (one hopes inspired by Johnston) took Anderson on in 1876.

† This was 'Tom' Lingard, the 'Rajah Laut' (or 'Ruler of the Seas') hero of Joseph Conrad's *Outcast of the Islands* and *Almayer's Folly*.

barque *West Indian* and the trader who had first discovered the entrance to that river, was now dealing exclusively with Guthries' as his consignees. They had helped him in a time of trouble; and Lingard did not forget. $7,000/- it had cost to settle Perriaya the Chetty's mortgage; and if it had not been for Guthries' he would have lost his fine *West Indian*. She had already been taken over by Perriaya on a bill of sale dated 1st June 1875; and it was a grateful Lingard who was able to pay the money down in hard cash on 3rd August of that year and take her back.

The buying and selling; the Singapore properties and the land agencies; the trusteeships; the normal, day to day commerce of Guthries' continued to keep pace with this growth. Two new events, one quite small and one later to be of some interest and amusement, were now attracting the occasional glance of Mr Glass.

The first was the arrival in Singapore of a likeable young character, Thomas Heslop Hill, who had been a coffee planter in Ceylon until a disease had destroyed his crops, and who had recently acquired an acreage of jungle on the island of Pulau Ubin in the eastern arm of the Johore Strait. On this – if he could be provided with financial assistance – he wanted to experiment with a few seeds of coffee, in this new and blight-free land.

Glass liked his attitude and recommended him to Guthrie and Scott, who advanced him the wherewithal and gave him their blessing.

The second event occured in June of the previous year, 1876. A splendidly enterprising English explorer, typical of Queen Victoria's magnificent reign, Henry Alexander Wickham by name, had returned to London from his adventures in Brazil, bringing with him aboard the ship *Amazonas* certain contraband (as seen from the Brazilian angle) in the shape of about fifty sacks, or say 70,000 seeds, of two South American types of tree which produced a gummy juice not unlike the Malayan 'caoutchouc'; these trees being known to botanists as Hevea Braziliensis and Castilloa.

Wickham had caused these seeds to be planted at Kew Gardens, where about four per cent had germinated; and of these the Superintendent of the Singapore Gardens, one Mr Murton, had acquired specimens to the number of twenty-two.

The amusement was occasioned some nine years later by

the reaction to this unimportant event of a Mr H. N. Ridley, the new Gardens Director.

That enthusiast, shortly after his arrival, had embarked upon a positive crusade on behalf of these miserable seedlings, boring everybody in the Club and indulging in fantasies of their being 'the salvation of Malaya', to the extent that he became widely known as 'Mad Ridley'. To keep him quiet he had been allowed to plant out nine or ten of them behind the Resident's house in Perak – at that time Mr (later Sir) Hugh Low, who was luckily a qualified botanist himself – together with one Castilloa for good measure; and on the same visit Ridley had superintended the planting of three or four more seedlings at Klang in Selangor.

* * *

Abandoning this pleasing picture of botanical zeal, the scene now shifts to a day when Mr Heslop Hill, the coffee planter, had decided that he really must look for a job or starve. Things were not going at all well; and his coffee-plants on Pulau Ubin were a failure.

Fortunately there was plenty of work to be done in the Native States. Before long, Hill, in muddy boots and torn breeches, was superintending the construction of cart tracks from Kuala Lumpur to Rawang in Selangor; in Perak from Bidor to Kuala Kangsar; and later at Seremban in the state of Sungei Ujong.

Good men are indeed hard to keep down. In recompense for his exceptional services the Selangor Government granted him certain fine patches of jungle at 'Batu Caves', 'Kent' and 'Weld's Hill'. Sungei Ujong gave him the lands of 'Bukit Nanas', 'Linsum' and 'Siliau', as well as a block later to be incorporated into a larger property known as 'Linggi'. Perak granted him two excellent areas known as 'Kamuning' and 'Changat Salak'.

Now he would plant coffee – on good land that would really pay.

At this period occurred a disastrous failure in all European tin mining interests throughout Malaya, amply justifying Guthrie and Company's initial hesitation regarding the Selangor Tin Mining Company. It was caused by inadequate prospecting and the use of too much expensive machinery. None but a certain John Muir on his mine up at Rawang – with his rich land and primitive 'Chinese' mining methods – was able to survive the storm.

This resulted in a massive shift of interest from tin to the more attractive prospect of planting first pepper and later Liberian coffee. The great acreages of these, rapidly opened, may be said to have provided Mr Heslop Hill either with good company or with many competitors, depending upon which way one likes to look at it.

Being a sociable soul and an optimist, whilst coffee prices boomed, Mr Hill probably took the former view.

But Brazil, from which the rubber seeds had been stolen, was soon to take its revenge.

Throughout the fat years from 1886, when the coffee plants first came into bearing, up to 1897, Hill and his companions flourished and thought little of the world's affairs beyond the distant jungle mountains. Their neatly kept estates and their charming thatch-roofed houses filled their lives.

Then came the shock. Prices that had remained steady at a satisfactory $47/- per 'pikul' (133 lbs) ever since 1894 suddenly slumped to a miserable $19/-. Brazilian coffee was flooding the market, Malay's 'coffee days' were numbered and its plantations doomed.

Few gave a thought to Ridley's ridiculous 'rubber', about which he had been prating every since his arrival in 1886. Then along came one 'Tim' Bailey, who had interplanted Hevea seeds (initially to form windbreaks) between the rows of coffee on his estate which later became part of the 'Highlands and Lowlands' properties near Klang in Selangor; and a belated scramble to do likewise occurred, in which Heslop Hill participated on all his far-scattered holdings.

This move – to be followed far and wide as the years went on – was only just in time to save Malaya's economy.

Its phenomenal success transformed the face of the country from north to south and expanded Britain's commercial interests in Malaya to giant size.

* * *

In the year 1896 the firm of Guthrie and Company, under the guiding hand of Thomas Scott and John Anderson, had finally decided to move forward firmly onto the mainland. They had accepted the 'agency' of no less than five coffee estates in Selangor and two in Negri Sembilan – these being among the estates owned by Thomas Heslop Hill, who was at that time busy planting up experimental patches of rubber between his coffee trees on all his many holdings.

Then, suddenly, the bottom fell out of the coffee market. Heslop Hill was now suffering agonies of doubt as to the future of his rubber trees – which he was convinced 'would never give any juice'. He had therefore thought it wise to put his property of 'Kamuning' up for sale.

This estate in Perak totalled 6,000 acres, with heavy stanniferous deposits and several opencast tin-mines in full operation. On it Hill had already planted four hundred acres of coffee and a little pepper, both of which were now in full bearing; and among the coffee, one hundred and twenty acres of rubber had recently been successfully interplanted.

John Anderson, Thomas Scott and a well known Kuala Lumpur millionaire named Loke Yew jointly purchased this fine property for themselves at the auction; which was therefore added to the list of Guthries' agencies in the following year, as was also a further coffee property in Selangor named Ledbury.

Thus the two partners of Guthries' for the first time became landed proprietors in the Native States. So too the firm itself from the year 1896 began to take firm root on the Peninsula.

BOOK FOUR

THE FLOWERING

CHAPTER I

TAKEN AT THE FLOOD

By the beginning of the twentieth century Guthries' had been in business on the mainland of Malaya for four years.

They were agents for a range of rubber estates; and John Anderson was part owner with Thomas Scott and Loke Yew in the large property of Kamuning in Perak. Although not yet providing much grist for Guthries' mill, these new interests were patches of light in a gloomy scene, for British business in Singapore was facing hard times.

The entrepôt trade was meeting vigorous competition; and all eyes were now beginning to turn towards 'The Peninsula', where the four States of Perak, Selangor, Negri Sembilan and Pahang had been grouped together in 1896 to form the 'Federated Malay States', with Sir Frank Swettenham as their Resident General.

Whether this limited amalgamation was in the best interests of Malaya in its growth to nationhood, or whether some wider scheme embracing all the Native States should have been devised, is a much discussed question. It is always easy to criticise in the light of subsequent history – and it should not be forgotten that Britain's chief rôle in Malaya was not that of a Father Christmas, but to bring peace out of the chaos, and to trade. First things first. Queen Victoria's ideal of making Malaya into a self-governing nation – the basic object of the Malayan Civil Service – would come, if it came at all, much later. What can certainly not be denied is that the 'FMS' (as it soon came familiarly to be called), was an immense administrative advance; and one that provided a vitally needed channel for the entry of commerce and capital, and so for the development of the whole country.

In October 1897 Guthries' had been invited by the Resident General to become 'Commercial Agents in London for the FMS Government'. Although this offer, which was accepted by the firm, was later withdrawn on the grounds that 'it might be regarded as interference with the functions of the Crown Agents', it is interesting as indicating Guthries' foremost position, even at that early date, in the rapidly developing mainland.

For British business firms in Singapore, the formation of the FMS was not before its time. The Dutch had been improving their shipping facilities; and since 1891 vessels had been calling for Straits produce at no less than fourteen ports in the Netherlands East Indies, of which the largest were Belawan and Macassar.

From the Straits Settlements tin was still the greatest export, whilst the trade in gambier had greatly declined by 1900. Pepper continued to be a significant item of merchandise, but spices in general were increasingly being shipped from the Netherlands East Indies direct to Europe and America and so bypassing Singapore.

The tide of fortune was beginning to turn against the Straits Settlements. Such trade as still existed was now meeting keen competition from the Germans, who were undercutting the freight rates of all British shipping lines and offering long term credit at low interest. Their secret Consular reports to the German government on every aspect of commerce formed by far the most accurate and comprehensive pool of information on Far Eastern affairs at that time in existence.

To off-set these misfortunes, the FMS – with its new demand for every description of import – was a godsend. Guthrie and Company were lucky to possess their landed and 'agency' interest on the mainland, where rubber trees, some now ready to be tapped, were already in evidence among the unprofitable coffee.

It is improbable that the firm was yet aware of the significance of these young trees to its future, but it is from this time that it first began to divide its trunk into two separate but interlocking branches. These were to be the essential complements to each other over the years, each one supplying what the other needed.

Events were also soon to cause the formation of a third body, in London, which would grow in time into the central directorate of all the firm's many activities. These three bodies were to face new challenges in difficult times and eventually to move forward into great prosperity – all three remaining together for as long as it was convenient to continue their mutual association.

Meanwhile in 1900, matters were not going well. Exports, upon which so much of the firm's prosperity depended, were down. Imports were certainly increasing heavily – but so were the overheads.

In order to keep pace with so many new lines of importation, Guthries' had been forced to expand; some might say, to over-expand. But for the energy and genius of John Anderson in abandoning unprofitable trade and concentrating on success – and in re-framing the whole structure of the firm with an eye to floating Malayan rubber companies on the London Market – it is doubtful whether Guthries' could have survived the first five difficult years of the twentieth century.

Anderson's rapid arrival to the leading position in the firm deserves some explanation.

In 1900 James Guthrie had died at his home in Tunbridge Wells; his loss being keenly felt both in London and Singapore. Thomas Scott was now an old man, sending news of failing health from his home in Angus – a house whose strange name 'Auchenreoch' had already become the telegraphic address of Guthries' in Singapore. Glass had left in 1892, together with Alexander Johnston, who had also become a partner in the firm at the same time as Anderson, in 1876.

James Guthrie's son Alexander, the heir to the 'Guthrie Empire' whose arrival in 1870 had curtailed Greenshields's future and swept his stake from the board, had died in 1878, leaving Scott free to foster the interests of his enterprising young protégé John Anderson; who thus became Scott's only partner and the driving force behind all the firm's business in Singapore and throughout Malaya.

True to Scott's hopes, Anderson was not long in showing his mettle. He had soon visited Bangkok to encourage that important aspect of Guthries' trade; and had then been appointed Consul General for Siam in Singapore.* In 1896 he became a member of the Singapore Legislative Council and – not content to remain a quietly attentive 'back bencher' during his first period in office – had made no little stir by opposing the Government on a question of land tenure in

* At this time John Anderson married Margaret, daughter of Admiral Bush of the Siamese Navy and well known at the Court of King Chulalongkorn. She died suddenly in Singapore within three years.

Malacca on the very first day he ever sat in Council. Over this a positive dogfight had broken out, in which this belligerent newcomer had led the non-officials; who were only defeated in the end by the inevitable 'official majority'.

At the next meeting, however, Anderson showed he was not one of those who think it their duty to oppose at any price. He proposed a motion to increase the fines for falsifying weights and measures which was heartily supported by the officials.

But, perhaps not surprisingly, he lost their backing once again when it came to his next motion, which was to increase the Council's non-official representation.

After that, and one more violent collision with the officials over the regulations for appointing legal advocates, Anderson washed his hands of government affairs and successfully continued to mind his own business for the next eleven years.

It was not until 1907, when the Governor himself invited him, 'as one of the most level-headed and respected citizens of Singapore', to return to the Legislative Council to head a commission of inquiry into the question of the opium trade throughout Malaya and Singapore, that the voice of John Anderson was once more to be heard in the Government of the country.

It was in matters of commerce and of 'the agencies' that the forceful hand of John Anderson can most clearly be discerned.

By 1900 a great change of the firm's policy had occurred. 'Shipping Line' Agency work was now slashed to the bone, being a very small profit-bringer; only two lines of ships remaining on the Company's books.

The 'trading' section of the firm would now concentrate on imports for the planters on the mainland, who were in need of all manner of stores and machinery. Jump in at once then and collar the best agencies. Not only that, but open an agency in Penang under the name of C. S. Seng and Company for local sale to the mainland of paint, cement, ales and stout, steel and bicycles. Acquire the agency for the Government of British North Borneo. Establish a footing in Sumatra by taking on the agency for the Pekan Bahroe Planting Company. Induce Scott to open a larger office in London to handle the home agency business. Finally, start up a branch in Australia for the collection and sale to China of sandalwood.

Rather than draw up a list of all the new agencies acquired by the firm since 1876, let it merely be said that, whereas at that time there had been three banks whose work in Singapore was carried on by Guthries', there were now, in 1900, no less than six. The insurance business remained unchanged at five agencies. Shipping was reduced to the Shan Line and Eastern and Australian Mail Steamship Company, served by two coal agencies – the old Cory Coal of long ago, plus the Wallarah Coal Company of Australia. Finally, by an immense change of emphasis, there were in 1900 no less than twenty-three new 'general agencies' held by the firm, whereas there had been none at all twenty-four years before.

These concerned tin-mines, gold mines, tobacco estates and tapioca plantations, as well as sugar, flour, cement, explosives, tea and coffee machinery, office furniture and safes, whiskies, beers, wines and spirits, canvas, Jeyes' Fluid and Lipton's tea.

John Anderson's reason for all this new business was of course the vast opportunity for trade provided by the opening of the FMS. The development of tin mines and plantations had caused a massive increase in the population of the Peninsula, and an avalanche of Chinese and South Indians had latterly been pouring in at the rate of over a hundred thousand a year.

Even so, whilst new warehouses were built to hold goods for the mainland of Malaya, the old godowns on Collyer Quay still dreamed peacefully of cordage and of aromatic oils.

The light still filtered through the cobwebs onto sacks of pepper and of cloves. Caoutchouc and guttapercha, nutmegs and benzoin, still came in through the wide doors on labouring backs to scent the evening air, as they had done long ago.

The Straits Produce Department, in short, still survived; and still supplied a small helping of bread and butter to a firm now outgrowing its nursery days and acquiring a taste for caviare and champagne.

* * *

On the mainland of Malaya, by 1900, planters were already beginning to take a serious interest in this new crop called 'rubber'.

The tree itself, 'Hevea Braziliensis', belongs to the family of trees and shrubs known as the 'Euphorbiaceae'; the largest and most widely diffused of all the Linnaean groupings. The family ranges from such small and familiar plants as the poinsettia and 'catstail', through the tapioca and castor oil plant to the enormous Macaranga tree, a single one of whose leaves is large enough for a baby's bath. The exhausted students of Dr Carl von Linné might well be excused for suspecting that the genus 'Euphorbiaceae', with no common feature apparent between one member of the family and another, was merely a blanket term to cover every plant too troublesome to classify.

'Hevea' is a fairly large deciduous tree of small pale-coloured flowers, whose sweet scent soon tends to grow rancid and overpowering.

Its foliage consists of leaflets springing finger-wise from a single stem to the number of three a leaf. The leaves grow in rings of five, jutting out from the branch like the spokes of a wheel to form a foliage-structure composed entirely of massed bunches of small circles reminiscent of a sketch by a pointilliste painter. The seeds resemble three chestnuts hanging together in a grey, woody pod – from which, on sunny days, they are ejected in all directions in a fusillade of small crackling explosions.

Except in the far north of Malaya, where the Trades bring a touch of winter drought from the plains of China, these trees, in the timeless equatorial land of their adoption, have almost forgotten the seasons, and flourish better in their new South-east Asian home than they ever did in Brazil (in which place, if their descendants are returned to it, they now pine and die).

Their value to man consists in the milk-white sap or 'latex' that exudes from the outer bark when delicately cut with a knife – a bark of ash-grey with dappled flecks of red and smooth as a faun's pelt.

A rubber tree takes about six years to become strong enough to be cut, or 'tapped', without serious damage to its growth. By that time it is perhaps twenty feet high, with a trunk diameter of six inches at eye level, which is normally kept branchless up to from seven to ten feet from the ground.

Many systems of tapping have been tried over the years, the ideal being to extract the greatest volume of sap from the tree without weakening its growth, whilst arranging matters – by careful cutting of the bark, so as not to damage the living tissue or 'bast' – so that the wound heals and the bark renews itself to form a smooth skin once more, which may be tapped again in future time.

Towards the end of the nineteenth century rubber had begun to cause considerable interest in Europe and America.

Originally the French mathematician La Condamine, when measuring the arc of a meridian in Brazil in 1736, had brought this strange stuff to the world's attention as a substance used by the natives for making waterproof boots and for covering their tents and clothes against the tropical rain, but little notice seems to have been taken.

Priestley, in 1770, is said to have introduced 'india rubber' into Britain, at which time inch cubes of it were on sale in London at seven shillings and sixpence each.

One Mackintosh, in 1824, who had been unsuccessfully attempting to produce a waterproof shooting jacket by drenching it with mineral oil, met and joined forces with a scientist, Thomas Hancock, who was using Brazilian 'india rubber' dissolved in naphtha for the same purpose. They then patented a process for the production of these rather messy articles and made a few sales.

Charles Goodyear of Massachusetts in 1843 patented a means of rendering rubber permanently elastic though dry and no longer sticky, which he called 'vulcanisation'; and from that time on Brazil began to supply an increasing tonnage of 'Para' rubber to the world's markets.

It was however Dunlop who eventually turned the scale by inventing the 'pneumatic' tyre in 1889.

By this invention that benefactor of humanity made an end to the shattering inter-crural thumps suffered by an entire generation, as they trundled over the cobblestones on their penny-farthings and, later, bicycles in a growing horde. The future of rubber as a world demand was assured.

Towards the end of the century the first motor cars, too, were already to be seen on occasional roads; and Brazil was exporting between twenty and thirty thousand tons per year of this precious 'india rubber'.

* * *

It was at this same time that ex-coffee planters in Malaya were examining the few rubber trees that had been planted by Tim Bailey, Thomas Heslop Hill and others; some of which were now old enough to be tapped. From the amount of sap they gave, it seemed that a good stand of Hevea should be able to produce no less than three hundred pounds of dry rubber per acre per year. At current prices there was good business in this.

E. V. Carey of Klang, and the two brothers Charles and Robert Meikle of an estate known as Wardieburn near Kuala Lumpur, had followed Tim Bailey's lead and planted rubber seeds between their coffee trees. These trees were attracting the interest of the two young brothers Kindersley who had joined Meikle some years before as 'creepers' or apprentices – to the extent that they had bought land of their own near the village of Kajang in Selangor in 1894 together with a part of the coffee property of Inch Kenneth at the same place; on which, by 1896, they had planted up a whole five acres of rubber.

Then the rush began.

Everybody was planting rubber as fast as they could. Rows and rows of the tall Hevea seedlings began to wave their leafy tops between the coffee shrubs on estates throughout the country. New clearings appeared in jungle edges. Cart tracks wound their way across the swamps and through the mountains to new lands, where forests were being felled and timber burnt to make ready for the new great ruler of the East, whose name was Rubber.

Years were to go by before the first bale found its way down to Singapore; but long before that the agency houses had begun to reap the rewards of Western entry into Malaya.

There was first of all the tremendous stimulation of foreign imports, caused by the demand for goods of all sorts by the planters themselves and by the rapidly increasing labouring population brought in from India and Ceylon by the British India Steam Navigation Co and from China by the Shan Line. But beyond that, an entirely new avenue of progress was opening for the Singapore merchant firms.

To plant up a rubber estate, even on the modest scale of a hundred acres or so, needed more capital than most people could afford. Jungle felling, preparation of the land, building of labour lines, engagement of labour, water supply, sanitation, medicines, purchase of seeds, manure, fencing, draining and the erection of some sort of habitation – all had to be thought of and paid for in hard cash, before the ad-

Sir John Anderson

Rubber tapping old style

venturous planter could resign himself to settling down for a whole six years of waiting before the first drop of latex trickled from his trees. During the whole of that time quit rents had to be met, the young plants tended and an extensive labour force paid.

Clearly this was a matter more for a limited liability company than for an individual. It was at this point that the agency houses were able to step in with timely offers of assistance.

Within a short time it became the practice for these agency houses to undertake preliminary negotiations for land with the State Governments; and, on invitation of groups of planters, to assume full control of their landed affairs.

A prospectus would then be drawn up and a limited liability company floated by their head office in Britain.

The advantages of this system to all concerned were very real.

Seen from the angle of the planter, he was now a shareholder in a properly organised business with a solid financial backing. He was free at last to develop his property in peace without the haunting fear of bankruptcy always peering like a spectre over his shoulder. He would earn a fair recompense for his hard and lonely life if things went well, and be helped over the worst pitfalls in his path should matters pan out badly. And a 'hard and lonely life' it was.

From the standpoint of the agency houses the system also held out excellent prospects. They would take a large holding of shares in the new company at par, and would become the Eastern agent for the London board of directors, among whom would of course be at least one of their own partners. The supply of every sort of agricultural implement, machinery, tool, fertiliser, building material and household necessity both for the estate as well as its labour force would then become the exclusive business of the agency firm.

Lastly, though this aspect developed slowly, for the rubber industry itself – and so for the future of all Malaya – the agencies' supervision of groups of estates; their centralisation of bookkeeping, finance and general management; as well as their system of employing private persons, often from outside the firm, as 'Visiting Agents', to unify procedure and encourage new techniques from estate to estate, were of essential service to the development of the whole industry. Their pool of centralised knowledge was to be of vital importance to all Malaya in the years to come.

As the writer of the work *Resources of the British Empire* was later to remark, 'Though there was, as has been seen, a rubber boom, its course was extraordinarily free from the financial scandal usually attending on such a phenomenon. Of fraudulent companies there were none, and of hopeless propositions from the start very few indeed. Seldom during a period of capital influx into an industry can a cleaner record have been achieved. These results can be put down to the fact that the leading part was taken by sterling, old-established East India Merchant Firms.'

* * *

Anderson venerated Thomas Scott – '*the* friend', as he once wrote, 'in his life'. But, especially toward the end, that did not prevent the latter's becoming, as was the Cross of Lorraine presented by General de Gaulle to Winston Churchill, 'une lourde Croix'.

Scott was now an old man and very much 'set in his ways'. He was the senior partner of Guthries', and also of Scott and Company, which had now moved to Number 5 Whittington Avenue, Leadenhall Street, and which was to all intents and purposes the London office of the Guthrie firm.

For several years it had become clear to John Anderson that this division of the firm into two halves, with the weaker, but senior, half in Britain, was an anachronism. The firm should be represented by an office in London in its own name. Moreover, with the chances now coming their way of floating rubber companies on the London market, it was obvious that, in order to attract public confidence, the two firms, combined as one, should become registered as a Limited Liability Company.

Thomas Scott was in no frame of mind for that sort of talk. The private company of Guthries' had been good enough for him, for his brother-in-law James and for James's old uncle Alexander. He had his son Robert to think of too; and succession was an important matter in a family concern. Turn the whole business into a Limited Liability Company and find oneself pushed around at board meetings by heaven knows whom, just because of this new-fangled rubber or whatever it was, that might be no more than a flash in the pan? Never!

So the unhappy tangle continued, as arguments between the generations sometimes do; youth eager – age reluctant; the young man with his eyes on the future – the old with his thoughts in the past.

Scott had been back to Singapore in 1899 for a short while. Anderson had tackled him then and later in 1901, when the latter was on leave in London on a working holiday connected with affairs in Australia as well as in Malaya – a furlough made glorious for him by his meeting and marrying his second wife, a Miss Winifred Ethel Dunbar Pope – but the old man had remained obdurate. Nothing was to be achieved whilst the senior partner was alive.

However, inevitably, 'the old order changeth'.

Mingled with the shock of losing his old counsellor and friend, there must have been in John Anderson's heart a not unkind tinge of relief when the news reached Singapore that Tom Scott had died at Auchenreoch on the 26th June 1902, that now the great firm of Guthries', which Thomas Scott had guarded so well, could at last once more move forward.

John Anderson acted quickly – and he needed to. He made rapid visits to London once more. Meetings were held with Mrs Sophie Guthrie, James Guthrie's widow, and with the Scott family headed by Robert McNair Scott and his mother Elizabeth née McNair (a far cry now from those wild chases round the deck and the laughter in the bo'sun's swing; but her heart and spirit remained young and unbroken, and she was a beauty still); with the result that Guthries' and Scott and Company joined forces as a Limited Liability Company on the 28th of February 1903, with its Head Office in Singapore. A London office remained at Number 5 Whittington Avenue and the combined firm was registered as 'Guthrie and Company Limited'.

But this did not come without much hard bargaining.

The newly formed company was capitalised at one million Malayan dollars, half being held by John Anderson and half by the Scott family together with Mrs Sophie Guthrie. Some three hundred thousand dollars of debenture or preference shares were to vest in the Scotts with Robert McNair Scott (till then a practising doctor of medicine) as London Director – to balance which, John Anderson was made Governing Director of the whole concern for the period of his lifetime, with very large powers indeed.

Now the firm could progress. Anderson hurried back to

Singapore; but before doing so there was the organisation of the London office to arrange.

Henry James Duncan Padday, the old General Manager of Scott and Company, together with Robert McNair Scott, would hold power of attorney from Anderson. So would two others who had proved themselves in the old firm of Scott and Company. These were Robert Murray Bell, an excellent young man of business who would provide the experience Scott needed; and John Emil Taleen, keen as his middle-European name, who knew his job thoroughly, exercised a masterful control over his staff, and who would continue to direct the increasingly important export department – this now being mostly cloths, foodstuffs, tin plate and machinery for Malaya.

Douglas William Lovell would be in charge of the sale of Straits produce in London; and Arthur William Stiven was useful in all departments and would have particular charge of staff and accounts. Both were old Singapore hands and new-comers to the London Office.

The rest of the staff could carry on as before; and so, too, could the curious practice of importing tinned pineapples into Britain from Malaya through Taleen's Export Department, and other such anomalies.

John Anderson was not the man to worry about logic provided the system worked.

CHAPTER 2

THE LINGGI STORY

Back in Singapore, Anderson threw himself into the new future opening for Guthries'.

Just before the firm became a Limited Liability Company in 1903, a property known as Changkat Melentang had been added to the agency list, as well as three coconut and fruit holdings on Singapore island, two of them belonging to Chinese and one – the coconut plantation of Pongol – to Anderson himself.

But it was not until immediately after this that two really important landed affairs came into the firm's control.

The first consisted of the Cheviot and Glendale estates in Negri Sembilan. These were mixed coffee, coconut and rubber properties owned by two former officers of the Singapore garrison, a Colonel the Honourable Charles Lambton and a Major Leathers, to whom was later added a third party, Mr F. Lambton. The estates were put in Guthrie and Company's charge in 1904.

The second large agency was that of 'Linggi', which also came to Guthries' in 1904, and whose history shows what small margins of luck and good management divide the undertaking which succeeds from that which fails. It tends also to modify any impression that the majority of estates were able to benefit by the first great 'boom' in rubber in the early years of the twentieth century.

Such is far from the case.

Fortunes were made only by those few properties with large acreages of rubber already mature by 1909 or at latest 1911, when the demand for rubber had exceeded the supply and a pound of it would fetch half a sovereign or more on the London market. In other words, only properties lucky enough to have bold and farsighted directors in England and brilliant managers in Malaya as early as 1903, or at latest 1905, were able to reap the vast profits of the boom years.

To take the case in point, 'The Linggi Liberian Coffee Company Limited', with an authorised capital of £7,500, had been registered in London in 1895 for the purpose of acquiring 1,000 acres of land in the State of Negri Sembilan, in order to plant coffee.

Charles Malcolm Cumming, a coffee planter of the locality, together with two neighbouring planter friends, had proposed the formation of this large property to a certain Mr Bishop, a bank manager; with the result that a Company – comprising five London businessmen, a surgeon, two barristers, a surveyor and various others – had been formed. A thousand acres of vacant jungle land were acquired for $4,000/-. Cumming and Bishop were the chief shareholders and land titles were duly issued by the Dato Klana (or chieftain) of Sungei Ujong in Negri Sembilan.

In spite of this good beginning, 'Linggi' was to have a rugged infancy.

Coffee prices fell disastrously in 1898, as has been told.

Cumming had wisely been planting up areas with experimental rubber from the beginning of the estate's opening in 1896; but when, in 1898, the shareholders had been asked to subscribe a further £3,000 for this 'rubber' experiment to be pushed forward with all speed in order to counterbalance probable future losses on coffee, they had failed to respond.

It had only been by Cumming's cutting down his own salary to practically nothing and taking on contract work from Government to build roads, that he had been able to continue his experimental rubber planting – a task which he completed on about three hundred acres leased for experimental planting along the Negri coastline, near the small village of Port Dickson.

Results of these trial areas persuaded the shareholders to authorise the planting of the first fifty acres of rubber on Linggi estate itself in 1902 – and Cumming's courage had eventually had its reward.

In February 1904 samples of Cumming's experimental plantings of 1896-7 were sold on the London Market for four shillings and fourpence per pound; and a much relieved board – who could now at last see, as Cumming had always predicted, where their best future lay – agreed that pending future developments 'arrangements would be made with Messrs Guthrie and Company to meet Mr Cumming's monetary requirements for running the estate, on the strength of reimbursement when the produce is sold'.

Even then the fate of Linggi still hung in the balance. Unless more capital could be raised the board would need to sell out.

This was put to the shareholders at an Extraordinary General Meeting in February 1905, with the forceful argument that 'rubber was now sure to be an increasingly profitable crop due to the rise of the motor industry' – a proposition that, fortunately for them, was generally accepted by those present. At the same meeting the name of the company was changed to 'Linggi Plantations Limited'. Guthries' were appointed Agents in the East and Secretaries in London; and Dr R. F. McNair Scott, the London Director of Guthries', was appointed to the Linggi board.

After that, matters began to move. The financial crisis was over, and in March of the same year John Anderson in Singapore was empowered to purchase for Linggi a further large property nearby named Ulu Sawah.

In May 1905 the estate of Kanchong was also bought by Linggi; and by the end of that year the nominal capital of the totally reconstructed company was raised to £50,000.

Guthrie and Company were by now heavily involved financially with the workings of the Linggi firm. A formal 'agreement of agency' was therefore signed between the two companies at the end of 1905 by which Guthries' were in future to have a commission of two and a half per cent on all sales of rubber and on all purchases of supplies.

* * *

The example of Linggi – its uneasy beginnings, the doubts and hesitancy of its shareholders, the precarious balance of opinion between supplying more capital on an untried venture or selling up – is typical of all the many Malayan agricultural undertakings at that time. Those who stuck to coffee, and were afraid to launch into rubber until crop returns had been further proved (and they were many) either went out of business or missed the boom.

Linggi's history is representative only of planting companies who had progressive managers at the right time;

whose shareholders chose boldly to finance the planting of rubber before 1903; and who had employed an experienced agency house in Malaya to supervise their business.

In 1898 Guthrie and Company had become the agents for Mr Heslop Hill's plantation at Batu Caves as well as Mrs Hill's land at Bukit Nanas. Under them these estates, together with Klang Lands and other properties, had then formed themselves into the 'Bukit Nanas Syndicate'; of which Guthries' continued as agents.

In November 1907 Linggi Plantations Limited, also on the advice of Guthrie and Company, bought up that Syndicate for the sum of £40,500 plus a total of 230,000 shares in Linggi of two shillings each. These shares were allotted to Heslop Hill, John Anderson and R. F. McNair Scott in the proportions of 112,000, 112,000 and 6,000 respectively. It is easy to see from this how interested the firm had by then become in rubber, not only as a Company, but also on the personal front of its Managing Directors.

In January 1908 John Anderson, now Governing Director of Linggi's Agents and a large shareholder in the Syndicate which that Company had just absorbed, became a member of the Linggi board.

Having purchased the estate of Beaumont in Selangor for $20,000/- in October of the same year, Linggi decided in December to buy up Kamuning, of which Anderson and Loke Yew had been the owners since the death of Thomas Scott. Loke Yew sold his shares to Anderson and the estate was bought by Linggi for £105,000 paid into John Anderson's hands. Guthrie and Company Limited, agents for the vendors as well as for Linggi, were paid in addition two and a half per cent of the sale price for their work from both sides.

No sooner was this done than Guthries' on behalf of the Linggi board, in September 1909 floated Kamuning estate once more on the London market as a separate company, for which Linggi received a sum of £132,500 (being 105,000 shares of one pound sterling each and £27,500 in cash), with the right to nominate three directors to the board of the new company with one of them always to be Chairman.

Thus the rubber industry grew; and thus the fortunes of John Anderson and of the firm of Guthrie and Company Limited grew with it.

To give details of all the other properties of which Guthries' became agents during the first decade of the twentieth century would merely repeat, with variations, the Linggi story.

In 1905 the export of rubber from Malaya was one hundred and four tons.

On the 14th of March 1907, the *Straits Times* remarked that 'within the last few years there have not been many products the demand for which has increased so enormously as the demand for rubber . . . Rubber is of the utmost importance.'

In that year the export had increased to nine hundred and two tons.

Three years later, by 1910, the export of rubber from Malaya was 5,439 tons – whilst by 1914 (a mere four years on), it had reached the astonishing figure of 196,000 tons; amounting to fifty-three per cent of the world's total supply.

Estates able to take advantage of this meteoric boom in rubber paid dividends of up to 375 per cent in the case of The Selangor Rubber Company and 237½ per cent in that of Linggi in 1910.

Though holding no monopoly of good fortune, Guthries' were agents, shareholders, sellers of rubber and general suppliers to at least their fair share of the best of Malaya's rubber estates during the years of the boom.

* * *

To talk of a business but not of its staff is to describe a clock without speaking of its machinery. Any story of South-east Asia that tells only of events and the doings of historical figures, while ignoring the human *masse de manœuvre*, is as empty as a drum or a dead sea-shell. Unless it takes account of the middle class of citizens whose roots are in the peasantry, whose sons became leaders and who rose through British commercial enterprise, it will have failed to disclose the source of energy which made such progress possible.

Some of the captains and officers have already been met; now to speak of the engine room artificers and the crew.

Since the earliest days of this history these 'senior ranks' throughout the Straits Settlements had been first the hard-working Chinese, secondly members of the Portuguese and Dutch races of Malacca, and more recently the astute and loquacious sons of India, the Madrasee Hindoos – all three of which groups provided the essential 'clerisy' of commerce as well as of the administration of Government.

The sailors, the outdoor overseers and the craftsmen were generally the Malays. Daily paid working men consisted of Chinese and South Indians, with a few Malays and Eurasians.

To represent them all, four individuals – two now and two in a later stage of this story – will be chosen. The first two represent the clerical class upon which the success of Malaya has been built; and the third and fourth stand surety for the working men whose toil and fortitude are the flesh and bones of Malaysia.

* *

Gan Eng Seng was one of the many sons of a poor Chinese family living on the outskirts of Malacca. His 'Gan' forefathers had emigrated to Malaya from the Fukkien Province of China, which, as good Hokkiens, they never forgot; though their motherland had been a harsh parent to drive them away from her by starvation.

Their new home of Malacca had proved less, but only a little less, unkindly; and at sixteen years of age young Eng Seng, whose name may be translated as 'Timely Opportunity' or 'Lucky Chance', said goodbye to his old home, squared his shoulders and made his way to that great town they spoke about called Singapore.

Lucky for him that he worked his way down the Malacca Strait in the one particular 'Pukat' that he did. Lucky to be told to off-load a bale of gambier into a godown on Collyer Quay called Guthries'. 'Lucky Chance' indeed to stumble at the entrance and hurl himself and his load in a heap at the feet of Thomas Scott. Plucky little Eng Seng was given a job in the godown on Mr Scott's instructions; and when Mr Scott engaged a man he did not forget him, but watched his progress and kept in touch.

It was six years after this, in 1867, that in speaking of that same godown, this history mentioned a handsome young pigtailed Chinese aged about twenty-two, whom Watson pointed out as 'Gan Eng Seng'; who was attentive and pleasant to look upon, but who was not expected to appear again in this chronicle and in whom nothing was seen out of the ordinary.

Truth to tell, he was summed up wisely. There was nothing extraordinary about Gan Eng Seng. His short biography is touched on here merely to outline a segment of the human element with which this story deals and to show the stuff of which the Chinese race is made.

Eng Seng made himself irreplaceable. He grew to know the godown better than the palm of his hand. He knew everything that was in it, where it was, how much it cost, where it came from, where it was going to, how long it had been there and how much it weighed. From sweeper to tally-clerk, to assistant storekeeper; to storekeeper itself – the busy, confident little figure of Gan Eng Seng climbed the ladder of success rung after rung; till at last a day came when he was given the post of Chief Compradore to the great firm of Guthries' – and at the same time became labour contractor for the rapidly expanding Tanjong Pagar Dock Company under the chairmanship of Thomas Scott.

From that time on, riches were his to command. And he used them well.

Recollecting how James Guthrie had started a school for poor children in Tanjong Pagar and noting how much interest Tom Scott always took in it – and remembering, too, his own unlettered and penurious childhood – the very first thing Gan Eng Seng did with his new wealth was to start a free school for the poverty-stricken Chinese children of the poor quarter of the town, in an area known as Telok Ayer.

Soon, too, he became the owner of large tracts of land to the east of the town, where he built a fine house for himself and his family among his fruit and nutmeg orchards. He entered as a partner into no less than fifteen Chinese trading concerns on the island; became a leading member of Mr Pickering's Chinese Advisory Board; donated thousands of dollars every year to hospitals and the needy; and founded a school for the poor in his ancestral village of Sam-Toh in the far-away province of Fukkien in China, which he frequently visited till his death in 1899 to pray at the tomb of his forefathers.

A great man. And a great benefactor.

In passing the famous Gan Eng Seng School in Singapore today, it is pleasant to pause awhile as the healthy laughing children come pouring through its doors, thousands strong, and to say, 'Well, Eng Seng – and you, too, Tom Scott – you did not do a bad job; either of you'.

* *

Ruy de Araujo (pronounced A-rose-o) the 'Bo'sun' was probably the first European since the ancient Greeks ever to set his foot upon the soil of Malaya, when he jumped over from the bow of the long-boat at Malacca to hold her steady whilst young Captain Despartes stepped ashore. They were the first to land on the Malay peninsula from Admiral Sequeira's small expeditionary force to the Far East in the autumn of 1509.

From that moment of destiny in South-east Asia – through Araujo's two-year-long imprisonment in a bamboo cage hung over the street until rescued by Alfonso de Albuquerque, and through centuries of diverse fortune and much adversity – the name of Araujo has remained as a permanent feature in the Malacca annals.

Shortly after the founding of Singapore, sucked into the vortex of that new Settlement as by a goldrush, came young Joachim de Araujo in search of fortune – at about the same time as John Sergi, also from Malacca, whose name has already been mentioned. What he did, and whether he found what he sought, is uncertain. All that is known is that he returned to Malacca in 1832 to marry Belmira de Sta Maria, the daughter of the highly respectable Senhor Carlos de Sta Maria and his wife Isabel Nuñes.

They returned to Singapore and in due time had seven children, of whom the second, Simon Jonathan Araujo, born on 28th October 1849, concerns this story closely. It is he who, having altered the spelling of his name to 'Aroozoo' (to the confusion of his biographer) became the office boy in Guthrie and Company's office in 1865 – that is to say two years before his cheerful and cheeky countenance was first observed by the reader when visiting Greenshields at that place.

Young Simon rose in the service of Guthries' to become chief clerk in 1876, by which time he had already married Regina Brown, the daughter of William Brown* and his wife Catherina, both of Penang.

Simon Aroozoo and Gan Eng Seng were close companions throughout all the many years of their work together in the firm. Simon, following the lead of his brilliant friend, became a considerable landowner too in the course of time, with roads and schools named after him, and descendants – trading

* William Brown, the grandson of David Brown of Lanarkshire in Scotland, was the first large landowner on Penang Island.

and professional people of note – who are now among the leading families of Malaya and have taken an important part in the social and educational life of Singapore for more than half a century.

The above two may be taken to represent the best of all the thousands of clerks in Malaya, whose faithful and often unrecognised services have oiled the wheels of progress. They have kept the engines turning whilst the engineers planned and the working men created a garden from a wilderness to make that country what it is today.

By the time old Simon retired in 1922, after fifty-seven years of duty with the firm, Guthries' had become a tradition with the Aroozoo family, into which brothers, sons and nephews entered themselves as a matter of course to work their way upward to success in life.

British commercial enterprise may have good reason to feel proud of a record in which so many local men and boys have used it as a support – have climbed up it as though up a beanstalk – to pour their wealth and energies for a century and a half into the building of two modern nations in South-east Asia.

CHAPTER 3

PROSPERITY

Before the outbreak of war in August 1914, the Government had been very much inclined to let commerce, of whatever nationality, go its own way within all reasonable limits. Within those limits it was anxious to afford encouragement to British enterprise; the Government of the FMS being particularly forthcoming in its offer of a helping hand to the promotion of British commerce.

Present-day students of Malayan history often cavil at this attitude of the FMS Government, claiming it to have been unfair to Asian interests. But when seen against the background of its times it was a perfectly correct and proper policy to adopt. There was every reason to assist British enterprise and no reason not to.

Britain's object in intervening in the Peninsula in 1875 had been to bring about a condition of peace and good government; first so that British trade and commerce might flourish and, secondly, so that the many afflictions of the local populace might be allayed. Both these objects had been attained in a remarkably short time. Good fortune – and a deal of good housekeeping – had even enabled the FMS Government year by year to pay for all the rapidly growing social services from duties and taxes on the country's commercial resources.

But Government's policy of assisting British enterprise never discouraged the growth of trade among the Asian population. Indeed, the majority of Asian businesses in their thousands – Chinese and Indian plantations and tin-mines as well as their shops and offices of trade and commerce – originated during this period. But the time had not yet come when the FMS Treasury could expect much contribution from these sources of revenue in its task of paying for the medical and health services, the construction of roads and railways and the provision of schools. These therefore largely needed to be financed from Customs duties on the imports and exports of British commerce – which the Government had thus no hesitation in supporting in every way it could

The FMS Government strongly favoured the opening of tin mines, the planting up of estates and the establishment of commercial offices by large and well financed British business firms; and saw no reason whatever to make any bones about it.

As a result, by 1910 the FMS was in a very prosperous condition indeed. Taxes on the export of rubber and tin, and on the imports needed by a rich and growing community, had provided the revenue for a network of roads and other public works unique in Asia. A railway system had been completed connecting Singapore with Penang and later with Bangkok. A Health-and-Medical Service, better than in most European countries at that time, had been established which would begin a successful campaign against smallpox and cholera with later victories over beri-beri and malaria. Finally, the State Primary Schools, opened in almost every 'Mukim' (parish) of the FMS, obeyed an educational policy that can only be criticised on the ground that it was designed solely for the Malay section of the country's multi-racial population.

This progress, brought about largely through the success of the rubber and tin industries, was already causing Malaya to stand out from among its neighbouring countries like a lighthouse.

Departments of Agriculture and Fisheries, Drainage and Irrigation, Forestry, Mining, Geological Survey; the administration of the Law; the Police; and the general economy of the country as shown by the country's fishing, farming, mining, timber extraction, local government, urban and rural, and industrial development, should also not be forgotten. Each one of these, together with Ordnance Survey, Harbours, Veterinary affairs, Game preservation, Animal husbandry and a host of others, were already the function of a specialised cadre of government officers under the control of trained administrators belonging to the Malayan Civil Service.

In these conditions Guthries' flourished exceedingly.

C. S. Seng's 'Agency' in Penang had developed to the point where it could be replaced by a full-scale Branch in 1905. Another Branch had been opened in Kuala Lumpur in 1909 with subsidiary Branches in Klang and Port Swettenham; and a Branch was also to be opened in Medan, in Sumatra, in 1912.

Guthries' had by now become Agents for no less than six more rubber estates in Borneo and a further one in Sumatra. They were Agents of four more Insurance Companies, two more Banks and the Singapore Electric Tramway Company. They represented Rudge motor-bicycles and Swift, Stoneleigh, Rambler, Herreschoff and Daimler motor cars.

This success was not brought about without much hard work and many difficult struggles.

From 1910 the export of rubber from the Malay States became not only the most important individual item of trade, but one which, by itself, supplied more revenue to the FMS Government than the taxation on all other imports and exports added together.

Every aspect of rubber's economy, from production to shipping and final use of the finished product by the buyer, had therefore become a vital interest to the Singapore Agency Houses.

* * *

One of Guthries' chief worries was the cost of shipment – the 'freight rates' – which had been drawn up by a ring of shippers in 1897 so as to secure a monopoly of freight from Singapore to the United Kingdom.

This monopoly, known as the 'Straits Homeward Conference', was supported by Boustead and Company, Patterson Simons and some others. It had been firmly opposed by John Anderson in 1897, in 1902 and in 1907; in the last of which years Guthries' had raised such an outcry that a Royal Commission was appointed to inquire into the whole affair.

Though the Commission's report was not particularly unfavourable to the shipping ring, John Anderson's minority report opposing it was enough to persuade Parliament in 1910 to approve the 'Straits Freights and Steamship Bill', which greatly modified the 1897 'Conference' and removed most of its worst evils.

Damage to Singapore's trade had, however, already been caused by the 1897 'Conference'.

Buyers in Britain and Europe were finding it cheaper to buy rubber from the Netherlands East Indies, where it could

Rubber tapping modern style

Simon Aroozoo

Gan Eng Seng

be shipped in 'non-Conference' vessels, and so the whole rubber trade was in danger of slipping out of Singapore's grasp.

Also, because of the high freights, it was much more expensive to ship rubber from Singapore to London and Europe (governed by Conference rates) than it would have been to ship it to America or Russia, where the Conference rates did not run. Both these countries, as well as Australia and Japan, were now buying increasing quantities of rubber. But as matters stood they could only buy it in London, which had been the leading world Para Rubber Market long before the first seedlings had been planted in Malaya, being a great financial centre with special services for weighing and sampling, warehousing and trans-shipment. America and Russia – to say nothing of Japan and Australia – were therefore becoming furious at the high prices imposed by London's monopoly and at the long double voyages the rubber had to make. They would gladly have taken their custom elsewhere if only enough rubber had existed anywhere else to satisfy their needs.

But more rubber was being exported from Java and Sumatra every year, so the situation was annually becoming more dangerous. Something had to be done about all this; and John Anderson decided to take action.

There was only one thing to be done. Rubber must be dragged out of the hands of London and offered for sale in Singapore, for shipment direct to all consumer countries wherever they might be. This step would lower the sale price by cutting down the expenses of insurance, warehousing, double freight and double handling and so ensure that Singapore kept its leading position in the rubber trade.

Once he had made up his mind, for Anderson to think was to act. As Chairman of the Singapore Chamber of Commerce, Anderson laid his plans. Rubber traders must agree to set up a local market – a 'Rubber Exchange' – where samples of rubber would be displayed in public and where various lots of physical rubber could be bought at auction. Whatever London might have to say – and many objections were sure to be raised – they must get busy at once to lease a suitable building; engage an adequate staff; and buy and install weighing machinery. Every rubber shipper must set aside as much rubber for local sale as could be spared over and above the London contracts already entered into.

The Singapore Chamber of Commerce was not long in drawing up a set of rules; and the first Rubber Auction was held in Singapore in 1911, at which lots were put up for sale by Guthries', Patterson Simons, Bousteads', Barlow and Behn Meyer.

As a result of London's efforts to stifle the growth of the Singapore Rubber Exchange, it was not in fact until after the outbreak of the War in 1914 that the full benefit of selling direct from Singapore came to be appreciated. From that time on the growing demand of America, Japan and Russia for rubber was met increasingly from Singapore; and the War might have taken a different course if those allies had not been able to keep themselves conveniently supplied.

* * *

The 1914–18 war also brought another significant change to the trade of the Straits Settlements. This was the temporary but complete obliteration of German competition in the Straits' trade and commerce. German business was replaced by that of the Americans and, to a growing extent, the Japanese.

After the war, and a short but very active period of rubber buying, the market slumped; many estates were offered for sale at low prices – and these both the Americans and the Japanese were able to buy up extremely cheaply, thus securing an even firmer foothold in the country and in Malayan commerce and industry.

In this post-war situation a complete change of policy occurred at home. Commerce was no longer to 'go its own way'. The theory of 'Empire Trade', or 'Imperial Preference', came to the fore; the thought behind this being 'an Empire developed as a single economic unit', with internal free trade as the ideal. Great Britain and the Dominions were to be the manufacturers of industrial goods, whilst the Colonies and Protectorates were to be the suppliers of raw material.

But in the situation then existing the theory of Empire Trade, so far as Singapore and Malaya were concerned, was foredoomed to failure. In order to overcome competition from European, American and Japanese firms it had been necessary for British Agency Houses to force their export of rubber into those countries rather than into Britain, which had resulted as a rule in the purchase, in return, of those countries' goods (rather than Britain's) for importation into Malaya.

By 1925 the annual value of Malayan rubber exports was sixty million pounds sterling, being therefore greater than the total exports of Ceylon, Nigeria, Gold Coast, Southern Rhodesia, Mauritius, Trinidad and Jamaica taken together.

Parliament was now awake to the importance of this trade, and for the first time fully appreciated the extent to which the Singapore Agency Houses had become the vital links in Empire commerce. Hence the latter were now continually being reminded of their 'Imperial' obligations and exhorted to find new openings for British manufactures.

But – as has just been remarked – ever since 1918 the tendency among Singapore Agency Houses had been to turn to sources of supply and demand *other* than the United Kingdom or Commonwealth countries. With the best will in the world, Guthries' and the other Singapore Agency Houses were unable to comply with Parliament's exhortations if they wished to continue in existence. The stream of commerce, now running in completely new channels as a result of the war, had made 'Empire Trade' impossible for Singapore – at least as far as slavish observance of 'Imperial Preference' was concerned.

Growing tension in regard to this matter came to a head at the Ottawa Conference in 1932, when the FMS adopted 'Preferential Duties' as a policy of Imperial co-operation, whereas Singapore declined to do so.

* * *

It was the firm of Guthries' which led the outcry of the merchants against these 'preferential duties' at the Ottawa Conference. In the same year it was they too who, for the same reason, stoutly opposed a proposal by the Governor, Sir Cecil Clementi, to form a Customs Union between the Straits Settlements and the FMS. Guthries' stated that 'We need both our Empire and our Foreign trade and, if preserved from interference, can maintain them both without prejudicing in any way genuine Empire expansion'.

Finally, it was Guthries' who fought to the last ditch against the 'Textile Quota' bill, whose passing by the Singapore Legislative Council on 11th June 1934 had such an adverse effect on the mercantile houses of Singapore.

The Textile Quota bill was designed to limit the importation into the Straits Settlements of Japanese textiles, whose worldwide distribution was damaging the trade of Lancashire. Parliament in Britain had therefore caused action to be taken in Singapore to restrict the modest imports of these into the Straits Settlements (which was a fairly easy step to insist upon), whilst refraining from doing so with their much heavier importation into Hong Kong, the West African Colonies or any of the Dominions, where such insistence would have been difficult. The bill was thoroughly unfair and unsound, in short; and it was typical of the Singapore Merchant Houses' fighting spirit that they raised such a prodigious though unavailing hue-and-cry.

But of course what had really been happening all this time – creeping quietly in like a tide whilst Tweedledum and Tweedledee fought their savage little battles unawares – had been something too deep-seated for any business house, or any Government, to mend. The whole trade of Singapore had been falling more and more into the hands of the Japanese.

During the 1914–18 war, Japan had first been able to compete with Britain in exporting cotton and rayon, bicycles and tyres, flooring and wall tiles, wire nails, staples and such hardware into the Straits and the FMS. Post-war, with the rise of Japan as a manufacturing country, all these goods, and commodities of many other descriptions, were landed at Singapore by the large Japanese merchant marine, which had replaced the German lines. These goods were now taken into the godowns and import offices of such important new business concerns as Mitsubishi Shoji KK (Limited) or the Mitsui Bussan KK (Limited), for retail distribution throughout the whole Peninsula.

Finally, in 1930, the worldwide depression in trade had compelled many countries to abandon the Gold Standard.

Britain took this course in September 1931, at which time one hundred Malayan dollars were worth between 76.5 and 93 yen in Japanese currency. A few months later the Japanese suddenly depreciated their own currency to the extent that it took 196.5 yen to equate with one hundred Malayan dollars! Flooding the East with cheap cloth, piece goods and manufactured articles of every description, from then on Japan was able to capture the major part of the entire Oriental market – a flood which was not to be stemmed for a further fourteen years; and then only temporarily and by the harsh arbitrament of arms.

CHAPTER 4

VEGETABLE AND MINERAL

By 1910 Guthries' main interests were in rubber and general trading.

Nevertheless, other commercial lines, highly prosperous to it at one time, should not be forgotten.

The first, the collection and export of sandalwood, arose out of the firm's commerce in Straits produce. The second was none other than that age-old business of South-east Asia, the mining of tin.

* *

Sandalwood, the 'Chandana' of the ancient Sanskrit-speaking peoples of India, had been exported from South-east Asia for thousands of years, the tree being thought by some to be the 'Almug-wood' used by King Solomon in his building of the temple of Jerusalem. However that may be, sandalwood was certainly taken to India and the Near East in pre-Christian times from Malaya, which is believed to be its place of origin; and it has also been in much demand in China for many centuries.

Both India and China use the smooth yellow timber of sandalwood for the carving of sacred objects; and for burning as incense, when powdered down and set in gum, in the form of 'joss sticks'. When distilled it produces an oil used in medicines and as a base for scents; but it is chiefly famous for its sweet amber smell when a paste of the powdered wood is spread over face and thighs, to drench the skin with long-lasting perfume as soon as it is warmed by the body beneath.

Sacred the little Santalum, Sandalwood or Chandana tree must certainly have been to the first primeval wanderer who stumbled across it, as it remains to his descendants today. Its scent alone would have ensured that, to say nothing of its extraordinary habit of feeding solely from the roots of surrounding vegetation, taking nothing from the soil for itself. Timor, Sumbawa and Sunda had exported it for hundreds of years, and towards the end of the nineteenth century the trade in this wood through Macassar and Singapore had grown so great that it exceeded the sources of supply.

At this stage – in 1895 to be exact – young Anderson first recollected Eucaria Fusanus, a tree of the same Santalaceae family as sandalwood, to be found fairly freely in the more fertile parts of Western Australia. Small though he was when he had been there, his eyes and ears were very sharp and he had a retentive memory. Eucaria Fusanus was slightly different from sandalwood, as he knew; but in smell, composition and effect its derivatives were every bit as good as the latter's and practically indistinguishable from them. From Fremantle northwards, he remembered, all along the coast and far inshore as well, these trees, locally regarded as 'sandalwood', and so named, grew in fair profusion.

Let the Wallarah coal people therefore suggest the name of someone to investigate on the spot and report as soon as possible on the prospects.

Charles Murphy, the man chosen, was not long in sending a favourable account of the 'sandalwood' forests near the coastline north of Fremantle; and in the following year 1896 a Western Australian department was opened in the firm's office in Singapore with Murphy in charge and two young men, C. E. Strode-Hall and J. Snodgrass, as his assistants.

Though sandalwood had been the original cause of this move of Anderson's, the duty of these three was to drum up every form of trade they could between Guthries' in Singapore and the west coast of Australia. The trade included timber, sago, tobacco, rattans, 'Rajah' brand pineapples, oil cake and a material called 'Crash' (a form of cloth in bolts of twenty-four yards length) as exports from Singapore, against the importation of pearls, mother of pearl, bêche-de-mer and trochus shell from Australia into Guthries' Singapore godowns, either for local sale or re-export.

The three salesmen used to travel out to Fremantle, and then up and down between there and Broome in the far north-west, aboard such vessels as the little old *Saladin*, *Sultan* or *Karrakatta*, whose long funnels and straight bows are still to be seen in the postcards so gaily sent home by those who took part in the goldrush to Donnybrook.

* *

About this time there came to the fore two men who were to decide the destiny of Guthries' first Australian venture; their names being Duncan Paterson and Alexander Ross.

Paterson had joined Guthries' in 1885 as an assistant coal and shipping clerk. Ross had been taken on from home two years earlier, in 1883, in the considerably more elevated capacity of assistant manager, with his name duly printed in the Singapore *Annual Directory*, though admittedly at the bottom of the list of assistant managers.

Now, in 1898, Ross was to be seen as the Senior Assistant, ruling the office, very much in the good books of Thomas Scott and junior only to that august London figure and to the latter's partner, John Anderson, in Singapore.

Paterson, too, was on the road to success, for he had just been selected by Anderson for the key position of Manager of a new branch of Guthries' to be opened in Fremantle.

The stage was set for a battle royal that would involve not only Paterson and Ross, but the two partners one against the other; that would have repercussions even after the death of Scott in 1902; and that would ultimately result in the downfall of Guthries' first business in Australia.

* *

On the 10th of February 1898, Duncan Paterson with his wife and infant daughter arrived in Fremantle. After two months of working furiously – bicycling down to his one-roomed office in town early each morning from cheap furnished lodgings and never doing less than twelve hours work a day – Paterson had already laid the foundations of a highly prosperous business. Pineapples and tobacco were selling well; contracts had been entered into for the supply of sugar from Singapore to every brewery in Fremantle and Perth; a beginning had been made in a new trade of jute direct from Calcutta. Anxious feelers were also being put forth by Paterson for the import of goods direct from Thomas Scott and Company of London rather than through Guthries' head office in Singapore. Above all, he was able to report to Anderson in April 1898 that in the matter of sandalwood he was off to a very fine start indeed.

In spite of adverse comment from Mr Ross of the 'Singapore Office' he had found it necessary, in order to break into that business at all, to agree to setting up a joint account, on a fifty-fifty basis, with a firm called J. and W. Bateman, in respect of all sandalwood exported. Batemans' had the sandalwood trade entirely in their hands, and if one wanted to do business, this was the only way to do it.

Setting up the office, moving into better quarters, the purchase of furniture and the engagement – again against the wishes of 'the head office' in the shape of Mr Alexander Ross – of a cashier as well as a general clerk, occupied the remainder of 1898; at the end of which time the new Australian venture had cost a sum of about a thousand pounds more than it had made.

By June of 1899, however, the Fremantle branch of Guthries' was doing splendidly with the gold mines of Calgoorlie and Calgardie – in kerosene, castor oil, cotton waste and explosives. It was selling five thousand cases of Malayan pineapples a month with large contracts for next season's delivery, and it had shipped two thousand tons of copper ore from Ballowballow to Swansea at a commission of one shilling per ton, with more contracts coming. By mid-year of 1899 it had also become the owner of five pearling luggers.

By this time, too, it was beginning to import direct from Scott and Company of London such things as anchors, chains, coal-tar, coke, oakum, copper rods, galvanised bars, cotton waste (baled by Rigby, Wainwright and Company) and many other items from iron nails to fencing wire, netting and linseed oil.

An import trade had begun with California in canned fruit, prunes in four and seven pound tins and apples in barrels. Indian teak was coming from Rangoon; carpets from Bombay; tea from Ceylon; cigarettes from Malta and cigars from Manila. Whisky was being supplied from Scotland and explosives from Dr Nahnsen and Company of Germany. The branch was also doing a good business with the eastern States of Australia in all lines of produce and was the agent for several companies of insurance, including the Triton Insurance Company and the World Marine.

Sandalwood was now being purchased by the firm independently, as well as through the agency of Batemans'. A successful export of Jarrah wood had been begun to the Tanjong Pagar Dock Company on behalf of a Messrs Gill and MacDonald.

In short, surveying the general scene, Paterson was able to write, in the most conservative manner possible, that 'if we sit tight and keep things running smoothly, last year's debit of £1,000 should be more than wiped off by the end of 1899'.

* *

But all this time something was going badly wrong.

The Singapore office was perpetually interfering, misunderstanding telegrams, failing to send in accounts and generally proving itself obstructive and troublesome. In addition to this negative attitude there were signs of a positive intention to destroy. To begin with, there was the matter of Guthries' own monopoly brand of 'High Life' cigars, which Paterson discovered to his astonishment were now obtainable by the Australian retailer direct from the head office in Singapore at cheaper prices than they were issued to his branch in bulk!

Secondly, there was the much graver question of the sandalwood shipments. As soon as Paterson had begun this export in conjunction with Batemans', he had asked the head office in Singapore to credit his Fremantle branch with a commission of five shillings a ton, which would only just cover the cost of labour, overtime wages for office staff, fees for the accountants etc, without gain of any sort to the Branch.

He had also suggested that on shipments of sandalwood to China and Europe the Branch keep the profits for the benefit of its future business, all the work having been done in Fremantle and the cargoes never having been within a thousand miles of Singapore. 'Singapore', as Paterson remarked in a later note of protest and appeal to Anderson, 'had had no more to do with these shipments than St Petersburg.'

Both suggestions were turned down abruptly, Ross calling Paterson's attention, in 'a tone of disparagement totally undeserved', to a remark said to have been made by Thomas Scott that 'Fremantle was never intended to have any share in the profits of the sandalwood business'.

This was depressing news indeed, but worse was to come. Paterson had engaged a certain Mr Amsberg, aged twenty-four, who had been in local commerce since he was fourteen years old and had what Thomas Scott used to call 'the minor trade' (groceries and so on) at his fingertips. As Amsberg had been most useful in Fremantle, he had been transferred by Paterson to Singapore in order to buy the type of goods that he – and only he – knew to be the best selling lines in Fremantle. Ross was furious at this overstepping of his authority and refused to have any dealings with Amsberg.

Paterson thereupon begged Anderson or Scott most urgently (and for the fourth time during one year) to pay Fremantle branch a visit, which they had never seen, in order to learn of the situation for themselves; but the 'Head Office' appeared to have so many pressing duties for them to perform that they were neither of them able to get away.

Worn out with worry and overwork, Paterson thereupon fell dangerously ill, after having written to Anderson that 'the Western Australian Department [in Singapore] does *not want* to run things so that Fremantle will pay'.

* *

The first crisis came when Paterson was already better and back to work. Anderson had written to say that any expansion of the Fremantle branch was not desirable; and that with Paterson's ill-health the time had come to curtail several of its less paying activities.

Paterson was baffled. It seemed to him certain that somehow or other Anderson in Singapore had misunderstood the situation or had not been presented with true facts on the profitable business being done by the Branch at Fremantle. He therefore wrote him a long letter and added that he had already engaged an assistant, a Mr F. Barrymore, to tide the branch over whilst he had been on sick leave and had now engaged him on a more permanent basis to handle the increasing work of the firm.

Alexander Ross saw to it that his protector, Thomas Scott in London, should be informed of this high-handed action on the part of Paterson; and a sharp division of opinion between the two partners occurred. It only remained for the 'Head Office' to deny all responsibility for the total loss of forty-four tons of Fremantle sandalwood whilst off-loading in Singapore – and the fat was in the fire. Batemans' had had enough. If that was the way things were going they would dissolve partnership.

The joint sandalwood business was now making two thousand pounds clear profit a year to each firm; and there was every reason for the Guthrie-Bateman combine to continue if at all possible.

At this time a tangled correspondence broke out between Paterson and Anderson, all much confused by the introduction of a fresh subject into the already turgid mixture.

Paterson's contract with Guthries' was to terminate at the end of 1900; and he had stated that with the responsibilities shouldered by him in Australia he would only be prepared to continue beyond that date if given the promise, after a further three years, of a partnership.

Anderson was by no means willing to grant this – first because even to propose such a step would madden Thomas Scott; and secondly because it was Anderson's determination to convert Guthries' into a Limited Liability Company as soon as possible, in which organisation Partners do not exist, but expensively salaried Directors do. Anderson had no wish for more of that particular category of person than those with whom he knew he was already to be saddled.

Letters grew heated; telegrams followed – a spate of telegrams – to the end that Batemans' washed their hands of any further dealings with Guthries' and dissolved their partnership.

Paterson resigned. And at last Anderson made a rushing visit to Fremantle.

* *

Thomas Scott died on the 26th of June 1902, the news not reaching Anderson in Singapore until the morning of Tuesday the 1st of July. It was, however, on that very same day that Mr Alexander Ross, the Chief Assistant Manager, found himself summarily dismissed from duty with notice of legal action served upon him for breach of his contract, in that he had been working for or with a firm of Messrs Shrager Brothers whilst still in the employment of Guthrie and Company.

John Anderson's visit to Fremantle in 1901, and the surprising disclosures made to him there, had at last opened his eyes to the truth.

A much relieved Paterson had withdrawn his resignation; and Anderson had bided his time until he could deal out telling retribution to the traitor in the camp – an act of justice which he was generous enough not to take whilst his poor failing old partner Scott remained alive. But the damage was done. The Bateman partnership was at an end; and from now on the Fremantle branch of Guthries' must struggle on as best it might.

* *

Deprived of the sandalwood nest-egg Guthries' Australian business, though at last permitted to retain its own profits, floundered into difficulties. Paterson's old trouble – a tuberculous lung for which he had already once had treatment at Davos – broke down again in late 1902 and compelled his temporary transfer to the London Office. During his absence the unfortunate Barrymore attempted to reactivate the collection of sandalwood, by the branch 'going it alone' in competition with Batemans'; and at the same time entered into a series of disastrous forward contracts which left the bank balance of the branch in a much depleted condition.

Paterson returned to Fremantle in September 1903 to find little left in the Profit and Loss Account of the satisfactory £29,000 that had been there on his departure. By stringent economy and heavy reduction of staff, however, he succeeded in converting that figure to slightly over £53,000 by the end of 1904.

Such prosperity was enough to turn anyone's head. Sandalwood had actually had scarcely any part in it. The luck had been running largely with pearls, the Siebe Gorman diving apparatus and a type of explosive for the gold mines called 'Devil' brand, in addition to the growing volume of business with the eastern Australian States as well as Europe and America. If only Paterson could once more bring back the old sandalwood business also, there would be a fortune indeed.

Batemans' had no quarrel with Paterson. If he were on his own they would co-operate with him willingly. A great future would undoubtedly open for him if he were an independent man.

Correspondence then broke out between him and Anderson in Singapore about this very point. Paterson's conditions for remaining with Guthries' were perfectly reasonable in the light of the attractive alternative before him. But, now that the Fremantle branch was dealing largely with London firms and was retaining its own profits, Anderson saw no particular advantage to Guthries' in agreeing to them. The parting of the ways came on 9th February 1905, when Paterson resigned from Guthries'. In due course he established a business in his own name and made a very handsome fortune.

Having suffered a series of heavy blows from that time forward – badly taken down by their agent in Calgoorlie over explosives, £10,000 loss through a fire, £25,000 loss through an investment in 20,000 tons of chaff which the firm held too long, and its unlucky entry into contracts for the sale of onions from the Eastern States immediately before the onion prices sky-rocketed by fifty per cent etc – the Fremantle branch of Guthries' went into voluntary liquidation in 1908.

It should be added that one more effort was made by Guthries' to enter the Australian sandalwood market – this being in 1910, when a business was opened in Fremantle under the name of 'Guthrie and Company Limited, (New Firm)', a certain John Hector being the Manager. The heyday of sandalwood was, however, over by that time; and this second attempt was also closed down, with some loss, in the year 1912.

* *

It would be satisfactory to say that the experience gained by these first two endeavours was of essential value in later years, when the time came for Guthries' once more to launch itself upon the Australian market. The fact is, however, that the former ventures and the successful Australian trade of today are so entirely different in every way that these old lessons have now no special relevance.

All that can safely be assured is, first, that of all things learnt, the most important was the need for the closest possible daily, even hourly, contact between the top executive échelon and the man on the ground, coupled with repeated visits for informal talks on every single aspect of affairs. The second was the inescapable conclusion that every living entity, including a business, has an optimum dimension at any given time, beyond which its growth is merely a cause of trouble and is of benefit to no one. The ideal to be achieved – and which has been achieved – is the closest possible friendly association between a family of independent business concerns, mutually co-operating for the security of their shareholders.

Guthries' had made much profit from sandalwood at one time – and had attached much importance to it; but the most valuable benefit that ever came Guthries' way from sandalwood was their learning of that ideal.

* * *

No true history of Malaya could be written without mention of the metal Tin, the essential stepping-stone used by Man in his ascent via the Bronze Age from the neolithic cave. Nor could any firm of traders as long resident in the East as Guthrie and Company be expected to have abstained from so attractive, if speculative, a gamble as 'Mining' throughout the whole course of its career. The wonder indeed is the modest extent, rather than otherwise, to which that firm had at any time become involved in it.

Extreme caution had certainly dictated their attitude to Tungku Kudin's offer of the shares in the Selangor Tin Mining Company in 1873, as has been mentioned. It is true that in 1889 Guthries' were Agents for the 'Pahang Central Tin and Exploration Company Limited', this being the first time the firm had interested itself officially in any mining venture; but there is no evidence that it put any money into the concern or ever did more than act as the company's representatives.

It was not in fact until 1890 that Guthries' finally decided to take any active part in that seductive game – and even then, strangely enough, it was not tin with which they first became concerned (as might have been expected on the part of a Malayan business), but gold.

* *

In the early part of the year 1890, a certain Henry Norman had landed in Singapore from a small coastal steamship and had made his way to the office of Messrs Guthrie and Company on Collyer Quay. He had travelled on foot, by native prahu, bullock-cart and pony all the way from Yala across the Siamese peninsula to the insignificant west coast township of Ra Nong near the Burmese border, then down to the island of Ujong Salang ('Junkceylon'), or Bhuket, as the Siamese say; and had thence come on to Singapore by sea. Tired, dirty and distinctly short of that most necessary of evils known as 'coin of the realm', Henry Norman yet gave no impression of distress or failure, for in the inner pocket of his shabby alpaca frock-coat there had reposed a creased and grubby document of no small importance and value.

So at least it had certainly seemed from the expression on the face of Norman's friend, Louis John Robertson Glass of Messrs Guthrie and Company, when that excellent man of business had somewhat gingerly fingered the original – which appeared to be written in Siamese – and had then thoughtfully examined the attested translation – 'Permit to prospect and to mine for gold and/or other minerals in the Hill known as Temoh in the district of Yala as at the plan attached etc.'

'Yees – verry interesting – signed by the Chow Phya Boladeb, I see – that means the Director of Land Development, doesn't it? – of Southern Siam. So that is why you went to Ra Nong. Yes. And then these are your prospecting results over the last eighteen months; spot bores at five-chain intervals to begin with, followed by close boring in the two selected areas you have marked in blue – I see.'

Steamers took some time to reach England in those days – but as soon as it was possible in the nineteenth century for such an event to occur, those same documents were in the hands of Thomas Scott in London; and were forming the subject of a conversation between him and his financier friend, the Honourable Mr Cachick Paul Chater. A telegram was sent to Glass in Singapore – 'Chater offers purchase half share Temoh Gold Mine ten thousand dollars'; to which a speedy agreement was dispatched by Henry Norman, thus concluding the deal.

No sooner done than Chater and Scott together floated a company named 'the Temoh Gold Hills Limited' on the London Market, to which the public rapidly subscribed an initial capital of no less than one hundred and twenty-five thousand pounds sterling.

History does not relate whether Mr (later Sir Paul) Chater continued his interest in the gold-mine. Nor does it say whether his partner Henry Norman, possessed now of pocket money to the extent of $10,000/- together with shares in the mine convertible at par to cash amounting to some sixty thousand pounds, dutifully returned to Temoh – or whether, as might seem more probable, he high-tailed it out of the East just as quickly as he knew how. All that remains is the fact that the Temoh Gold Hills Limited paid dividends; and that Guthries' continued as the company's Agents until the mine was worked out.

* *

It was Temoh gold which first drew Guthrie and Company's attention to Southern Siam; without which introduction it is possible that the firm might never have come to interest itself in the subject of this section, which is tin.

It so happened in the year 1904 – in other words at just about the time the gold of Temoh was petering out – that part time investigations were being carried out on river flats adjacent to Ra Nong. Gold was not discovered in significant quantities; but Tin was. The questions then arose as to whether it was worth mining – and, if so, by what means.

In those days alluvial deposits of tin were worked by washing – that is to say, the tin-bearing earth, sand, clay or whatever it was, having been dug up by hand, was mixed with water and then pumped up to the top of a long wooden ramp, down which the laden mixture flowed – the tin, being heavy, lodging in various slats placed at regular intervals on the way down. As the pumping was usually performed on the capillary system, the basis of which was an endless chain operated by a gang of twelve or more men working at a treadmill, the operation of an open-cast tin mine was slow, expensive and extremely troublesome.

In London John Anderson decided to seek the best advice available, both as to the prospects of deriving profit from the tin near Ra Nong, as well as the best method to be employed in extracting the ore if the prospects seemed good.

Luckily, among his London acquaintances was no less than the brilliant E. T. McCarthy, the well known consulting engineer. 'Why yes,' said the latter, 'on low-lying river flats, in a country of intensely heavy rainfall, what you obviously need is a boat, not a quarry. What you want is to let the water in, not keep struggling to keep it out. Half the trouble with these open-cast Chinese mines is that they are always getting flooded; and then it takes months of labour to pump them out before work can begin once more. Why not tackle the problem from the other end? Rig a bucket-dredge over the side of a large pontoon of some sort and eat your way into the tin-bearing area from the river or wherever you build and launch it? Something like a steam-dredge at a harbour mouth in fact. I'll draw up the specifications for you and design you one.'

So it came about that a company named the 'Renong* Mines Limited' was floated in 1906 to carry out detailed prospecting and planning for tin mining by the then unique method of employing a mobile pontoon or dredge. Upon the formation of its successor, the 'Renong Dredging Company', in November 1908, the first tin-dredge ever to work on land in South-east Asia was shipped out in sections and assembled on the river flats at Ra Nong.

By a strange quirk of fate a marine dredge for coastal tin had begun operations not far off at Tongkah harbour only a few months before the Renong dredge was installed; but the credit for tin-mining on land by dredging rather than by tunnelling into the earth or by open-cast quarrying must go to 'The Renong Dredging Company' and to their agents Messrs Guthrie and Company, through whose financial backing E. T. McCarthy was able to give free rein to his genius in designing the prototype of all the many dredges that produce the majority of Malaya's tin today.

* *

To continue the history of the mine itself, the 'Renong Dredging Company' re-formed itself into the 'Renong Tin Dredging Company Limited' on the 1st July 1913, when the construction of two more dredges was undertaken. All three dredges continued to work the river flats of Ra Nong until 1918, when the two newer ones were dismantled and re-assembled at Rasa in Selangor, where a large patch of riverine land had been acquired on mining lease from the Selangor Government. The original dredge remained working at Ra Nong until 1927, when the tin came to an end and the dredge was sold.

At Rasa matters proceeded well until disaster struck both dredges in 1921.

The upper Selangor river, always a turbulent and unpredictable stream, had been growing increasingly unmanageable for several years as a result of the clearing of mountain jungles around the newly opened health resort of Fraser's Hill. During the wet season of 1921, after a cyclonic rainstorm, a sudden flood of immense proportions dashed down

* 'Renong' means 'Ra Nong', of course.

the narrow valley, carrying all before it; swept away anchor-cables and moorings; and, catching both dredges broadside on, capsized them both as they rode to their headlines.

These vast steel monsters having sunk without trace in deep water and under fathoms of black ooze, the insurance underwriters had no hesitation in indemnifying Renong Tin in full and in abandoning the 'Wrecks' to the Company. Mr Nicholls, the manager, however, was not prepared to give in so easily.

He called in Guthries' Engineering Department; and between the two of them they proceeded to right the great hulks in their submarine position and then gradually to raise them once more to the surface – a remarkable if costly feat of engineering, whose best monument is the sight of these floating factories, filled with clamorous noise and brilliant lights and busy men, still grinding and screeching away by day and by night in their muddy lagoons at Rasa to this very day.

Since late in the thirties Renong has also possessed a further dredge that used to be seen east of Kuala Lumpur, working in a small valley known as 'Gombak'; and is now busily employed north of that city on the plain of 'Jinjang', where it has eaten through trunkroad and railway, reconstructing both with replacements of better quality on improved alignments.

At Rasa more land was acquired for mining in 1935; and two dredges are now working over the valley where the district capital of Kuala Kubu used once to stand until that same evil stream, the Selangor, rose in even more terrible wrath in 1926 and erased it from the eyes of man for ever.

To the story of Guthries' adventures in the world of Tin are now therefore added the interests of the historian and antiquarian, as paving-slabs, gravestones, inkpots, spoons, forks and crockery of all descriptions – scooped up from forty years ago and from under as many feet of heavy mud and sand – emerge once more in the buckets into the light of day.

As in the past, Guthries' still cherishes its share in the development and operation of Malayan tin, as one of the most interesting of all its many-sided activities.

CHAPTER 5

OPIUM

John Anderson was a prominent figure throughout Malaya during the early years of the twentieth century. He was the most outstanding personality in the rubber industry, upon which the development of the FMS depended; and he was at the same time principal spokesman for the entire Straits Settlements business community in its struggles with the Government on matters of trade policy.

Yet it is probably by neither of these things that he will chiefly be remembered, but rather by his chairmanship of the Commission of Enquiry into the Opium Trade, to which he was appointed by the Governor of the Straits Settlements in the year 1907. His brilliant carrying out of that assignment was to lead, more than anything else, to his being knighted in 1912.

Opium smoking had been general among Chinese, Indians and South-east Asians long before any contact had been made between them and the races of the West. For many centuries before the formation of the East India Company in 1600 it had been the practice among Eastern potentates every year to auction the monopoly of running brothels and gaming houses, as well as of selling to the public such commodities as pork, intoxicating spirits, and especially opium – upon the revenues of which sales they and their governments often largely depended. The successful bidders at these auctions, known as 'Farmers', were entitled to buy (or, in the case of brothels, to 'hire') the commodity they were farming at wholesale rates; and to sell it to the public at retail prices which, in theory at least, were controlled by the Government.

The East India Company had continued this system; and upon the transfer of the Straits Settlements from India to the Crown in 1867 the new Government of the Straits had inherited this source of revenue from its predecessor.

Auctions were held in fair conditions; the opium (mostly

from India) was of good quality; retail prices for sale to the public were strictly supervised; the farmers themselves engaged and employed their own service of preventive officers known as 'Chintengs'. Beyond that point the Government did not concern itself. In spite of comment from various quarters that 'The Straits Settlements lived on its vices', the Government did not at first appear to see any good reason to amend this procedure; or, perhaps more likely, it was unable to discover any practical means of abandoning it.

From 1867 until 1908, when action was taken on the Opium Commission's recommendations, between forty-five and sixty-six per cent of the total annual revenue of the Straits Settlements had been derived from the yearly auctioning of the Opium Farms alone. But conscience – that uneasy tyrant who will never leave the lazy British in peace for long – had been stirring up a fuss about opium ever since Lord Ashley, the Earl of Shaftesbury, had moved a Resolution in Parliament condemning the trade as early as 1843.

During the nineties, in South-east Asia, a group of Singapore missionaries, together with certain progressive younger Chinese, had begun to express strong 'anti-opium' sentiments; and these came to a head in 1898, when the *Straits Magazine* of June of that year published an article by a Dr Lim Boon Keng of Singapore calling for the formation of an 'Anti-Opium Society'. Rapid note of these signs of awakening Oriental concern upon the subject of opium was taken in Britain, where an organised 'Movement' against the traffic in opium had been gathering momentum since 1874. Inspired by that organisation, anti-opium Resolutions had been moved in the House of Commons in 1875, 1883, 1889, 1891; and culminated in 1894 in the setting up of a Royal Opium Commission at the insistence of Sir R. Laidlaw and Mr Samuel Smith, MP. Thus the Singapore agitation in 1898, small though it was, was certainly well timed.

Out East, matters had then tended to hang fire, possibly due to financial interests among the many Malayan Chinese who were involved in the trade – and it was not until 1906 that the tide appeared at last to be turning in Malaya, as it had long done in Britain, against continuance of the opium 'Farms'.

* * *

In the year 1898 two interesting events occurred; one in the Straits Settlements and one at home.

In Singapore that same Dr Lim Boon Keng who had just written to the *Straits Magazine* had been joined by a newly qualified medical practitioner called Dr Suat Chuan Yin, who had for some time been making it his duty to preach against the evils of opium, and who eventually combined forces with a Mr Suen-Sze-Ting, Consul-General for China no less, in opening a small 'Refuge' or rehabilitation centre in the latter's garden for those suffering from the opium habit.

In Britain a Liberal Government was now in office, under Sir Henry Campbell-Bannerman, whose Secretary of State for India, John Morley, had just publicly stated in Parliament that 'if China is sincere in desiring to restrict the consumption of opium . . . His Majesty's Government would co-operate, even though it might cost some sacrifice'; so it is probable that the events in Singapore and London were interconnected. The action of the Consul-General in opening his 'Refuge' was perhaps as much inspired by orders from Peking as by his own natural benevolence. The progress of the anti-opium movement from that time on provides an insight into the differing racial characteristics at that period between East and West.

In Singapore, the 'Refuge' – now supported by public subscription and able to move into larger quarters – was soon known by the pleasing appellation of 'The Anti-Opium-Smoking Lodge of the Charitable Institution for the Fostering of Virility'. Thirty seekers after increased virility were lodged free of charge; and a guarantee was given that they would be cured of the opium habit in a fortnight. This was achieved by the simple expedient of depriving the inmates of opium; administering sleeping draughts; and the sub-cutaneous injection of morphia (alkaloid of opium) to any who might feel slightly depressed.

In short, in true Celestial fashion, the gesture – and a very graceful gesture too – had been made. An opportunity had been provided for the attainment of merit by the exercise of generosity. Both patients and benefactors had been spiritually improved by the experience and no one was any the worse.

In the West, on the other hand, matters ground on in sadly pragmatical and unromantic manner.

In 1906 America – that eager beaver in everybody's business – had invited Britain to a 'joint International

Commission of Enquiry into the Opium Trade in East Asia'. In 1907 Britain had agreed, provided the 'production of native opium in China was included among the subjects tabled for investigation'. The Straits Settlements Government was then required 'to institute similar enquiries in the Straits Settlements as well as the Federated Malay States' – all the above being couched in that dry and niggardly manner so distressing to Oriental urbanity and so dampening to the flaming torch of Britain's starry-eyed if badly briefed idealists. (Enthusiasm for distant causes – provided they were distant enough – was of course rampant in Britain even then). In March 1907, in the far-away mining town of Ipoh in Perak, the first 'Anti-Opium Conference' had been held. As a result of this, by exempting Anti-opium Societies from fees under the Societies Ordinance, the FMS Government had first tacitly given its approval to the cause of reform.

In compliance with the Secretary of State's directions, the Singapore Legislative Council approved the appointment of a Commission of Enquiry. John Anderson was appointed Chairman of the Commission, his fellow members being Mr Tan Jiak Kim, Dr David Galloway, the Reverend W. F. Oldham (Methodist Bishop of Singapore), Dr W. R. C. Middleton (Principal Health Officer to the Singapore Municipality) and Mr E. F. H. Edlin, an Advocate and Solicitor.

* * *

The task before these men was formidable; for the Commission had not only to investigate the entire matter of the opium trade from production to consumption, but had then to advise what to do about it. The facile answer 'nothing' would no longer do, as that restless demon aforesaid was already roused.

Wiser than other bodies in later years, the Commission realised that prohibition would merely drive the traffic underground. It was also aware of the awkward position in which it found itself. More than half the annual revenue of the Straits Settlements depended on the opium trade; hence any recommendation for its continuance would be sure to be interpreted as 'kowtowing' to Government convenience.

In short, the Commission would be wrong, whatever recommendation it made.

However, braver than later-comers, in this situation the Commissioners carried out their self-imposed burden with praiseworthy indifference to public opinion.

No less than 34 meetings were held, 22 being in Singapore, 5 in Penang and 7 in Ipoh and Kuala Lumpur; at which a wide section of the public were interviewed, ranging from doctors, lawyers, businessmen, priests, clergymen, shopkeepers and mine owners to padi planters, rubber tappers, mining coolies and rickshaw men, to a total of ninety-four persons in all.

Arising out of all this Mr Anderson was able to give an incisive summing up, to the effect that consumption of opium appeared to be limited to the Chinese, 'who were well capable of looking after their own affairs, and should be encouraged to do so'. In short, the Chinese were not children, to be molly-coddled. If they wanted to take opium there was no earthly reason why they shouldn't; and certainly no earthly means of stopping them in any case. Opium smoking in moderation would seem no more dangerous to health than the use of tobacco, provided it was well prepared and free from adulterants.

Let the whole system of 'Opium-farming' be abolished, and a monopoly for the preparation and sale of opium be vested in the hands of the Government itself – so safeguarding the Government's Revenue whilst ensuring that good opium was sold to the public at fair prices. To this thoroughly businesslike recommendation were added the further clauses that the cost of opium should be the same in the Federated Malay States as in the Straits Settlements (FMS opium had been much cheaper until then) and that 'measures should be adopted for the ultimate extinction of the opium traffic'.

These last clauses, with others concerning the management of smokers' saloons and the suppression of opium in brothels, made it necessary for the Government to set up a Preventive Service of its own in replacement of the opium farmers' privately-employed 'Chintengs'.

It was that Service – maintained by revenue from Government's monopoly in selling opium – that was well on the way to eliminating the drug traffic from all Malaya until the fateful year 1945, when Britain decided to proscribe the consumption of opium by legal edict.

Thus the Government's monopoly of opium-selling necessarily came to an end. The Preventive Service – having no longer any ostensible reason for its existence and certainly no further revenue to support it – was paid off. And so it has come about that opium of dangerously poor quality is now openly smoked by old and young in every town and village throughout the land.

BOOK FIVE

STORMY HARVEST

CHAPTER I

AN INCONSPICUOUS NEWCOMER

The early years of the twentieth century made little impression on Number 5 Whittington Avenue, London EC. Here, for a year or two after Scott and Company had merged with Guthries', the caller, puffing his way upstairs and passing through the firm's gloomy portals, would have noticed no change in the sedate course so long pursued by that old 'East India Merchant House'.

There, in the inner office, still reigned the solid Mr Padday, soon to be retiring after many years in Penang and London. Beside him was Mr Robert Murray Bell, already obviously in command in spite of the occasional appearance of a handsome young doctor with his man-about-town air named Robert Frederick McNair Scott – who was in fact the senior London shareholder and Anderson's co-director.

There flitted Mr Emil Taleen in his shirtsleeves; pencil and paper in hand as he pounced hawklike about the Export department – a nightmare to junior clerks and the scourge of office boys. ('Piece goods, Lipton's tea and Ayala champagne for Singapore. Cotton waste, wire and Watson's dynamite for Australia. Gillingham's cement, Marshall's gas engines and Jeyes fluid for the FMS. Check all weight specifications, bills of lading, invoices. Carry over into day book and cross-refer with serial number of order in each case together with letter of credit.')

There too was to be observed the grey-haired presence of Mr Douglas William Lovell of the Produce department – much taken up with the latest shipment from Singapore of rice, tapioca and pearl sago, together with a parcel of Malacca canes and some citronella grass, for all of which warehouse space had to be provided at short notice. Fortunately cloves, nutmegs and mace, as well as such essential oils as patchouli and ylang-ylang, found a ready advance market in the City and caused no storage problem, which was a great relief.

Mr Lovell had also recently escaped another headache – boxes and boxes of that extraordinary stuff 'rubber' from C. M. Cumming's experimental plantations near Linggi in Negri Sembilan – which Lovell had passed on to young Duncan McNaught to handle. A good job the boy had made of it too – sold the first lot at the 1904 February auctions for four and fourpence a pound; and now more coming in and prices still rising. That young man would be in charge of a new department, the 'Rubber sales department', in a few more months; with little Jimmy Moffat (great great grandson of old Billy Moffat of the *Scaleby Castle*, by all the Powers that be) as his assistant. McNaught was to become a great expert on rubber; and, in time, to leave Guthries' to set up a successful rubber broking business on his own. James Moffat was later to rule the 'rubber sales' for many years with W. M. Leach to help him.

Also to be seen coming and going between the general office and the sanctum of the great Mr Bell was the stooping figure of Arthur William Stiven, in charge of Accounts; together with the youthful square-cut form of the 'personal assistant' to the former, the energetic Mr Alfred Hammond.

Arthur Stiven fades into the recesses of the Accounts department. There, running his pencil down a long list of figures at a side desk, sits a young man – the sixth leading personality in the tale of Guthries' – at sight of whom the presiding spirit of this history has good reason to catch its breath and pause.

John George Hay was, in fact, by no means alarming to look at. Rather prepossessing than otherwise, he was of medium height, thin, with a longish nose and a fair complexion – striking the attention, if at all, in no way other than in the alertness of his eye and the possession of rather fine hands.

Young Hay, later not only to wield such a powerful influence over Guthries' but to become leader of the entire worldwide rubber producing industry, had started life modestly, as many another famous Scotsman had done before him. Immediately-antecedent family fortune is a matter of little account in Scotland, where all blood is good. In a better integrated society than is to be found in England, boys from the croft, the manse, the shop and the castle look each other proudly in the face, trail their coats and fight each other, rough it and ruffle it with the best together in university, school or Princes Street. For there 'the rank is but the guinea's stamp; the man's the gowd for a' that!'

John George's father, Peter, was a Hay; in other words he belonged to one of the oldest and noblest clans in Scotland. The fact that he was also the unsuccessful proprietor of a small village shop at Burntisland in Fife was not as important to his neighbours as a fanatical religious enthusiasm on his part that set him at once among the country's 'characters'. 'Insured with the Almighty', as he maintained, Peter Hay, a sort of Scottish Mr Barrett of Wimpole Street, spent his days longing for the Heavenly Father to rescue him from this Vale of Tears – an unwordly concentration on the afterlife which certainly created his repute as a speaker at the Sabbath meetings of the Kirk, but which was no doubt responsible, too, for his lack of success in matters of business.

George, as John George Hay was always called by his family and friends, was born on the 1st of February 1883, the seventh child of a total brood of ten – a determined individualist ever since he first 'landed on his feet' at the earliest possible moment by emerging into the world legs-foremost. First at Burntisland and later in Aberdeen he had been brought up in the midst of a ravenous family by a shrewd and ever improvising mother, who was never too busy to be able to reserve a special smile for the boy who took so closely after her. He needed her protection if ever a child did – a highly strung lad, beset on the one side with the terrors of Hell fire for putting his hands in his pockets or whistling on Sundays, and lulled on the other by midnight visions of himself as a Cambridge undergraduate; from which he would awake in bitter disappointment to find it was only a dream.

With precocious eloquence, he once gave an 'end-of-term' recitation on the stage of his primary school at Aberdeen. 'When I grow up, and if I can, I want to be a clergyman', young George had declaimed, standing up very straight and wriggling his toes; just one of those walks of life, as Fate would have it (of all the many his friends and enemies were later to wish him) to which he never did in fact attain.

George joined a draper's shop at seventeen and in due time won a diploma in accountancy at night-school; after which he was accepted at Aberdeen railway station to fill a clerical vacancy. An acquaintance of his in the railway office, one J. I. ('Jiddy') Dawson, who had left for a better job in London and had joined Guthries', heard of a post going in the Accounts department of that firm that would just suit Hay – wrote to him about it – and there he was at last, aged twenty-one, a London businessman as from the 21st March 1904, employed by the well known East India Merchant House of Guthrie and Company in the capacity of Assistant Cashier.

* * *

In those days the Accounts department had just been put in rather grumpy charge of a new growth, recently foisted upon it. This was the 'Companies department', which had come into being as a result of John Anderson's whirlwind re-arrangements in London and Singapore after Thomas Scott's death. This 'Companies department' was designed towards the flotation of these new rubber companies on the London market that were making such a stir. The taking on of the Linggi Liberian Coffee Company in February 1904 had been the excuse for it, with more work of the same sort coming later; and a thorough nuisance it was altogether, what with the shortage of space, the two departments having to share a typist and nobody knowing anything much about company law.

As soon as Hay had settled in, one of his first jobs was to go into the new 'Companies department' (where the shared typist used to sit) and dictate a weekly letter to Singapore on the question of bunker coal. Here was shortly afterwards to arrive a gay young spark named C. B. Hester, aged nineteen, who quite fell before the spell of John Hay's flow of words and was to wonder ever after where on earth, in so short a time, he could possibly have got all his facts from. He would brief Singapore each week on the supply situation and on the current price of ships' fuel at every coaling station throughout the world; until Hester began to wonder whether it was not all just a clever bit of showmanship.

But that was not Hay's method, as the world would find out in time. Two of Hay's secrets of success were lightning intake of information and comprehensive grasp of the overall picture. But these could only have been achieved by intense concentration and attention to detail. It was this power of 'pin-pointing' the mind that gave him a clearer view of affairs than could possibly be derived from any clever skimming of the surface. The facts he gleaned sank into the recesses of his brain below the conscious levels of his thought – from which deep sea bed were to flash out in years to come those gleams of intuition which baffled his colleagues, which it irritated him exceedingly to explain and which amounted to genius.

When he lacked the material of facts on which to base his actions, however, he was of course just as liable to make mistakes as any other man. He nearly made a serious one at the very beginning of his career.

The Accounts department was not by any means the 'showpiece' among Guthries' departmental activities. Staid and conservative, the fusty old office with its pernickety book-keeping cut a poor figure beside the dashing and clatterbang 'Exports' or the romantic 'Produce department' with its Eastern smells and swashbuckling maritime air. And as for the 'Head Office' itself, all bird's-eye-and-maple and shining mahogany, with young Alfred Hammond under Bell's very nose all day and as smart as a new pin – why, that was the place to get on in the world and make a name. The way poor old Stiven would come crawling out of his hutch to see the boss five times a morning was enough to make the very ledgers hang their dog-ears in shame. Hay grumbled that he could moulder away here the whole of his life and never get anywhere. He must leave the Accounts department as soon as possible.

Mr Berry, of the firm of Lewis and Mounsey, Chartered Accountants, busy with Guthrie and Company's books, shook his head at this attitude. 'You are making a mistake, my boy', he said. 'You stay here. With the new Companies department as part of the Accounts work, this will soon be the most important section of Guthries'. You watch it. And if you will take my advice you will learn up all you can about company law. There will be a lot of work for Guthries' coming in that way soon.'

It was a lucky day for Hay – and for Guthries' too for that matter – when young master George listened to that piece of advice.

*   *   *

Mugging up on company law kept Hay heavily occupied during his first year with Guthries'. There were the daily accounts to do; the weekly letter to Singapore to write; and now an Extraordinary General Meeting to organise on behalf of the Linggi Liberian Coffee Company Limited in an attempt to raise more capital from the shareholders. As far as Hay could see, the only hope of achieving this – and so of avoiding the necessity of winding 'Linggi' up – was to convince the public that in this new produce called 'rubber' they were on to a good thing. But it was no use talking loosely about it. Facts and figures were what counted – and they must be at one's fingertips. More work therefore; first in the rubber sales department with Duncan McNaught and later at Daimler's for an estimate of future rubber consumption in the manufacture of motor tyres, so that the Chairman's speech would have enough real meat in it to win the shareholders over.

George Hay's weekend bicycling trips with Fred Hammond, down to Brighton and all along the cliffs to Newhaven, would have to be postponed.

No sooner had this momentous meeting been brought to a successful conclusion in February 1905 than Hay found himself already regarded as the firm's expert on matters of company law – saddled with the technicalities of changing the Linggi Company's name to 'Linggi Plantations Limited'; drafting the terms of Guthries' appointment as 'Agents' to Linggi in Malaya and Secretaries in London and of McNair Scott's appointment to the Linggi board for the lawyers to put in polished form.

But Linggi was only the beginning.

The tide of interest in rubber was about to set in – and to grow into a roaring flood – as that wise old witch-doctor Berry, of Lewis and Mounsey, had rightly smelt out and prophesied.

The Companies department was hard at it day after day. In addition to repeated meetings, there was all the work to do of preparing the floating of Colonel Lambton's and Major Leathers's fine estate of Labu as a limited liability company in 1907. There was much hard work in all this new business, to say nothing of carrying on the Accounts department itself – of which Hay had been promoted to Chief Cashier in that same year.

However, it was not until the following year, in 1908, that

work began upon what was to prove Hay's first challenge and his first real opportunity. He had already learned to place complete faith in his own competence – a stalwart quality whose attendant defect was his increasing disinclination to trust to the ability of others. He never really had confidence in anybody except himself to do a job well – he never learned to delegate – and from this there grew not only a 'distance' between him and his companions, but a mounting pyramid of labour whose apex gored his shoulders to the end of his days. Only one with such flooding ambition as to swamp the friendly 'give-and-take' of life would have needed to bear the burden he insisted on carrying.

* * *

One day in 1908 a certain Mr J. A. MacGregor, of Seremban in the Malay State of Negri Sembilan, who was the senior partner of a firm of advisers to the planting industry ('Visiting Agents') known as Messrs MacGregor, Mansergh and Douglas – later to be known as Mansergh and Taylor's – suggested to his friend John Anderson in Singapore that Guthries' might do worse than make a bid for the three poverty-stricken properties of Sua Betong, Sengkang and Pasir Panjang, over which MacGregor and his firm held controlling interests.

The plantation would take a heap of money to develop.

Here was rubber selling for seven shillings a pound and not a single tree on any of the estates yet ready for tapping. Costs were going up by leaps and bounds – and what with one thing and another it might be just as well for MacGregor, Mansergh and Douglas to sell out now if a decent offer were made.

Anderson had followed his 'hunches' before and found no reason to regret having done so. He had one now about these estates – in spite of the fact that on the total area of over thirteen thousand acres there were said to be less than eight hundred planted with rubber, and all still too young to be tapped for at least another three years. Much of the rest appeared to be nothing but a rolling plain of empty land – 'one of the biggest open wastes in the FMS' – as it was described in 1911 by Mr (later Sir) Eric Macfadyen, who had been engaged to make a report on the company's properties – 'an open lallang prairie'. It is only necessary to recall with what horror the planting community mentions the word 'Lallang' – that deep-rooted grass that eats up all the good in the soil and is the deadly enemy of the rubber tree – to realise the courage John Anderson must have possessed to follow his 'hunch' in this case.

Back in London, Hay's duty was to draw up the Prospectus for the new company to be launched, named 'The United Sua Betong Rubber Estates, Limited'; a task which he undertook with the same single-minded devotion that hallmarked every action in his life. John George Hay was always in earnest. Whether it happened to be golf, fishing or cricket, he would give his whole attention to whatever he was doing as though to a battle upon which his life (or, more important to him, his reputation) depended. He could never bring himself to take second place. Not to be first burned Hay up and went against his very nature. As a newcomer to the art of cycling he had even overborne the objections of his good-natured friend Hammond and insisted on taking the front seat of his tandem; with results – as they whirled their way down the steep hills of Sussex – that may well be imagined.

Young men often take themselves seriously; and there was nothing strange in this attitude on his part at the age of twenty-five. In his case, moreover, that tendency had been played upon and strengthened by a stern upbringing which had had no place in it for the ability to smile at life or to laugh at himself. Though success would bring these gentle gifts to him in time, both his nature and his background endowed Hay, in compensation for their lack in his youth, with a power-house of energy that would send him surging to the front in whatever he undertook – and that enabled him, in its first flush, to produce a Prospectus that was a model of its kind.

United Sua Betong was duly incorporated on the 15th of July 1909; with an authorised capital of £70,000 in £1 shares, of which 57,000 were issued there and then. The first Chairman was Sir William Hood Treacher, late of the Malayan Civil Service; Guthrie and Company were appointed Agents and Secretaries, and Mr John George Hay, a signatory to the Prospectus, was detailed as the person to undertake the latter duties.

CHAPTER 2

THE BOOM

In speaking of 1909, John Anderson might well have paraphrased Macbeth – 'so foul and fair a year I have not seen'.

On the one hand the boom was just the beginning. Rubber was selling for 12s 6d a pound; and an original two-shilling share in Linggi was now worth seventy shillings. Kamuning Estates, sold to Linggi by Anderson for one hundred and five thousand pounds' worth of Linggi shares when they had been at par, had just been floated as a separate company once more, in which new concern Anderson retained the above shares and was credited with the sum of twenty-seven thousand pounds sterling in addition. Both these companies – as well as some dozen or so other large rubber concerns by now included on Guthries' Agency-list – were under agreement to deal solely through Guthries' in all matters of buying and selling; and also to pay that firm a commission of two and a half per cent on each item of such business undertaken. And Mr John Anderson held half the shares of Guthries' in his own name.

On the other hand, there never had been such an irritating series of misadventures as seemed to have broken out in the London office as well as in Singapore. In the East, that necessary but maddening business of the dismissal of Ross for ruining the Australian venture in 1902 had left a bad hole in the book-keeping side of the staff. A certain W. W. Macmillan, with accountancy experience, had seemed a good substitute for Ross in Anderson's opinion; and he had been posted over the head of poor old Lim Koon Tye, the firm's chief Asian book-keeper, who had every expectation of being given the senior appointment. After that there was nothing but trouble.

Macmillan was soon promoted to General Manager, one of the main duties of which position was to control the firm's portfolio of investments. Lacking local knowledge, and at odds with the Chinese staff (who were capable of advising him and would have done so had they not been hurt at his overstepping Lim Koon Tye), Macmillan was soon in difficulties. In early 1909 he made a dangerously large forward-purchase of tin in expectation of a rise in price. The market fell disastrously instead. Guthries' suffered heavy losses which seriously embarrassed the firm. This was all bad enough – but worse was to come.

A Chinese land-owner in Perak had instructed his lawyer in Singapore to sell an important property of his known as 'Heawood', and had given him the usual power-of-attorney to do so.

At this time, Robert McNair Scott, the London Director and fifty per cent shareholder in Guthries', had decided to come out to Singapore with his mother to obtain first hand knowledge of what Macmillan had been up to in his outrageous speculation in Tin. Over this an acrimonious correspondence with John Anderson had already occurred. The Scotts arrived in Singapore on the 20th of March 1909, to find that Macmillan had been permitted by Anderson to leave for good on the 18th. An unhappy period in the directors' relationship then ensued until Anderson left on holiday for home on the 12th of April.

It was some weeks after this that the Heawood tin and rubber property was advertised for sale.

Robert McNair Scott in Singapore and C. M. Cumming, of Linggi estate fame, together acquired an option on it and proceeded to float a new company on the local market, which they named the 'Elphinstone Estates, Limited'. A Mr A. E. Baddeley of Guthries', soon to become General Manager of that firm, was appointed to the 'Elphinstone' board of directors as Chairman. Meanwhile – quite unaware of this – John Anderson, by then at home in Scotland, had also heard that Heawood estate was for sale. With his friend Gibson he therefore registered and floated 'The Heawood Tin and Rubber Company Limited' in Glasgow, with Robert Murray Bell of Guthries' London office on the board.

Thus there were now two companies claiming the right to purchase 'Heawood'; each headed by one of the fifty per cent shareholders of Guthries' and each also with a high-placed representative of that firm on its board. A more explosive situation could scarcely be imagined.

Ill-feeling, already boiling between the two shareholders, grew to such a pitch that for a time matters reached a complete deadlock; the Scotts' attorneys refusing to pass Guthries' accounts at the Annual General Meeting. In the end 'Heawood Estate' of Glasgow made a firm 'take-it-or-leave-it' offer to 'The Elphinstone Estate' of Singapore, which the unhappy Baddeley considered really should be accepted for the sake of peace. Elphinstone Estates went out of business. So a rearguard action on the part of the Scott faction began in the face of John Anderson's heavy guns, which was to end in the Scotts' eventual disappearance from the pages of Guthries' history.

Robert McNair Scott and his mother left Singapore for the last time in September 1909, to continue a tangled argument over Macmillan's ill-starred speculations and over a counter-charge made by Anderson as to the Scotts' use, or misuse, of Company's funds during his absence – a sound of battle that rolls inconclusively into the distance and so out of this story at the point where Anderson was driven to offer McNair Scott and his mother virtually half his kingdom for their shares in Guthries', in order to be finished with this insufferable situation for ever. The offer was accepted; Anderson became the sole shareholder in Guthries' (apart from certain small holdings by employees); and Robert McNair Scott continued as Director and later Chairman of Linggi Plantations.

Nobody had won the argument and both were heartily thankful it was over. The storm had also cleared the air and made Guthries' future progress more easy.

John Anderson returned to Singapore in April 1910. He now had complete control over the entire range of Guthries' business, which was what he had always wanted. From now on he would do the steering himself, without having to argue or consult with anybody. Anderson had no intention of staying out in the East for longer than he must. He had lived there since he had been a child of seven and had been to school in Singapore. He also knew the country and the people as few men have ever known either. But for that very reason the East had never cast over him the spell it so often seems to exercise upon those who come to it later on in life. To him, the 'land of his adoption' could never be Malaya – indeed it would much more likely be London. And there was no denying the fact that he was now fifty-eight years old. Nevertheless, there was a mass of work still to be done.

Sendayan estate in Negri Sembilan, Tangkah estate in north Johore and Bukit Kajang estate in southern Selangor had all just recently been floated as limited liability companies by Guthries' London office; and these needed constant nursing during the first year of their life under Guthries' control as Agents.

Lambton's and Leathers's property near Labu in Negri Sembilan was another problem. A large piece of land nearby had been planted up by them with rubber; and the Labu estate was now exhausting its reserve funds in maintenance and manuring costs of these seedlings. The new area should therefore be floated-off as a separate estate to call in fresh capital from the public – a work which would be carried out at once under the new estate name of 'Cheviot'. No sooner was this done and Cheviot floated in London by John Hay and his Companies department, than an estate near the coast of Negri Sembilan named 'Lukut' (which had been awkwardly thrown in as a division of Linggi some short while previously) was seen to form a more logical part of the newly acquired agency over Port Dickson estate in the immediate neighbourhood. Hence a considerable reshuffle had to be undertaken to bring this about in the shape of a new combined property, in future to be known as 'Port Dickson-Lukut' estate.

More work for Hay poured into the London office week by week from John Anderson's teeming brain. Kimanis estate was floated towards the end of 1910, and the last great effort of the year was the combination, on the advice once more of MacGregor of Mansergh and Taylor's, of various scattered Chinese rubber holdings in Negri Sembilan near the village of Temiang. 'Disunited Temiang', as it was dubbed by the staff, duly came into being as 'The United Temiang Rubber Estates Limited' on the London market in late 1910, floated by Guthries' and as Guthries' last 'Agency' acquisition for that year.

So the work went on.

In Singapore, A. Hood Begg from Aberdeen, a capable man of business who had opened the Penang branch in 1905, took over as General Manager in 1910, with Baddeley as his deputy. H. W. Noon was in charge of piece goods; Hay's dour Aberdeen friend J. I. Dawson had now been out East for the last three years and was doing well; V. I. Horne was learning in the rough-goods department before going on to open a branch in Klang. Young D. M. MacGilvray had been in Singapore for a year. He would soon be joined by two other recruits for Guthries' named Butterworth and Dunn.

In London until 1909 Robert Murray Bell remained in charge, with G. T. McEwan ruling a totally reconstituted Export department which he had splendidly built up and organised. The Produce department importing from the East under William Leach had dwindled to a trickle; or rather had remained as large as ever, but was now lost between the giants of 'Exports' and 'Rubber sales' – the latter of which still remained in the capable hands of Jimmy Moffat. The third new colossus, the Companies department, now the largest department of all, still bowed to its young John George Hay; while its staff congratulated him on his marriage in July 1910 to a Miss Constance Maye Leveritt, a close neighbour at his lodgings at Forest Hill.

Over all his empire a leisurely Anderson shone benignly; and, to complete the solar analogy, made his way splendidly towards the West in the beginning of 1912. For his outstanding work in Singapore and Malaya, John Anderson, on his arrival in London, was knighted by His Majesty King George the Fifth.

In that forgotten world all was safe and secure. In straw hats and blazers, in punts on the river, the young 'nuts' of the day looked forward through many years of sunshine to an assured future in the professions, the armed forces or the ancient, rock-like merchant houses of the City of London. So it had been beyond living memory. There was no reason why it should not go on in the same way for ever.

But 1912 merged into 1913; and 1913 into that fatal year, that fatal day, whose very sound (more like a deep bell than a date) still strikes chill into the hearts of those alive today who knew that time – the 4th August 1914.

* * *

Both Malaya and Guthries' survived – indeed thrived upon – the holocaust of the first world war. It was as though Fate had reserved them for a sterner experience in later years; and had contented herself meanwhile with branding them both with one mere lash from the whip of Mars.

Yet even that one branding stung; and it has not yet been quite forgotten by either. It happened in this way.

Wednesday the 28th October 1914 had stolen calm and clear over Penang; the first fingers of an equatorial dawn disclosing certain warships lying peacefully at anchor in that island's placid harbour. There had been much jollity ashore on Tuesday night; and now the watch aboard the Russian cruiser *Zemchug* and the two French destroyers *Pistolet* and *Iberville* were soporific, to say the least of it. Several senior officers of all three vessels had been away on shore leave overnight and had not yet returned to duty – a fact which had given the junior officers and crew the chance to entertain a number of Penang's enchanting little houris in their cabins and mess decks throughout the sultry hours of darkness.

A British Royal Naval cruiser, HMS *Yarmouth*, was expected to join them some time during the morning watch for combined exercises; and lo and behold, there was *Yarmouth* coming in now under her white ensign, turning in a wide arc to starboard and coming up to her station in the naval anchorage.

Then all hell broke loose. Down with the white ensign, up with the German 'Doppeladler' and over with the fourth 'funnel', carefully constructed of dunnage and burlap and painted 'crab-fat' grey. Captain Carl von Mueller gave the order and the German raider *Emden* poured a lethal succession of broadsides into the Russian cruiser close alongside. *Zemchug* was done for. She listed over and sank at her moorings in under fifteen minutes, taking with her almost a third of the 355 who had been on board. Pausing only to sink the gallant little French destroyer *Mousquet*, as she came nosing her way into harbour in the half light from off-shore patrol, *Emden* made away to the north-west and disappeared.

A la guerre, comme à la guerre. When *Emden* was eventually battered to bits herself by HMS *Sydney* off Keeling in the Cocos group of islands, her navigating officer, the swashbuckling Lieutenant Jules Lauterbach who later commanded the German raider *Möwe*, remained alive and free. Von Mueller had placed him in command of a captured British vessel, *Exford*, to lie off Cocos-Keeling with coal for *Emden* to refuel at sea; and when *Exford* was captured by the British *Empress of Japan*, Lauterbach and his dare-devil prize crew of *Emden* sailors were taken to Singapore as prisoners of war. The reckless courage and resource shown by *Emden* officers and crew during her short but glorious career might have warned Singapore of the type of men now committed to its charge – but neither the local Government nor the military were yet thinking in particularly warlike terms and both had still much to learn.

At the outbreak of war all German nationals in Singapore had been interned in the Teutonia Club – their own splendid edifice now known as the Goodwood Park Hotel. They were permitted to take their servants with them, to operate their own bank accounts and to buy goods and send messages wherever they wanted. People sent them flowers and fruit, paid them visits and found it quite impossible to cease to regard them as friends.

It was into this typically English atmosphere of 'Alice in Wonderland' that the Straits Government now saw fit to introduce Lieutenant Lauterbach and his sailors – personalities of a type such as 'James Bond' and 'Total War' have recently made commonplace throughout the world, unfamiliar as they were in those more gentle days.

The two senior German internees were Mr Diehn of Messrs Behn, Meyer and Mr Jessen of the Eastern Smelting Company. These two, in their patriotism for Germany, did what would now be thoroughly understandable, but what appeared then to be beyond belief. On behalf of their country they took part in an Eastern plot to murder her enemies among their fellow Europeans.

Emissaries of Germany's Muslim ally Turkey had been attempting to contact Diehn and Jessen since the beginning of the war; and had also been active among the colony's Mohammedan trading community. Their intention was to stir up trouble between them and their Christian overlords; and to inflame ill-feeling till it burst out into rebellion. A prominent Indian merchant named Kassim Mansoor had just been arrested and condemned to death for high treason in connection with that plot; and beneath the smiling surface of the Straits Settlements there flowed dangerous undercurrents indeed. The emissaries' intention had been to recruit Diehn's and Jessen's assistance in fomenting ill-will between the Moslems and the 'infidel' British – though in justice to those two Germans it must be mentioned that there is no evidence of their actual complicity in the attempt until the arrival in their midst of the *Emden's* prize crew from the captured *Exford.* After that – pooling their resources of knowledge on the one side and daring on the other – they made good progress.

Singapore had quite recovered from its fright over *Emden* four months previously, when that raider, before she had been destroyed, had sunk no less than eighteen vessels in the Bay of Bengal and Indian Ocean alone. Now she was gone; and soon after, on 9th December 1914, almost the entire German fleet under Admiral Graf Spee had been defeated off the Falkland Islands; leaving Singapore with no possible enemy action to worry about. So business was booming and everything was 'back to normal' – bridge parties, dances and picnics on holidays.

As for defence, there was the Army of course. There was not much 'Navy', to be sure; only the old gunboat *Cadmus*, lying alongside at Keppel Harbour, with a total complement of about eighty men. The army, to tell the truth, was also in a somewhat attenuated condition. Normally the military defences of Singapore, apart from the Forts under the command of a detachment of Royal Garrison Artillery, consisted of two battalions – one being from a British regiment and the other belonging to the Indian Army. At the outbreak of war in 1914 these had been the 1st Battalion of the King's Own Yorkshire Light Infantry from Britain and a detachment of 1,200 officers and men of the 5th Light Infantry regiment from Bengal. But the King's Own Yorkshire Light Infantry had left for the front at the end of 1914; and now the 5th (Indian) Light Infantry was off to Hong Kong on the 16th February aboard the troopship *Nore*, already at anchor in the roads.

The scene is now set for Monday the 15th of February 1915 – a public holiday, being Chinese New Year; and a grey rainy afternoon.

The rank and file of the 5th were almost all Pathans and Rajputs – Mohammedans from the Ranga district of Bengal, in the vicinity of Cawnpore. It was a good regiment, which had remained staunch during the Indian Mutiny. The battalion had been stationed in Singapore for a long time; and although there had been rumours of dissatisfaction over a matter of promotion and at leaving for Hong Kong, nobody had taken it very seriously. It seemed odd to the officers that there should have been such a fuss, and such a growth of unpleasantness in the barrack lines, during the fortnight before leaving – and they had therefore decided to pretend not to notice anything amiss and to 'play the whole situation down'. So after the 15th of February there would be no military force left in Singapore at all except the Volunteers – and a detachment of the Johore Forces about two hundred strong, sent over to Singapore on the 14th and already in quarters in Tanglin Barracks.

As for the poor old 'Volunteers', they were of course a joke, as always. During the *Emden* period these were found insufficient to man the Forts, so a new corps known as the 'Singapore Volunteer Rifles' had been formed. Then the local recruitment for 'Kitchener's Army' had begun; and most of these had sailed from Singapore on 11th November 1914 with the 1st Malayan Contingent, for France in 'the New Army'.

Apart from a few garrison artillerymen and engineers, that left nothing but a small detachment of the 3rd Sikhs; a few 'Malay States Guides' (a Sikh regiment locally recruited many years before in Malaya) in much disfavour for obeying Kassim Mansoor's plot by refusing to go to East Africa and now virtually in detention; and a remnant of the Singapore Volunteer Corps together with a few members of the Malay States Volunteer Rifles under training. To this assortment was now added the best joke of all – 'a perfect scream, my dear' – a corps of poor old 'Veterans', trudging along in the dust without any special uniform and most of them never having handled a rifle in all their lives.

In the light of this distinctly slender arm of defence for Britain's greatest Eastern fortress, it seems a little strange that in a time of war the military staff at Singapore should have uncomplainingly allowed two Japanese cruisers to depart on the 13th and the French cruiser *Montcalm* to leave the port the very day before the Indian regiment was also scheduled to embark for Hongkong.

In spite of the rain, everyone was making the best of the 'Chinese New Year'. Dunn and MacGilvray of Guthries' shared a seaside bungalow down at Pasir Panjang. They had invited quite a party to bathe in the morning and stay for curry-tiffin; and now their guests had all happily departed with many thanks except for Butterworth, also from Guthries', who was staying for tea. Their Manager, James Robertson, one of the aforesaid 'Veterans', was gloomily marching up and down on sentry-go outside the Teutonia Club – a thought which gave undisguised amusement to the three young men as they lounged in shorts and open shirts over their tea. But it really was bad luck, they had to agree, as the Volunteers had been demobilised over Chinese New Year and nearly everyone was off, either to stay with friends in the Native States or at seaside bungalows, as they were themselves.

Up at Alexandra Barracks the last of the ammunition was being checked in at the Quarter-Guard ready for boarding the troopship *Nore* at dawn the next morning; Captain Boyce of the 5th Light Infantry marking each box as it was carried in by two sweating infantrymen and ticking off the number with the stub of a pencil in his regimental notebook.

Jules Lauterbach, together with Diehn and Jessen, had worked steadily and worked well. At 4 pm a shout 'down, Sir, with that rifle'. 'My God' – one shot straight through the heart; and Captain Boyce lay dead. Too late to go back now. 'Break out all the ammunition and distribute, as the Alemani (Germans) ordered. Quick – and then follow the instructions you already know.'

A full chronicle of events throughout that time may perhaps be read in some other book than this – though it must be confessed one knows not where. It has no business here at any rate.

All that need concern this story is the effect of the Singapore Rebellion on the firm and staff of Guthries'.

Merely let it be said that, in spite of most of the senior staff of the Eastern Extension Telegraph Station having been butchered, wireless messages reached the French cruiser *Montcalm* which off-loaded 190 men and two machine guns on Wednesday the 17th; reached the Russian cruiser *Orel*, which landed 140 men on Thursday; reached the Japanese cruiser *Tsuchima*, which brought 75 men ashore on Saturday the 20th; and reached Rangoon, from which place the 4th (T) Battalion of the King's Own Shropshire Rifles came rushing to land from the steamship *Edvana* in Singapore on the afternoon of Sunday the 21st of February.

By that time, out of a total of 815 mutineers, 615 had surrendered and 52 had been killed.

For the first four days it had been the despised 'Veterans', 100 Japanese civilians and the Volunteers who held the improvised line between the P & O Wharf in Keppel Harbour and Cluny Road to the east; and so protected the centre of Singapore.

On Tuesday the 16th of February it had been a force composed of 80 men from *Cadmus*, 21 Royal Garrison Artillerymen, 50 Volunteers and 25 European civilians of no organised party at all, but merely possessed of courage and some description of fire-arm, who had attacked, up hill, a well entrenched battalion of trained mutineers and defeated them, so releasing Colonel Martin, Commanding Officer of the 5th Light Infantry and his officers, who had been surrounded in his quarters all night together with 82 men of the Malay States Volunteers Rifles who had defended them from their own men. In the charge that routed the mutineers Captain Brown and his band of shotgun-bearing civilians had intentionally drawn the brunt of the enemy's fire whilst the men from the *Cadmus* and the Volunteer assaulted the hill.

It was Colonel Brownlow of the Royal Garrison Artillery who later made the sneering remark in his report that 'the armed civilians had sense enough not to make any very bad mistake', whereby he earned the most crushing rebuke ever suffered by a soldier in the civilians' reply that 'they regretted they could not return the compliment'.

But by now the navigating officer of *Emden* and his *Exford* prize crew, together with Diehn and Jessen, were no longer interested in the events of Singapore. They had been extricated from the Teutonia Club on the evening of the 15th, had escaped to Johore and had sailed for Java and the Celebes; whence – after a tremendous voyage – they arrived in Shanghai, where Lauterbach was given command of the raider *Möwe*. And so all came safely home to Germany at last.

And Dunn and Butterworth and MacGilvray of Guthries' were no longer interested either. James Robertson had been shot in the neck and left for dead at his sentry-post outside the Teutonia. He lived as a matter of fact; and in a short time recovered. The young men were not so lucky. They were shot dead as they sat on the verandah – or, in the case of Dunn, in attempting to escape from it; as also was Mr Leigh, the Manager of Guthries' 'Heawood Estate'.

CHAPTER 3

GROWTH OF A TITAN

Throughout the world the war dragged on, with its shattering toll of death and human suffering.

Torpedoed by U-boats, sunk by mines, a diminished British Merchant Marine brought what it could to a hungry England. A lean and chilly people husbanded their meagre rations, sitting huddled over diminutive stick fires and tramping – to keep the cold out of their cardboard-leather boots – to under-staffed and badly lighted offices. Restrictions on freight space – highly necessary ones too – had limited imports to the barest necessities. This was no time to deal in luxuries from the Far East. One thing from the Far East however was not a luxury – and that was rubber.

John George Hay had his war work. He knew where he could make his best contribution to an Allied victory and was perfectly clear-eyed about it. Rubber was the thing he knew about. Rubber was what the Allies must have to bring the war to a successful conclusion. Rubber therefore was what he would see they continued to get to the best of his ability. If anyone thought he was shirking his duty by not donning uniform and sitting in a comfortable mess at Aldershot, then let them.

From 1914 to 1918 he steadily sharpened his knowledge of rubber in all its aspects; and tightened his grip on the affairs of the Companies department. He was given complete charge of that department at the war's end in 1918, the same year in which he had been appointed to his first Directorship – that of the rubber estate of Beaufort Borneo, Limited.

For fourteen years he had been closely observing the growth of the rubber industry. Whether from that, or the technique he had learned in compiling the coaling statistics of long ago, or whether it was merely as a result of his passion for analysis through the study of detail, one cannot tell – but it was certainly at about this time that Hay was seen to emerge as

Renong dredges working at Rasa

Sir John Hay

the first man to view rubber from a global angle; the first rubber expert in the 'international' – as distinct from the domestic – field.

The facts he found were certainly interesting.

In 1910 there had been a million acres of planted rubber throughout the world, much of it still immature. This, at that time, had produced about eleven thousand tons of rubber, of which Malaya produced some five thousand tons. But eleven thousand tons was nothing to the amount of jungle or 'wild' rubber, as it was called, that still reached the markets of the world, mostly from Brazil. During 1910 this had reached the extraordinary total of eighty-three thousand tons, in response to the demand for rubber for bicycle and motor tyres.

Even so, the world total of 'wild' rubber and plantation rubber added together, ninety-four thousand tons in all, had not been enough to satisfy the growing demand. The price of rubber in 1910 had risen to 12s 6d a pound, or £1,428 per ton. And then a miracle seemed to have occurred – a 'miracle' that was in reality the harvest of determination and foresight on the part of Malaya's businessmen and dogged planters.

In 1914 – only four years after Malaya had been able to produce approximately five thousand tons of rubber per annum, and pretty proud of that fact too – in four short years it had increased its annual rubber production from five thousand tons to the astonishing figure of one hundred and ninety-six thousand tons – half the whole world's production of rubber and twice the amount of all the world's export of 'wild' rubber. This had been achieved without any significant increase in planted acreage, but solely through the young rubber trees reaching maturity.

It was not to be wondered at, therefore, that Hay spent much time brooding at his desk in the early part of 1918. Rubber was a Titan among the world's commodities. Its power must be harnessed and controlled, or it could ruin whole countries when its price declined. Planting had gone on throughout the war, especially in the Netherlands East Indies, where the Dutch had been bursting to 'catch up' with Malaya; and now the total planted area out East was four million acres – which should soon be able to produce over three hundred thousand tons a year.

What about the price when the supply exceeded the demand? In 1917 there had already been a noticeable drop; and now they were talking about 'voluntary restriction in production' among British firms in order to keep the price up. This was nonsense. Only a rubber restriction scheme on an international basis – and enforceable throughout the world – would meet the case when the need for restriction came.

* * *

The war was over; a short honeymoon of spending was over too – and a small boom in rubber had fluttered out in 1920 to a dismally sagging price of two shillings a pound; to be followed in 1921 by the quite unprofitable quotation of ninepence halfpenny. Four million acres of rubber were now in bearing; supply was exceeding the demand; and the industry was up against its first serious economic problem.

John George Hay was becoming known in the world of rubber. He had been made a Director of his favourite company – the United Sua Betong – in 1919. But he was not yet important enough to be consulted when the rubber producing countries formed a joint Committee and met in 1921 to discuss ways and means of improving the selling price of the principal export, as rubber had now become. The Committee worked hard; but – for a reason that will be explained – could find no common basis of agreement.

A fresh Committee was therefore set up in 1922 under the chairmanship of Sir James Stevenson, GCMG, of the Board of Trade, which reported in May of that year that no scheme could possibly be applied which covered only one or more of the producing countries and not all of them. Sir James and his Committee had been bumping the same trouble that had bowled out the Government-sponsored meeting of 1921; i.e. the Dutch.

In arriving at his opinion that no scheme would work without the co-operation of those tight-fisted folk, prudence had guided Sir James's footsteps. The Dutch East Indies were still on an extremely low wage rate. In places the peasantry – virtually serfs – could scarely claim to be on a 'wage rate' at all. It therefore did not suit Mijnheer to restrict the production and export of his rubber, when he could continue to make a profit out of it at almost any price. The fact that the rest of the world could not do so naturally just made him laugh.

In this situation it therefore seems incredible that any idea of such a thing as a 'restriction scheme' continued to be pursued. Nevertheless, in October 1922 Sir James Stevenson's Committee blandly announced that 'a scheme of Government intervention should be put into operation in Ceylon, the Malay States and the Straits Settlements'. In spite of the outraged comments of Anderson, Hay and a chorus of others, the famous 'Stevenson Scheme' was off to a galloping start – as the clearest possible example of a case (not unknown in Government circles) where slavish adherence to a theory has overridden common sense.

Undoubtedly the Stevenson Scheme increased the selling price of rubber. The restrictions on rubber exports imposed on Ceylon, Malaya and the Straits Settlements by their own Governments could not fail to have that effect. Together they did after all amount to two-thirds of the total world production. But this was a positive Fortunatus' purse for the Hollander. Without any restrictions at all he was now free to profit from the increasing prices by producing all the rubber he possibly could; buying it from the peasants for a pittance and selling it on the international markets of New York, London, Tokyo or Amsterdam for a mere fraction less than the restricted countries' quotations.

Planting up hundreds of thousands more acres of rubber from the introduction of the Stevenson Scheme in 1922 until the British Government was eventually induced, in 1928, to call it off; increasing his area in full tapping by leaps and bounds; over the years the smiling Dutchman grew fat and contented. He loved the Stevenson Scheme. His unhappy counterparts over the water, paying wages on a Government scale and forbidden to produce more than a severely limited quantity of rubber per month, did not blame him one bit. But they were green with envy.

Neither Sir John Anderson nor John George Hay was able to prevent the scheme's coming into force in 1922. It was largely the forceful representations of the latter, however, that persuaded Parliament in the end to rescind it in 1928.

* * *

The post-war depression caused a number of rubber estates to fall into difficulties. The value of land in Malaya dropped with the price of rubber; and many estates were forced to sell out 'at the bottom of the market'.

John Anderson's faith in the future of rubber had never wavered. The decline in price in 1920 and 1921 – so far from alarming Sir John – merely presented him with a chance to buy up more rubber land at 'bargain' rates; to consolidate his firm's position and to encourage its growth and expansion. A property upon which he had long set his eyes was a vast concern – the largest rubber company in the country at that time known as the 'Malacca Rubber Plantations Limited'; which had originally been floated in 1906.

The original shareholders had been a group of Malacca planters who had come together in 1905 to take out an option on the large rubber property of Bukit Asahan, in the foothills of the famous Mount Ophir. This was being offered for sale by its owner, a Mr Tan Chay Yan, one of the pioneer Chinese rubber planters of Malaya. They bought it – which shows courage or rashness – for £225,000; in spite of an exceedingly unfavourable report on its condition produced by W. W. (Tim) Bailey, of Selangor; floated a Company in London with an initial capital of £300,000 and immediately planted up a further six thousand acres of adjoining land which the newly established company had acquired from the Government.

From that time on it had grown rapidly, the estate comprising nearly twenty-five thousand acres by as early as 1909. Though the 'Malacca Rubber Plantations Limited' had hardly benefited at all from the great 1910 boom, it continued to expand all through the 1914–18 war; raising alarmingly large debentures at an interest rate of 6 per cent; issuing extravagant estimates of future prospects that in no instance were anywhere nearly realised; and in general sailing blindly ahead into shoal water with all kites trimmed to the gale of public optimism.

Then the awakening. The post-war depression exposed the weakness of the Company – its incoherent organisation on the ground and the lack of cash, due to improvident housekeeping.

This was John Anderson's chance – and 'Malacca Rubber Plantations Limited' were glad to abandon their splendid isolation and seek the shelter of so widespread and stable an establishment as Guthries', who became its Agents and Secretaries in 1920.

Then began a tremendous work of reform and retrenchment. Hay, who was elected to the board, was put in charge – the sure forerunner to a radical shake-up. The very first thing he did was to streamline the administration by closing down the unnecessary Malacca 'Town' office; abolishing the posts of 'supervisory-managers', reducing the number of managers from sixteen to six and deleting the post of 'General Manager'. Whereafter he cut down everyone's salary by twenty-five per cent among the staff and fifty per cent among the directors.

Having delivered that opening salvo the board was in a position to approach the public with a considerable degree of confidence; a step which they took by issuing at 96 per cent £150,000 of seven-year Notes bearing interest at 8 per cent.

The depression could now be faced. Labour-saving modifications in planting and production followed in quick succession; and by 1923 the company were able to issue 171,036 ordinary £1 shares to the public, which were readily taken up at a price of thirty shillings. With this new access of capital the seven-year Notes were there and then paid off in full. 'Malacca Rubber Plantations' was once more on course and well clear of shoal water.

From whatever problem it may have been that Hay had tackled and solved – and there were few in the world of business that ever defeated that dogged and intuitive brain – he never failed to turn once more in the end, with a sigh of relief, to his favourite hobby, the Company of all others to which he was most deeply attached – United Sua Betong. From his desk in Whittington Avenue he nursed that estate like a child. In 1923 he had advised the board to buy the property of Ampar Tenang in Selangor, which increased the planted area of United Sua Betong by several thousand acres; and in 1925 it was again by his unfailing persuasion and initiative that the directors and shareholders were brought to agree in purchasing an immense rubber-plantation known as Tanah Merah on the borders of Negri Sembilan. This single transaction doubled the size of Sua Betong, whose acreage was increased by it, in one stroke, from 15,597 to 33,665 acres – and was one of those triumphs of courage and confidence in the future of rubber that successive Boards of Directors always seemed to display under the mesmerism of John George Hay's leadership.

CHAPTER 4

TEA-TIME MUSIC

When the first war ended Sir John Anderson was sixty-six years old. The dawn of a disillusioned age found the old man still grasping the helm of Guthries', as it entered a new and uncongenial world. The business had made money during the war – a lot of money – and Anderson had thought it only right to draw up a 'bonus' scheme for all the staff in the East, in appreciation of their hard work and their lack of leave. He had sent them his decision in this matter, with a financial statement on which he had based his calculations for an adequate bonus for them all.

And now here was Baddeley, the General Manager in Singapore, together with every assistant empowered to 'sign by procuration', writing in to say they had not been given enough; contesting his figures; and having the impertinence to maintain that he had set aside 'far too much for deprecia-tion and reserve'. From a young man to honoured old age Anderson had been accustomed to being obeyed; to giving his orders and to taking command. He might well have given them nothing at all; sitting out there all through the war – and now to be flouted and argued with in the very matter of his own personal generosity was too much. And by Baddeley too – the very man who had sided with McNair Scott and made himself into the Chairman of that ridiculous 'Elphin-stone Estate' as soon as his back was turned in 1910.

'Ha, you thought I had forgotten, did you?'

'Hood Begg, pack your bags and go back to Singapore at once. You are the General Manager. Baddeley is sacked. And so are all the rest of them. Put Milne of Renong Tin in charge of Penang instead of Henderson; find replacements for John Robertson, Freeman, Noon and Hill Cottingham. Train up Macdonald to take over from you as soon as he is able; and then you come back here. Lucky that J. I. Dawson didn't sign this damned thing. Call him back from Medan and make him your assistant. He is a thoroughly safe and hardworking man, who might do well as General Manager later on.'

When it came to running a business, John Anderson knew what he was doing. He was a hard taskmaster; and some were to say an unmerciful one – but his loyalty was to the firm and he had no use for argument. Guthries' had need of such masters to bring it to the stage it had reached.

* *

Old age was fast creeping up on John Anderson; but he still knew a good man when he saw one. The need was for a qualified assistant in Guthries' Singapore Engineering department.

Alexander Guthrie's old firm has justly taken pride in the men and boys of Singapore who have risen through its ranks to positions of importance in that State and in Malaysia. It was now to become the stepping stone in an Englishman's advance to power in the international field.

Laurence Hartnett, during the Japanese War and afterwards to be Australia's Director of Ordnance Production and Ordnance Adviser throughout the area of South-east Asian defence, now Sir Laurence Hartnett, CBE, had called at Number 5 Whittington Avenue in answer to Guthries' advertisement one morning in the autumn of 1922. Two hundred and twenty other people had already answered in writing, but Hartnett tipped the liftman five shillings for the name of the boss and appeared before Sir John Anderson in person.

Trained at Vickers, and with a good 1914–18 war record as an officer of the Royal Flying Corps, Hartnett – quite apart from this initial show of initiative – was not an applicant to be sneezed at; and it was not long before he found himself in Singapore. Here he made friends with a pleasant young American named Graeme K. Howard, field representative of the General Motors Corporation, through whom he had soon obtained for Guthries' the Agency of Buick motor cars. A great line of progress then opened for the firm that might have led far, had Hartnett not left in 1925. Even as it was, his fluent and accurate use of Malay had already endeared him to a large section of the population – an example of 'drive' and vivid salesmanship which enabled him to sell Buick cars to every Sultan in the country; the Sultan of Perak, as Ruler of the senior State, even buying five of them in one afternoon.

Perhaps the most interesting event that occurred through Hartnett's unflagging enterprise was Guthries' sudden launching out into the field of broadcasting – a move taken as early as 1924, many years before such a thought had entered the head of Government or of any other person in the East. It started by the London office consigning a large number of 'wireless receivers' to Singapore on the chance of selling them there . . . a remarkable speculation, to say the least of it, at a time when there was not a single radio transmitter anywhere in or near Malaya; and one in which it is only possible to suspect the subtle hand of young Mr Hartnett himself. Armed with these 'receivers' he had no difficulty in obtaining Hood Begg's permission to set up a broadcasting station in the firm's garage in Grange Road; and before long many hundreds of delighted purchasers of Guthrie 'wireless sets' were regularly listening in to news items of local interest, music and talks.

No legislation existed at that time for all this; and a censorious Government soon stepped in to demand the station's immediate closure. But the Sultan of Johore was by now a 'wireless fan'. He invited the Guthrie Station to move to his 'Unfederated State', where it would be safe from governmental interference. This was carried out at once; and hearers throughout the country continued to receive their daily entertainment unimpaired.

Then began the very type of battle with the Straits Government that the Sultan most enjoyed. In a discordant obbligato to the sweet strains of Tea-time Music, a torrent of threats and counterthreats surged relentlessly across the Causeway being constructed between Singapore and the mainland State of Johore.

'Close the Station, or Government will take action.'

'What action?'

'Guthries' are in Singapore and can be made to suffer for this.'

'If you so much as touch them we shall stop the trains running through Our State to Singapore.'

In the end it was the firm of Guthries' itself that decided to put a stop to the game. It had been glorious fun, but the punches on both sides were beginning to have too much meat in them – and it was getting beyond a joke.

* * *

John Anderson had lived a hard and vigorous life – and he had never spared himself. At the age of seventy-one, in 1923, he saw that the time had come to hand over the reins. His long years in Singapore had aged him and then there had been the evil 'war years', followed by the post-war slump.* Young John, his elder son, was still a boy. Someone must be chosen to carry on the firm in all its many complicated activities. He must give thought to the choice of a successor.

Hitherto, throughout the whole history of Guthries' from Alexander right through to himself, the mantle of leadership had fallen automatically upon successors who were themselves proprietors of the business – and indeed until 1902, when Thomas Scott had died, upon members of one family. From now on, it would be a different state of affairs. Virtually all Guthries' shares were in his own name – and these would descend to Lady Anderson on his death. But manifestly she could not be expected personally to direct and control the affairs of the firm.

The time of change had come. After his death, the shareholder, Lady Anderson, must hold final power of decision at board meetings, whilst standing apart from the working of the business; and a Managing Director must be appointed to control the entire future destiny of Guthries'. The post would require intimate knowledge of the firm in all its ramifications, the highest business acumen, devotion to a concern in which he would not be the proprietor and lucid powers to explain his policy to one person – rather than to a body of shareholders, among whom a number of supporters to any sound suggestion may generally be expected. But who?

History was to show that there was in fact only one choice – John George Hay.

That remarkable Scotsman had displayed over the years a quality normally to be found only among poets. For him, the rubber companies – the children of his brain – had become 'forms more real than living man'. Quixotically generous though he had always been to his brothers and relations, indulgent and considerate to his own son and daughters and scrupulously just and humane to 'Labour' – that great army of working men and women upon whom the success of the

* In 1920 Guthries' had made a net loss of over six hundred thousand pounds sterling. It says much for its past conservatism, its bankers' faith in its future and its good name in the City, that it could absorb such a shock in its stride.

plantations depended – the fact remained that Hay realised his children and the world would best be served by the wholehearted giving of the centre of his affections to the one and only job he knew. Let the cobbler stick to his last.

That that same world at large, unaware of his private benevolence, might regard him as divorced from human feeling, unpredictable in his decisions, irascible, mean-natured, hard and heartless in his demands for a desperately high standard of efficiency, was no concern of his. The progress of Guthries' – of 'the estates' – was the outward expression of his duty to God and to man; and was to Hay what the call of his country may become to an ardent patriot. Of his senior executives he demanded their all – complete loyalty, unquestioned obedience, knife-sharp intellect and utter dedication. He drove them mercilessly – but none ever half as hard as he drove himself.

The fact that he evinced only slight interest in the Import-Export side of the firm's business, which he would refer to as the 'pots and pans', was not vitally important, as there were many good men to carry on the work in those departments.

Very definitely it would seem that it ought to be Hay who should logically be chosen to fill this uniquely difficult appointment. But logic is by no means the leading characteristic of mankind. Private distrust and antagonism, the deep-seated subconscious urges of the psyche, also play their preponderant part. This question of a successor was to bring to the fore that same 'reluctance to change' on the part of the ageing Anderson that had so added to his own difficulties in dealing with Thomas Scott in years gone by.

This history has already touched upon the rearguard battle waged by the Guthrie clan against the encroaching Scotts. It has followed the agony of Greenshields's failure to assume command – to capture an effective share in the control of the firm. It has seen how wave after wave of assailants – perhaps Watson, probably Johnston, unquestionably Paterson and certainly Glass – had broken and recoiled exhausted against the solid bastion of the 'Scott and Anderson' combine. It has witnessed the quarrel that in the end broke out between John Anderson and old Thomas Scott over the question of 'limited liability'; and it has described Anderson's eventual shaking off of the remnants of both the 'Guthrie' as well as the 'Scott' families, to become sole master of the firm, after the embittered duel over Heawood (or 'Elphinstone') estate. And, later, it will repeat the story of age's reluctance to give way to youth.

Now, full of years, the old bull elephant himself was to fight his last and lonely battle. What particular act or omission on the part of Hay finally caused these passions to flare up openly in Sir John Anderson will possibly never be known. Let it merely be said that a shadow had fallen between them ever since Hay had first begun to show his mettle, to display his restless strength and to stand full-grown between Sir John and the light of the sun; and that this darkness had deepened as Hay loomed ever larger on the firm's horizon and finally began even to crowd in upon Sir John and to jostle at his very heels.

It would not be fitting for the historian to indulge in details or in guesses as to the rights and wrongs of the actions taken at this time by these two great men one against the other, when close descendants of both are alive to this day. Suffice it to say that for one reason or another the ill-feeling between the two reached such a pitch that at last Sir John Anderson, roaring defiance at his upstart antagonist (the only man whose force and brilliance could match his own), appointed one Morrison to succeed him – and from his sick-bed ordered Hay to be sacked.

Thus, when Sir John (the Moses who had led Alexander's old merchant house to the Promised Land) died on 18th December 1924, it was Morrison who took over as Managing Director, with Lady Anderson as Chairman of the Board.

But events cannot permanently be bent from their course by such dramatic scenes; nor can the decision of a powerful and venerated leader, once dead, continue for long to hold the future in fee. In a very short time the faithful Morrison was compelled to report his total inability to run the business without John George Hay; and the latter therefore assumed the position of General Manager in early 1925 and became the owner of one-sixth of the business.

* * *

It was about this time, too, that a highly significant event in the development of the firm of Guthrie and Company occurred.

For many years the total range of the business undertakings

for whom Guthries' had been acting as Agents and Secretaries had become known familiarly as 'The Guthrie Group'. Though these concerns – rubber estates, coconut plantations, tin mines or whatever they might be – had already begun to bear the indelible stamp of the 'Guthrie personality' in their business procedure and methods of agriculture and of book-keeping and accountancy, they continued nevertheless to be completely separate and independent entities.

Though this was still to be the state of affairs for many years, coming events were to cast their shadows before. From immediately after the war these had been pointing to the folly of relying entirely on one major commodity. The depression in the early twenties had given not only Hay but the Government of the FMS a considerable shock. Both had therefore been casting about in their minds for some diversification of crop to shield them from the worst effects of another such depression. 'Have faith in rubber, certainly', they both said in effect, 'but by all means try an experiment in some other tropical crop as well.'

It was at this stage that Hay suggested a joint venture among some of the companies comprising the 'Guthrie Group', that was to have an increasing effect on Malaya's economy in the years to come.

'Elaeis guineensis',* the African oil palm, known as an ornamental tree in European conservatories from the mid-eighteenth century, had been planted as a crop in Java since 1859. By about 1906 the palm had spread to Malaya, where estate managers here and there had planted up a few trees in their gardens – but it was not until 1910 that planting on a commercial scale was begun, first in Sumatra and almost immediately afterwards in Malaya, at Kluang to be precise, in the State of Johore. Here quite a considerable little estate of these trees was flourishing by 1920.

Readily agreeing to Hay's proposal, certain 'Guthrie Group' estates combined to purchase this small property as the nucleus of a much greater area surrounding it, which they acquired from the Johore Government. A new company was formed called 'Elaeis', the largest single block of whose shares was held by United Sua Betong Estates; the planting of oil palms began in 1924 and, under the aegis of Guthries', a new agricultural industry took root in Malaya.

Important as this new development was to the firm of

* See Appendix C.

Guthrie and Company as well as to Malaya as a whole, its interest – perhaps its chief interest – to this history lies in the change it displayed in the nature of the 'Guthrie Group'. They were no longer a mere collection of estates that happened to employ the same firm of Agents and Secretaries. It was no longer a mere convenience that they happened to operate their business on identical lines and with identical account books. The 'Elaeis' venture was the first outward sign of their becoming a corporate body, with united interests and under a single overall command.

* * *

By 1928 Hay had enough on his plate to satisfy Gargantua.

Three years had gone by since 'the old man's' death. Everything since then had been Hay's responsibility; all must be borne on his shoulders alone. In 1927 he had become the Chairman of the United Sua Betong board; a position which gave him even more status in his fight with Parliament to rescind 'that first class disaster', as he termed it – the Stevenson Scheme; and when that came about in 1928 he was faced, as he knew he would be, with angry comment from many planters and colleagues in the rubber business.

The scheme had protected the price of rubber, while selling out the entire industry to the Dutch. It was a drug that had dulled the pain while aggravating the disease. Now that it was at last removed, the whole trade in rubber, from plantation to sale of the finished product, was laid bare to the unshielded economic forces of the world.

By now, in 1929, there were, in all the tropical regions of the globe, approximately seven million acres of planted 'Hevea', from which vast area the hitherto unapproached quantity of 862,000 tons of rubber was annually pouring forth upon the market – and selling at the modest but not entirely unprofitable price of tenpence a pound. But a world-wide economic storm was in the making – the shattering 'depression' of the early thirties – and matters could not continue long even at that low level.

In 1930 the price took another heavy dip – and by 1932 nearly 900,000 tons of rubber were being offered for sale at the ludicrous price of one and five-eighths of a penny per pound, or £15 3s 4d a ton. Such a fall was catastrophic.

CHAPTER 5

THE GREAT STORM

Out in Malaya in 1930 the sun shone gloriously on a magnificent countryside. From the air, where aircraft were beginning to thread their way in increasing numbers across the sky, one could now gaze down at the new Malaya. There – far below – were the rivers and the ships; the railway and the sparkling well laid towns – clean and knife-sharp roads slicing the map from north to south and from east to west as they dissected the greenery into admirably neat and well cultivated chunks. Everywhere, from one horizon to the other – in endless lines, close-packed and dead straight on the flats and twisting into satisfactory patterns as they followed the contours in the land – stood the regimented riches of Malaya; rubber, rubber, rubber, as far as the eye could reach – 3,500,000 acres of it in Malaya alone.

In the early 1930s on the plantations in Malaya there was a European assistant for every 250 acres of rubber. The head office of each estate was comfortably staffed with Managers, Deputies and Senior Engineers. Doctors in charge of 'Group Hospitals' toured their limited but densely populated areas on the watch for breeding grounds of the anophelene mosquito or for ill-kept labour lines. Young lawyers, chartered accountants and assistants in a wide range of commercial concerns jostled in their open sports cars among the sedate Argylls and Daimlers in the car park, as they hurried off to tennis or golf at a hundred country clubs.

By the end of 1933 a silence had fallen on the scene. Over empty house and weed-grown path, in the still and eerie billiard rooms, on the creaking shutters of the planter's abandoned bungalow, was written clear the sad word 'Ichabod', 'the glory is departed'. Rubber was not worth tuppence and the estates were on 'care and maintenance'.

John George Hay remembered the Stevenson Scheme. He knew very well what he was about. Let there be no talk of 'restriction' this time unless all joined in. Meanwhile he would rake those estates down from truck to keel and from stem to stern until they could ride out any known tornado. Racked with private heart-searching – for never let it be supposed he enjoyed hurting his friends, or that he relished unpopularity more than most men – Hay now turned to a duty he could not shirk. He knew what must be done. Wretchedly aware of the distress it would cause; and sick, sleepless with misery (which only his family knew), Hay had the courage to operate as a surgeon might amputate a son's limb without anaesthetic.

To the outer world he remained implacable; and appeared a mere brute. Young men can find other jobs – sack them. Well-to-do old planters with money in the bank and an elegant way of life in their country houses – away home with them. The hard men, the 'drivers', the managers of middle-age with initiative and a name for toughness – halve their salaries, cut down their car allowances, stop their home-leaves. They will never find another job so they will stick anyway. No dividends for shareholders – and directors get nothing. That would do for a start.

But the heart of the problem was wages. On rubber estates most of the work-people came from the Madras Presidency in the south of India and had been brought to Malaya by the 'Indian Immigration Department'. Although normally recruited by a 'Kangany' (or headman of a group of labourers) for daily-paid work on a specific estate, they were at all times free to change their place of employment if they wished. Free passages were given to them and their families from Madras, or from Negapatam in the far south of the Indian peninsula, whence they sailed to Penang or to Port Swettenham in Selangor. But free return passages were not given except in cases of serious illness, occasionally on the death of a parent or for some other grave personal affair, or finally on the expiry of their working life at about sixty or so, when those who had stuck it out over the years usually retired, respected and full of years, to their native villages in India. Those who wished to remain on in Malaya were welcome to do so.

The Indian Immigration Department derived half its funds from a levy or 'assessment' on the rubber companies in Malaya who employed Indian labourers, the amount of this collection being based on the average number of such persons employed by each company throughout the previous year at so much per head. The remaining half was met by the Malayan Government. The operation of the Department was in the control of officers of the Malayan Civil Service, while the administration of the 'fund' vested in a committee consisting of nominees of rubber-companies and Government officers combined.

Hay's second task was therefore to bring pressure to bear upon the Government, through the 'Fund' committee, for a radical change in the Indian Immigration Department's policy. From now on the Immigration Fund Committee should encourage the Department to be much more open-handed in the issue of return tickets to Indian labourers and their families – they should be permitted to leave Malaya at the Fund's expense whenever they requested and could show a good reason for going back to India on point of unemployment or insufficiency of income.

The effects of this more liberal attitude were soon apparent – though not without much outcry from India's politicians, already boiling for Independence and grabbing at every chance to sling mud at the Empire. The presence around him of thankful Indian families, home on Indian soil at last with their little gratuities, did not always shield the sweating young Malayan Civil Servant on 'Immigration' service in Madras from the brickbats of the mob – as half of them swore at Britain's treachery in forbidding them to go to the 'Eldorado of Malaya' and the other half berated that unhappy country's brutality in 'sucking the orange dry and throwing away the skin'.

But these were mere ripples on the stream. The great work of sending redundant labour back to its homeland continued; and soon it was possible for the estates to offer the remainder of their working population the alternative of going back to India, or of remaining where they were on very low monthly earnings; but with the attraction in the latter case of free quarters, water, lighting, schooling, medical attention and a plot of land for each one for the rearing of hens and goats and the cultivation of vegetables. The South Indian, if not carried away by political oratory, is a highly intelligent and sensible man. With boyhood's memories of the Indian climate and social structure, most soon decided which alternative to choose.

By 1933 'Wages', the heaviest item in 'Other charges annually recurrent', showed a dramatic decrease throughout

The fall of Singapore, February, 1942

Oil palm harvesting

the Guthrie Group; and Hay was free to turn his undivided attention to the international field.

* * *

Few men in private life can ever have occupied a more commanding position in public affairs than did John George Hay in the world of rubber.

If there was one good thing the Stevenson Scheme had done it had been to compel attention to the worldwide economics of the rubber industry; and, through Hay's knowledge of the workings of that Scheme, much influence had accrued to a body known as 'The Rubber Growers' Association', of which he was a member and later the Chairman. By 1930, therefore, as clouds gathered and the sky darkened before the storm of the great depression of the thirties that swept the world, Hay was to be seen, not in a ring-side seat at the impending battle of international wits, but in the centre of the ring itself among the leading combatants. 1930 was the beginning of a bad time – and the future was black.

The United States, Malaya's best customer, was buying less rubber. Wall Street had panicked, money was short and America's householders, with a wary eye to the future, were laying up their second cars, retreading their tyres and reducing the country's rubber imports in all ways possible. Surplus stocks began to accumulate; and the great industry itself, choked with its own supplies, was grinding to a halt.

Restriction of production, unpalatable as such artificial barriers to commerce always are, had seemed the only solution. But the problem had been, and still was, how to bring such a scheme about. As always, the Dutch East Indies presented the chief stumbling block. Unlike Malaya, with its modest population, limited area of intensive cultivation and excellent communications, the Netherlands East Indies was vast and inchoate. In proportion to the two populations, a comparatively minute 'Binnenlands Bestuur' (the equivalent of the Malayan Civil Service) admirably administered a hundred million people of differing tongues and races throughout an enormous island empire. In these conditions the production of rubber by the native small-holders, who formed a large proportion of the industry's producers, had seemed impossible even to calculate with any accuracy, let alone to control. The very acreages under native rubber – to say nothing of the probable output – were completely unknown.

On the large Dutch estates, however, matters were different; and in May 1930 Holland agreed to join with British interests in Malaya and Ceylon in organising a general one month's 'tapping holiday' . . . an experiment which proved hopelessly inadequate to stem the tide of over-production, but had at any rate shown the Netherlands' willingness to co-operate if only an effective means could be discovered.

At that time – in mid-1930 – the price of rubber had been sixpence a pound; but by June 1932, it was down to a penny halfpenny.

More discussions broke out in the Rubber Growers' Association therefore; but the problem of the Dutch East Indies still dominated all arguments, no solution was found and all that seemed possible was to let the economic forces continue to run their course. From now on, however, slowly and with many setbacks, the situation began to improve. Many factors were responsible for this. There was the decrease in production from estates whose costs were high and who had therefore perforce gone out of business. There was the decline in tapping among small-holders of the East Indies who were unfortunate enough to own rubber-plantations far inland, and whose transport costs made it not worth while continuing to collect their latex. Above all, there were signs at last that the storm was blowing over. In spring 1933 American and British consumption of rubber showed a definite trend toward recovery. The price rose to threepence; and now negotiations with the Dutch began in a much more favourable atmosphere.

Hay was overpressed with work following the formation of 'Oil Palms of Malaya Limited' that had grown as a much bigger brother to the Elaeis oil palm property in Johore and that had come into being in 1930. He had the direction of the entire Guthrie Group in his hands, being Chairman of almost every Company in it, and he was also – at an extremely tricky period in its career – the Managing Director of the firm of Guthrie and Company Limited.

None of these burdens prevented Hay from throwing himself into battle on the side of the Rubber Growers' Association, in a determined bid to find a basis of agreement for a scheme of rubber restriction. Such a scheme would need to involve three other rubber producing countries as well as the British possessions; the most awkward member of the whole squad being, as usual, the Dutch. Lucid argument, resilient optimism, immense patience – the three combined into a hypnotic power that rendered Hay's leadership unique in the world of rubber – at length had their way. In April 1934 the Dutch agreed to levy a tax on all small-holders' rubber at the ports of export, in lieu of attempting the impossible task of imposing a scheme for restricting their production. The result, in Hay's opinion – and events were to prove him right – would virtually be the same.

At that meeting in April, too, it was agreed that the Governments of the rubber producing possessions of Britain, France, Holland and Siam should impose a monthly quota on the export of rubber from their respective countries. These quotas were to be based on past exports, subject to an allowance depending upon the acreage of recently planted rubber not yet in production; and the whole Scheme was to be administered and controlled by a Committee to be set up between the various Governments to be known as the International Rubber Regulation Committee. Each government was to appoint one representative to sit on that committee; the Malayan annual quota was to be 504,000 tons, rising to 602,000 tons in 1938; the Dutch 352,000 tons rising to 488,000 tons; and the other countries less, in proportion to their planted area and prospects of acreage increase. The Scheme was to come into force on the 1st of June 1934 and end, unless all agreed to extend it, in 1938. The argument was over; and now it only remained for the technicians to work out the method of operating the scheme and to set it in motion.

There was no question now as to the chief voice in committee. Though British interests were represented by a Civil Servant, John George Hay was the real and effective leader. 'Socfin', the largest Belgian-French rubber combine in existence, sent Hay a telegram: 'in our joy our first thoughts of gratitude go to the architect of our revival'. The Right Honourable Sir Philip Cunliffe-Lister, Secretary of State for the Colonies, in a generous and true-hearted letter dated the 1st of May 1934, after a Cabinet meeting on the setting up of the International Rubber Regulation Committee at which Hay had been bidden to explain the matter, wrote: 'My dear

Hay . . . Let me also add my profound gratitude to you for all your help – indeed much more than help. For you are the architect and builder; and I was the builder's labourer. If I am in a tangle again I shall know where to look for help.'

A long line of predecessors over the years – Alexander Guthrie in his white stock, James in his grey beard and frock-coat, Thomas Scott and the recent shade of John Anderson himself – would nod with approval. The old firm had not lost its touch.

CHAPTER 6

THE FLOOD CONTROLLED

On the 1st of June 1934 Malaya set out to put its house in order. Seven months of 1934 were still to run. If full production of rubber were permitted, seven-twelfths of Malaya's quota for the year (304,000 tons) would be free to be exported by the 31st of December. But the International Rubber Regulation Committee had only agreed to full production for June and July, after which it was to be cut to 90 per cent for August and September, 80 per cent for October and November and 70 per cent for December. In other words, what was needed was the immediate setting up of a form of Bank, where each rubber estate in the country would be credited with book entries of its estimated annual output based on the previous year's crop returns – from which they would be able to 'draw' so much per month according to the varying percentages permitted to be produced.

Here was a different state of affairs from that miserable 'Stevenson' thing. This was a scheme that could be made to work.

Very soon a Malayan Rubber Regulation Committee came into being as the local overall directing body, with the Chief Secretary as Chairman. A Department of Rubber Control was set up, with a member of the Malayan Civil Service as Controller; and the nucleus of a bank-like organisation, well staffed by accountants and clerks, took shape in Clarke Street, Kuala Lumpur, to which statistics from all the rubber-plantations of Malaya began to pour in.

But what about the small-holders – the rubber planters of estates under a hundred acres – who together produced a third of the country's total export? In minor degree Malaya now faced the same problem that had so bedevilled the Dutch in the East Indies. To tackle this problem a considerable service was at once organised from among the ex-rubber planters, of whom not a few had been supported during the slump at a relief camp in Port Dickson set up by the Malay States Volunteer Force; and these new 'Rubber Regulation Inspectors' took up their gruelling tasks at once on a regional basis throughout the country.

Later historians unhesitatingly belabour the Malayan Government at that time for its failure to bring the small-holder into the 'Banking system' available to the large estates – claiming that this was a deep-laid plot to safeguard European interests against the encroachments of 'native rubber'. But Britain's back is broad; and its government quite accustomed to being wrong whatever it does. It bore in mind the fact that the small-holders' land was normally owned by a tribe of unregistered descendants of the registered owner, who was likely to have died about thirty years before – each claiming one seventy-seventh undivided share in three and a quarter acres. It remembered, too, that few small-holders had the faintest idea what a 'bank' was or what it did; and that even fewer could read or write. It knew that even those few who could read and write would be the certain prey of all the other seventy-six claimants if he dared to operate an account on their behalf, each one vociferously maintaining that he was cheating them and all stoutly refusing to empower him to act for them on any account. Finally it took note of the earnest wish of the small-holders themselves. 'Give us coupons, Tuan' ,they said; 'we understand coupons.' (Coupons were nice, too, because if you did not want to work you could always flog them.)

Overall, there was the question of speed. 'Had we but World enough, and Time . . .', sighed Marcus Rex, the Controller of Rubber. To organise a banking system for many hundred thousand scattered small-holders would take decades, not six weeks; and even then it would be hopelessly defective. Let a small-holders' representative sit on the Malayan Rubber Regulation Committee; and let the Rubber Regulation Inspectors' estimate of each small-holding's production verge on the side of generosity. Beyond that, what more could any human being do? So – under careful safeguards – 'Coupons' for the small-holders it was; and the system worked excellently.

The focus now shifts four years on; to England. The Restriction scheme's first four years had proved an outstanding success. Hay, as the most knowledgeable spokesman of the Committee's largest quota-holder, had won universal praise; and all participants had unanimously voted its extension for a further four years.

In December 1937 he had been awarded a rare distinction – the Honorary Gold Medal of the Rubber Growers' Association – to mark the 'deep feeling of gratitude for the arduous and highly efficient services he had given to the Association and the industry'. Almost immediately after this he had needed to pay a rapid visit to the East once more, to conclude a fresh agreement on the Committee's behalf with Siam, who was only prepared to continue with the scheme provided a larger export quota was permitted. Matters in Bangkok had gone well; and here he was, back again, immersed in the concerns of the 'Guthrie Group', of Guthries' itself and of the International Rubber Regulation Committee, at the beginning of its new four-year term of office. Back to work in the City; and to the sorting out of day to day problems of commerce in a world already becoming racked with apprehension and haunted by the approaching shadow of another war.

Governments are not always unjust. Their decisions – as Churchill was later to say of his own – have not always been wrong. Every now and then they chance to single out for the accolade of their approval one who, above all, has epitomised the essential spirit of their country; who has been the right man in the right place at the right time – the fulcrum upon which their forward thrust has depended.

On the morning of Thursday 16th February 1939 – to be warm and sunny later on, but now still cold and chilly in the early fog of a London winter – John George Hay, always a dandy when it came to the matter of clothes, is adjusting a white cravat, having attired himself in sponge-bag trousers and morning coat.

For the second time in the short space of twenty-seven years the old firm of Guthrie and Company, through its head, the leader of the East India Merchant community, was to be accorded an outstanding national tribute. John George Hay's name had appeared in the 'Prime Minister's List'; and at Buckingham Palace that morning King George the Sixth conferred upon him the honour of Knight Bachelor.

Sir John Hay had now reached the pinnacle of his career at the age of fifty-six. He and Sir John Anderson together had brought Guthries' forward from an old East India merchant house – albeit the earliest surviving and largest of them – to an organisation twelve times the size it had been at the turn of the century; to a position of unquestioned dominance in their spheres in London and throughout Malaysia.

But war clouds were gathering thick and fast. This was no time to relax, but to spur forward to a greater effort, and to an even greater challenge. If war broke out, rubber would be of vital need. This would be a global war – of that Hay was convinced – and it would be idle to hope that this time rubber could continue to be exported from Malaya as in the war of 1914–18. Not only must America, Malaya's largest rubber buyer, be persuaded to double her purchases in 1940 – and at a price at least as high as had already been reached under the influence of 'restriction' – but the whole policy of the International Rubber Regulation Committee must be diametrically reversed from one of restraint to that of a drive towards the greatest production possible.

Hay's name had become synonymous with 'restriction'. How was he now, in a flash, to carry the Committee with him in so dramatic a volte-face? A lifetime of training had hardened his leading characteristic of trusting his own judgement, and that of very few others. Many intelligent men had misunderstood his objection to the Stevenson Scheme in 1922; many more had reviled him when he had caused it to be withdrawn in 1928. They had not followed his refusal to have anything to do with restriction in the early thirties until all countries joined the scheme; and now that it was proving such a success in 1939 they would be baffled at his sudden decision to vote for 'full speed ahead' on production at the mere threat of war. 'Fatal to the prosperity of Malaya', they would exclaim; 'ruinous to the price structure of the industry.' Let them. In a steady stream of dictated letters and instructions, impatient of comment, regardless of criticism, Hay collected the compelling evidence of his case and of his statistics.

* * *

Suddenly the war was upon the world. Hitler's 'phoney war' of 1939 gave a breathing space, but in the spring of 1940 Hay was off to America, as the Committee's sole representative, to put the case before President Roosevelt and the United States Government. America is well accustomed to receiving all manner of propositions from all manner of men; but it is to be wondered whether it has often entertained as applicant one with such a proposal and with such an array of facts as were at the fingertips of the persuasive Sir John Hay. Luckily Roosevelt, who had just been re-elected to an unprecedented third term of office as President, had repealed the Embargo Act of 1937, was shipping invaluable arms and aid to the Allies and had issued an appeal to his people to make the United States 'the arsenal of democracy'. Hay's visit could not therefore have been more fortunately timed. His urgent plea – that America should go all out to buy every scrap of rubber in Malaya – was well in accord with the President's appeal to accumulate the sinews of war and deny them to the enemy.

Sir John was rapidly passed on to no less than the famous Jesse H. Jones, Federal Loan Administrator – the great 'Loan Ranger', as he was called – and between the two they drew up a concrete plan of action. A body would be formed called the 'Reconstruction Finance Corporation', which would join with the International Rubber Regulation Committee in setting up an entity known as the 'Rubber Reserve Company'. The Finance Corporation would attract revenue from the American rubber companies and lend it to the 'Rubber Reserve Company', who would thereupon guarantee to purchase from Malaya 100,000 to 150,000 tons of rubber before the end of the year as 'reserve stock'. The rubber manufacturers were at the same time to buy all their normal requirements of rubber on the open market as before, and to continue to lay down their own reserve stocks. The price was fixed at between eighteen and twenty American cents per pound (approximately fifty-four to sixty Malayan cents or between one shilling and fourpence and one and eightpence sterling – a very fair price at that time) and Hay managed to gouge an agreement out of Jones that if the American manufacturers failed to buy as much on their own as they had been accustomed to doing, the 'Reserve Company' would be obliged to buy proportionately more instead and so make up the difference. Hay deserves enormous credit for the force and brilliance of his negotiations.

Back in England Hay learned from Malaya that the

planting community's response to the appeal for 'all-out' tapping had been phenomenal. Massive supplies of rubber were pouring in.

Although the original agreement with America had only been signed on the 29th of June 1940, by no later than the 15th of August Hay was able to return to the charge; and a fresh agreement was entered into to cover the purchase of a further 180,000 tons in 1941, making a total 'rubber reserve' in America's hands of 330,000 tons. That should surely have satisfied any man – but not Sir John Hay.

Rubber production was away beyond expectation. By the end of 1941 there was still going to be an unexported stock of rubber in Malaya – out there at the end of a limb, with heaven knew what dangers to menace it now that Germany had made this fantastic breakthrough in Europe and was winning hands down all along the line. The lights were going out all over the world. U-boats had strangled European commerce and might soon cut Malaya's lifeline of trade across the Pacific to America.

In mid-1941 Hay was off to America again. 180,000 tons to America in 1941 were not enough – purchases should be increased by another 100,000 tons. The United States were now wide awake to the world's danger and trembling on the brink of armed intervention. The ever helpful Jesse H. Jones agreed to accept this heavy and unexpected extra purchasing commitment for his 'rubber reserve'. Sir John sighed with relief. Malaya's rubber stocks should now be cleaned out to the last ounce by the end of 1941.

The only fly in the ointment was that Jones had had his knuckledusters on this time and had lowered the price to between seventeen and eighteen and a half American cents.

CHAPTER 7

ON THE BRINK

Malaya still basked in the warm sun.

Only two roads crossed Malaya from west to east; one two-thirds of the way down its length, on the latitude of Kuala Lumpur – and the other further south again in the northern part of Johore, where the peninsula began to narrow down towards its southern point off Singapore. In addition to the Malayan railway up the west coast, a further railway line now cut northwards through this eastern jungle straight from Johore to the north-east corner of Malaya, where a small China Sea port known as Kota Bharu existed on the Siamese frontier. From there on it curved north-west through Siamese territory to rejoin the main line again at Haadyai, which was in road and rail connection with Malaya's west coast. A passable road, much intersected by rivers negotiated by hand-operated ferries, ran south from Kota Bharu to connect with the eastern ends of the two lateral roads – except during the monsoon periods of December and January, when it was generally flooded and unusable.

The outbreak of war in Europe caused every Englishman in Malaya to wish to return to Britain with the intention of 'doing his bit' and joining the armed forces. But very few could be spared – and those who succeeded in leaving their Malayan posts soon found that this was a very different war from the last one. Enthusiastic recruits were not wanted. 'Glamour' was out. A soured and realistic Britain had no longer any use for the romantic approach to hostilities. What it wanted was every man to shut up and get on with his job. He would be called quickly enough, as soon as he was needed. Those who had gone so gaily soon returned crestfallen; and all UK citizens of military age in Malaya resigned themselves to continuing their daily work, joining the Volunteer force or the Malayan Royal Naval Volunteer Reserve and poring over their wireless sets for news of events 'at home'.

Malayan defence against attack by an enemy had never been weaker than in 1940. At that time it was completely defenceless. An immense Naval Base at Singapore had been officially opened in 1938 in a somewhat incomplete condition, but not a naval ship was in it. After the Imperial Conference in London in 1937 Britain had decided to retain her fleet in European waters, sending warships Eastward only when necessary. Now the war had come, and all naval vessels were fully committed guarding Britain or on convoy work in the North Sea, the Channel and the Western Ocean.

Most of the land forces had been withdrawn to active service nearer home, leaving three battalions, a few detachments of the Burma Rifles and a scattering of Artillery to perform garrison duties here and there about the country. Then, after the fall of France, the Vichy Government in March 1941 gave Japan leave to move into south Indo-China, with its magnificent harbour of Camranh Bay, just across from Malaya. In April, Japan signed a pact of neutrality with Russia, thereby obviously freeing itself of northern worries so as to be ready for any eventuality towards the south. In June and July America imposed an embargo on the export of oil to Japan, which could only supply ten per cent of its oil requirements from its own sources; and froze all Japanese assets in the USA. In August, Konoye, the Japanese Prime Minister, sought an urgent meeting with Roosevelt. He was rebuffed; resigned – and was replaced by General Tojo the Army leader. It was obvious what was going to happen. Historians who were not there blame the British in Malaya at that time for their 'mental unpreparedness', for their incompetence, inefficiency and bungling, likening their state of mind to the blindness of their race in India before the Indian Mutiny. But what could they do?

Anxious Europeans pondered and discussed every facet of the nightmare menace as the net spread its web ever thicker and thicker around them – listening to their radios at all hours and ringing up their friends. They were under orders to stay where they were. They could not run away. Send their wives and families away of course – but a lot of them would not go. Many stayed, firmly determined to stick with their husbands whatever happened. They were by no means 'mentally unprepared'.

As the scene darkened, troops began to arrive at last; and by the beginning of December 1941 there were three weak divisions in Malaya – these being the 8th Australian division and the 9th and 11th Indian. A fable has grown and taken root that war-time military strategists were unaware that the jungle could be penetrated by troops of soldiers. Like many other facile post-mortem statements, this is of course completely untrue. They were painfully – all too painfully – aware of it. The trouble was not the permeability or impermeability of the jungle, but the fact that the jungle existed – and that they were on the defensive. The jungle was precisely the same as an immense smoke-screen, blanketing the eastern three-quarters of Malaya's land surface. An attacking enemy had all the advantages. He could pop out of it at any time, anywhere; and once he had withdrawn into safety of the tangled undergrowth he was as safe as if he were at home. To go in after him and ferret him out was worse than looking for a needle in twelve acres of hayfield.

The military officers at Fort Canning in Singapore, and those later in high command up and down the country, were not fools. With District Officers and Forest Officers they examined the terrain intelligently and with care. General Dobbie,* General Officer Commanding in Singapore during 1937, had been right. In a campaign in Malaya the attacking force would hold all the cards and wield the entire initiative.

If once an enemy landed. That was the rub. He must be prevented from landing. But how? There was no Navy; and a few Brewster Buffaloes and ancient Wildebeestes – which was all the Malayan detachment of the Royal Air Force had to boast – were not likely to be able to stop them either.

* * *

The outbreak of war in Asia on the 8th of December 1941 – Admiral Nogumo's attack on Pearl Harbour synchronised with the first landing of General Yamashita's 18th Japanese Division near Kota Bharu – and all the turmoil that ensued as line after line of futile defence broke and re-formed only to break again throughout the length of Malaya, has no need to be described in detail in this story. What is important to it is that well before dawn on that fatal 8th of December upon which those events began, the very first bomb to be

* This great soldier was later the hero of the defence of Malta.

dropped by Japanese aircraft on Singapore fell through the roof of Messrs Guthrie and Company's head office.

The delicate balance of history would seem to require no less. Drama could demand no more. The oldest and greatest commercial enterprise in South-east Asia – spearhead of Britain's thrust whose work for a hundred and twenty years had spread a network of Western prosperity from end to end of the Malayan Peninsula – had been chosen by Fate as the first sacrifice in the initial battle between East and West. Flames reached skyward, destroying the business heart and the records of over a century.

According to the canons of Greek tragedy this should be the end – complete destruction and the finish of the tale. But these events are still too near for such a clean line to be drawn – and it would not be the truth. A greater Guthries' was to arise from its own ashes in the fullness of time. And a further story must be told and a comment made before the fog of war clamps down over South-east Asia – and all the many struggling people in it – for many weary years.

* * *

Nadesan was the son of a Tamil coolie – of a south Indian daily-paid labourer on a rubber estate. When an exhausted detachment of the 11th Indian Division halted at Kamuning Estate of the Guthrie group, where Nadesan and his father worked, a section of the Madras Sappers and Miners attached to it had bivouacked overnight in Nadesan's labour lines. Nadesan consulted his bosom friend Perumal and they both decided to join – or at any rate to follow – the retreating army.

A fortnight later, when Colonel Whitman had taken them both on as recruits, the unit was involved in a rearguard action at the village of Bakri, in Johore, during the course of which Nadesan's and Perumal's section of Madras Sappers and Miners found themselves cut off by the advancing enemy and defending a hill in the falling dusk together with a half company of the 11th Indian. They had been told to defend the hill – and had been given no orders to retreat.

Colonel Whitman with a company from the south made three attempts to break through and rescue them, but Japanese in strength beat them off with much loss; and he was compelled to leave the small detachment at 'Bakri corner' to its fate.

These latter stuck to their posts and fought it out until those that had survived – only eighteen of them – were overrun. Wounded, many bayoneted in the stomach and all new to war, these survivors were lined up over a ditch as quickly as possible with bayonets pressed against their buttocks, forced to bend over, and were there and then one by one beheaded.

But not all. Unnoticed by the Japanese, Nadesan had dropped for cover into that same ditch as the rounding up and counting of survivors had been going on; and now there he lay, in fascinated horror, as his doomed companions began to line the side of the trench, almost directly above his head. Now or never was his chance to escape – to back away down the ditch to the safety of the mangrove swamp and the tidal waters of the river Muar. But suddenly there was little Perumal, with eyes of agonised appeal, gazing straight into his face from above; and as the fatal sword swept down Nadesan forced all his heart and soul into a contortion that yelled 'jump'. The last two inches of the sword slashed deep below Perumal's ear and jawbone and ground against the spine as he twisted and fell, the blood gushing from a gaping wound. The last heads rolled, and the yellow dwarfs retired chattering – to re-form and continue their lightning sweep south toward the town of Muar.

Within a second of their leaving the ditch, Nadesan had wormed his way forward through the bloodbath and seized the unconscious Perumal's head – to jamb it violently to the right and so close the brimming slice through half his neck.

Till midnight Nadesan remained immobile in the midst of the blood-smothered carnage, nursing the boy's head and holding it firm. Then slowly he dragged him down the ditch and to the side of the mangrove creek. Tearing strips from his shirt and binding Perumal's head as tightly to the right as he could, Nadesan proceeded to swim down to the creek and then out and up the Muar river in search of a boat. No sooner found – a mere 'jaloh', a dugout canoe – than he silently swam back with it to Perumal; eased him, still unconscious, on board; and so out into the stream. They had drifted safely past Muar in the dark; and a misty dawn found them well out at sea in the Malacca Strait, moving slowly to the south and away from the land as a northerly breeze picked up and Nadesan continued to use his single paddle.

With three and a half inches of freeboard; without food or water; how many days they drifted, or by what miracle Perumal survived, remains unknown.

Both unconscious, Nadesan quite naked and his clothes spread over Perumal to shield him from the burning sun and the night-time cold, they were eventually picked up by a patrol vessel of the Malayan RNVR. At the time of these events Nadesan was sixteen years old and Perumal fourteen and a half. Both lived and survived their later imprisonment by the Japanese.

Among the prouder records that this story has to tell is the fact that Colonel Whitman – or, more precisely, the shattered wreck of Colonel Whitman – who had kept himself alive through three and a half years of savagery with one purpose in view, refused to leave Malaya at the end of the war until he had exhumed and given honourable burial to each one of the Heroes of Bakri. Nadesan and Perumal were with him as treasured members of his personal staff; and the memory of those two boys and of Nadesan's heroic courage lives on as an inspiration to the few who still remember them.

* * *

Singapore fell on the 15th of February 1942 after a period of agony mercifully shortened by the moral courage of the General Officer Commanding, Lieutenant-General A. E. Percival.

It has been well asked how long the Isle of Wight might be expected to hold out, if all of Britain except that island had been captured by the Germans; if there were a million non-combatants infesting every corner of its surface and if its water supply came by pipe across the Solent from reservoirs in the New Forest.

Through absence of air cover the British warships *Prince of Wales* and *Repulse* had been sunk on the 9th December 1941; and Malaya had now neither air defence nor navy.

The British 18th Division had arrived on the 29th of January, survivors being picked up busily all day and most of the night by small vessels and sampans from the oily patch in the water where the converted liner *Empress of Asia*, which had carried most of them and their weapons to the East, had been bombed and sunk within sight of Singapore. With this access of strength, together with the arrival about the same time of the 44th Indian Brigade of young and untrained troops, General Percival was expected to repel landings along his northern, mangrove swamp coastline.

From the moment of the Japanese landing on the island in force on the night of 8th February, Percival was beset with telegrams enjoining him to fight the battle 'to the bitter end at all costs'. 'Commanders and senior officers should die with their troops. The honour of the British army and of the British Empire is at stake. I rely on you to show no mercy to weakness in any form. There must at this stage be no thought of saving the troops or sparing the population.' Yet by as early as 21st of January the Chiefs of Staff in England had ceased to nurse any illusions about the protracted defence of Singapore. They were already concerned about demolitions; and the question was now only one of 'how long?' Tens of thousands of troops and hundreds of thousands of innocent non-combatants were to be butchered for the mere purpose of making a satisfactory gesture. No possible good could come of it, as the conclusion was already foregone – but such is the military mind.

Fortunately, however, such are not all military minds. General Percival was ahead of his time. He was not only a soldier. His telegrams show him to be also an evolved and civilised human being. On the 13th of February he describes how the enemy has occupied the island, encircled the town and is now within five thousand yards of the waterfront, cutting off the water supply, bringing the whole town within range of artillery and making it unlikely that resistance could continue for more than another day or two at most. We are 'unanimously of the opinion', he says, 'that the gain of time will not compensate for extensive damage and heavy casualties in Singapore town. As Empire overseas is interested, I feel bound to represent their views. There must come a stage when in the interests of the troops and civil population further bloodshed will serve no useful purpose. Your instructions are being carried out, but in above circumstances would you consider giving me wider discretionary powers?'

How much more courage it must take a soldier to make even these guarded suggestions of surrender, rather than to commit battalions of troops and tens of thousands of terrified women and children to brutal destruction in order to save his face, only a soldier probably knows. The imputation of weakness would remain with Percival for the rest of his days – and he knew it. Moral strength of this order is rare, almost giving heart to believe that the days of Moloch and Baal are over and that slowly the world does move forward after all.

These and other communications convinced Churchill that 'it would be wrong to enforce needless slaughter, and without the hope of victory to inflict the horrors of street fighting on the vast city, with its teeming, helpless and now panic-stricken population'.

At 8.30 pm on the 15th of February 1942 Singapore unconditionally surrendered to the Japanese.

As old J. I. (Jiddy) Dawson from Aberdeen, the General Manager of Guthries', swam out alone from the burning city into the dark harbour on that desperate night, his last thoughts must have been of relief. He had stuck it out to the end. Everything was destroyed. His clever young protégé George, the now famous Sir John Hay, had seen to it that all the rubber which Malaya could produce had got out to the Allies. The cupboard was bare.

A sniper's bullet got him – and Jiddy Dawson became part of history.*

* There are two accounts of the death of the Honourable J. I. Dawson, member of the Singapore Legislative Council and General Manager of the firm of Guthrie and Company Limited – one as above and the other that he perished in the sinking of ss *Kuala*, which was destroyed by bombs from Japanese aircraft with much loss of civilian life, off the island of Pompong in the Lingga archipelago, south of Singapore. In this history the account of an Indian eye-witness – which may or may not be authentic – has been chosen.

BOOK SIX

PHOENIX

CHAPTER I

FLASHES FROM THE DARK

Little news percolated through to the outer world as the years dragged by. From Malaya occasional flashes of light illuminated a corner here and there, as small parties of brave men, air-dropped or sent in by submarine, radioed what news they could on their portable wireless sets from jungle hideouts.

Civilian internees, herded together like cattle, were on starvation rations and dying rapidly. Prisoners of war from the Services had been drafted to Thailand to build a railway; to Japan to work in carbide factories; to Borneo for road construction; had been sold to the Manchurian Railway Company (the Manchukuo Nakamura Tai) which had been compelled by the Japanese government to take up the contract to construct a railway from the highlands of Sumatra to Pekan Baroe on that island's east coast, in order to supply provisions to a starving Singapore. Axis submarines had been playing havoc with all shipping in Eastern waters, the Malayan food situation was critical, and it was only across the comparatively shallow strait between Pekan Baroe and Singapore (where it was thought submarines could not operate) that the slightest chance existed of maintaining a supply line of food to a city now skeletal with hunger.

The Nakamura Tai saw no hope of ultimate profit in this venture, even though they had been supplied with free labour, plant and rolling-stock by the military government. The expense of upkeeping so large a force of slave labour was immense. They were the 'overheads' and must be slashed, so as to reduce as far as possible the firm's certain losses. The efficient carrying out of this policy successfully reduced that undesirable item of expenditure at Pekan Baroe (to take only one example) by over two-thirds in under eighteen months.

Among the people at large, fear had been succeeded by apathy in the face of a catastrophe too immense to be grasped, let alone combated. The Malay half of the population were left without direction and hastened to make such arrangements as they could with the new arrivals.

The Chinese on the other hand remained, as they always had, with their emotions firmly fixed upon their motherland, China. China was still at war with Japan – and therefore so were they. This belligerency, this stubborn insolence on the part of the Chinese of Malaya and Singapore, infuriated the pompous little Japanese bullies inflated with victory, who thereupon mercilessly butchered men, women and children in thousands. Arising out of this bestiality, large parties of young Chinese men and women, burning for vengeance, banded themselves together in jungle camps throughout the Peninsula; and these began to prey not only upon the Japanese, but also upon the Malay villagers and government officials who were now of necessity working in co-operation with the invaders. Dragons' Teeth were being sown that would grow into a whirlwind of racial animosity, to be reaped with bitterness and tears in later years.

Throughout this time the smaller Indian population of the area suffered, as minorities often do, from all three sides. Cajoled by the Japanese into joining the 'Indian National Army', betrayed by the Malays for assisting the jungle fighters, they were killed by the latter for working with the Japs. The unfortunate Indian did his best to emulate all three wise monkeys rolled into one – pulling the grass over his head and seeing nothing, hearing nothing, saying nothing.

In the swamps of Sumatra, far away up the Kwai river in Siam and over the Three Pagoda pass, small groups of emaciated prisoners of war might be seen dragging at logs; harnessed to the chassis of broken-down timber-jinkers and lashed with whips – the ghost of Sandy Cranna, the tragic caricatures of Bennett and Gulland of Guthries' Singapore office and so many others – straining at the ropes, with bare feet bleeding and all doomed to death, their suppurating sores a nest of flies.

Richardson, Stark and Sly of the office had been killed in action before this nightmare started – and they were lucky.

Barnes, Baxter, Baxter-Phillips, Burns, Burnside, Crawford, Craig, Deighton, Gibb, Giles, Godfree, Godward, Gray, Harvey, Hogan, Hutchison, Mountain (old 'Sam'), Wooding, Wright – the grim cavalcade of fine men passes down to death and to immortality, as those who refused to give in; as gentlemen unafraid.

In the deep jungle Bob Chrystal, General Manager of Guthrie and Company's property of Kamuning Estate, wandered alone like poor Ben Gunn on Treasure Island; a bearded and tattered shadow, muttering to himself and moving slowly on hands and knees in his endless search for roots and slugs to keep himself alive, as he fought the burning torture of his duodenal ulcer. Months ago he had fallen in with the Chinese; but he had slipped away and shaken them off at last. Life with these men had proved impossible. They had now divided themselves into two warring gangs in the jungle. There were, first of all, those who supported the 'Kuo Min Tang' Chinese under General Chiang Kai Shek; and these had even had the advice of a few widely scattered British officers who were attempting to organise them into a more active form of warfare than mere passive resistance. Then there was the 'MPAJA' or 'Malayan Peoples' Anti-Japanese Army', also known as the 'Three Star' or later 'Five Star' troops, who were a far more highly disciplined and dangerous body of men; and all violent Communists. Their endless 'brain washing' and self-confessions had nearly driven Bob Chrystal mad.*

Both sides spent more time fighting each other than damaging the Japanese; and neither had any use for the assistance of a solitary Englishman. Rather than have to undergo any more of such tedious rubbish Chrystal had decided to take his chance to live or die alone.

* * *

Back home in London Sir John Hay cracked his whip and called what was left of his pack to heel. He had meant to go on to Malaya after America, but by a mercy of Providence civilian aircraft had been diverted from Singapore shortly before the surrender; so both he and his potential fellow prisoners had been spared an experience that might well have proved too much for either.

What must be done at once was to establish touch with

* For the Chrystal story see *The Green Torture, The Ordeal of Robert Chrystal* by Dennis Holman. Robert Hale Ltd. 1962.

every Guthrie employee at liberty; and to discover the whereabouts of every dependant of captured Guthrie personnel. They must be looked after. And don't run away with the idea that this is the end of Guthries', because it isn't. Now that America is in the war at last, everything is all right – we shall win this thing together. Everything must be centralised at 'Lotus' – a large Edwardian country house in Dorking which the firm had bought in 1940 – and we must start planning for the future. Shareholders, staff, dependants – all need encouragement.

And poor Lady Anderson needed encouragement too, together with heartfelt sympathy. John, the eldest son, a great tall fellow of considerable charm, popularly known as 'Panjang', which means 'long', had been living happily in Malaya for some time with his wife, Olive, when the Japanese war began. John was off, with a shrug and a smile, as a private in the Federated Malay States Volunteer Force. As the Japanese swept south he was caught up in an affray within six miles of Kuala Lumpur, on the main road to the town of Port Swettenham and there he met his end. Olive got out in time, but the tall, good-natured John lay in a ditch, with a Japanese bullet hole through his head.

The Guthrie empire would now descend, after Lady Anderson (by-passing the second son who died from tuberculosis contracted as a Major in Burma) to the third son, Keith, an officer in the Royal Air Force – to whom the sad news came whilst he was aboard a troopship from Egypt bound for Colombo.

* * *

The Eastern Exchange Banks Association, The China Association (for Hong Kong), an Association of all the undertakings with interests in Burma, The Rubber Trade Association of London, the British Association of Straits Merchants, the Rubber Growers Association, the Malayan Chamber of Mines, the Tin Producers' Association and all those connected with Malayan smelting interests had banded themselves together into a 'Joint Committee', with the object of forcing from the British Government a clear admission upon a vital matter of principle. Throughout the vast area covered by these interests, war damage had been tremendous and the loss total. What had not been smashed, burnt and broken in pursuance of the 'Scorched Earth' policy imposed by Government's orders, had fallen into the hands of the Japanese.

Every business house had contributed heavily to Government's compulsory 'War Risks Insurance Scheme'. On the 1st January 1939 the Chancellor of the Exchequer had stated in the House of Commons that losses and injuries of whatever sort caused by enemy action would be compensated from public funds – and now the British Government was not only suggesting that in view of the immensity of the losses in the East they might have to repudiate their debts under the War Risks Scheme (which was severely limited in its coverage), but were also in mind to hedge on the wider issue outlined by the Chancellor – claiming that his promise only applied to losses and injuries in the British Isles.

Sir John Hay was elected the Joint Committee's Chairman. Nothing can reveal that man's forcefulness so clearly as the letters he now began to write. In a letter to the Chancellor of the Exchequer referring to the War Risks Insurance Scheme he said: 'It can hardly be expected that people who have suffered the worst disasters of war, with all their terrible consequences and ruinous losses, who in good faith and trust in their Governments have paid fully and promptly the insurance premia required of them, should be prepared to accept passively the suggestions that the insurance is now of doubtful value or that the consideration of settlement be postponed to some indefinite time because of the uncertain solvency of the Insurance Fund . . . The measures necessary are an effective guarantee of the solvency of the insurance funds, a definite promise to set up machinery for the examination of claims and a fair and equitable settlement . . . Anything short of such measures would inevitably be regarded as a failure to honour obligations damaging to the repute of the Governments concerned, not excluding His Majesty's Government, upon whom lay the responsibility for the defence of the territories . . .'

On the wider front of payment from public funds of all losses and injuries incurred as a result of the war, whether covered by the Insurance Scheme or not, Hay fairly let himself go. 'Hostilities were not carried on in Eastern territories for the defence of particular interests or areas, but were part of much larger operations conducted on five continents and over the seven seas . . .' The general principle of responsibility for loss and injury must be made applicable to the Eastern territories under British protection as well as merely to the British Isles, for both had fought and suffered in a common cause; and the rubber, tin, oil, rice, silver, lead, wolfram and teak yielded by the East – and in the production of which the businesses he represented had faced danger to the point of death and ruin – were as essential to the war effort as Britain's arms and ammunition. There must be a clear and definite declaration of policy immediately, and an honest admission of Government's responsibility.

In reply to an unsatisfactory letter from the Under Secretary of State, Hay flamed: 'My committee have noted the terms of the Secretary of State's reply with profound disappointment . . . The remark that the Government find it impossible to deal with the matter on the basis of a simple statement of principle is a matter of no small surprise. The impact of war has fallen with disastrous effect upon the group of territories with which my committee is identified. Lives have been lost; freedom forfeited; people have been ruined; none has escaped loss. Against the background of these grim realities it is difficult to regard the Secretary of State's statement as an adequate or appropriate reply.' It was abundantly obvious that 'nothing can be discussed or settled except within the framework of a predetermined policy which will fix with certainty the question of responsibility for war damage.'

So the battle of paper raged throughout the years, against the darker scene of total war. The vision of Sir John Hay, hurling the barbed invective of his stinging prose in broadside after relentless broadside into the face of a British Government that could not escape him, twist and wriggle as it might, presents a fitting and forceful climax to the ancient and traditional battle between the business community of Singapore and Malaya and the mass weight of bureaucracy. He is old Sandy Guthrie fighting for 'free port' status; he is nephew James at the time of the Currency tangle; he is both of them together fighting for the transfer of the Straits Settlements to the Crown; and he is the entire Guthrie team in one as they force the issue of Governor Ord's replacement and so make way for development and progress to enter the peninsula of Malaya. As had happened before, it proved too much for a hesitating, overpressed and reluctant government.

The many thousands of commercial undertakings and private persons throughout Asia whose war claims were honourably dealt with by the British Government in time to come have cause to be thankful to Sir John Hay and his refusal to give in.

CHAPTER 2

THE LITTLE JACK HORNERS

Mankind having shown no disposition to behave itself, God interposed His finger in the year 1945. A weapon of devastating destruction was put into men's hands, so that henceforth they might proceed in the knowledge that indulgence in one further world war would result in their disappearance from the scene.

The 'Mark I' demonstration at Hiroshima might appear at first sight somewhat arbitrarily chosen but its falling certainly brought the Eastern war to an immediate halt and saved a great many more lives in South-east Asia than it destroyed in Japan. To the prisoners of war it was an undoubted blessing.

Throughout this time the Colonial Office had been by no means idle. A number of Malayan Civil Servants had been exempted from the 'call up' during the war in Malaya, owing to the essential nature of their duties. Some of these were on short leave or in conference in London when Singapore fell to the Japanese. Others, either in the fighting Services or not, had successfully made their escape immediately afterwards. Assembled by the chances of Fate and the fortunes of war, quite a number of these administrators found themselves in July 1943 organising the future of Malaya at what was known as the 'Malayan Planning Unit' in the stuffy chambers of the Colonial Office. By the time the war ended in 1945 their plans were complete.

In the atmosphere of unreality which every staff headquarters in the world seems fated to engender, it appeared perfectly obvious to these planners that now was the ideal time to make a fundamental change in government policy. The entire administration of Malaya should be streamlined. Singapore, as an international port, should be set apart on its own, under continuing Colonial Office control. The four countries comprising the Federated Malay States and the five countries, hitherto under loose British protection and known as the 'Unfederated States', should all be combined into an entity to be called the 'Malayan Union'; into which the small colonial possessions of Penang and Malacca should also be thrown. Throughout the whole area, elections would be organised as soon as possible; and every adult inhabitant of the country would have a vote, regardless of his race. A new Malayan Civil Service would have to be recruited of course, as all administrators now in prison would certainly be wrecks on their release – probably mere slavering idiots – if in fact any survived at all.

It was an attractive idea; and it took care of everything – a simplified structure of government, a rapid approach through elections to the granting of independence to Malaya in accordance with Queen Victoria's edict, a just reward to the stalwart Chinese, a slight rebuff to the Malays, 'who had played in with the Japs'.

Unfortunately it overlooked two important points. The first was the attitude to this proposal of the Malay half of the population, whose only home was Malaya and who were the only people in the Peninsula with whom Britain had ever entered into any treaty obligations – among which had been, incidentally, the undertaking to 'defend Malaya from enemies' – and the second was that the Malayan Civil Servants who survived imprisonment were by no means any more idiotic than they had been when they were captured – indeed most of them proved to be considerably less so.

They emerged from their years of slavery a tough and thoughtful band of dedicated reformers – men whose wits had been sharpened by bitter hardship, who had formed lifelong friendships with the country's simple people and upon whom abstinence had wrought its usual miracle of clarifying the mind. This glib 'Malayan Union' scheme – so cleverly cooked over the gas fires of the Colonial Office and chattered about at cocktail parties whilst they were slaving like beasts of burden – would never work. It ignored the fact that Man is an intensely 'territorial' animal; and that the Malayan peninsula is the homeland of the Malays. Certainly the Chinese half of the population must ultimately have a fair voice in the country's affairs, but that must come gradually and by a graceful act of understanding on the part of the Malays as hosts. Such advances must take root slowly in the minds of the people until they come to be accepted – they must arise, as it were, 'from the inside'. To impose them on the country now – and from an 'outside' power – would be dangerous folly.

* * *

As the war neared its end in 1945 the head office of Guthries' down at 'Lotus' had become exceedingly busy.

In his position as Chairman of the Joint Committee on Eastern business affairs, Hay had evolved two blue-print schemes for action when Malaya was liberated. The first was to form a 'Malayan Rubber Estate-Owners' Company' which would organise and handle the whole problem of the estates and their rehabilitation on a co-operative basis; and the second was to employ the 'British Association of Straits Merchants' set up in London during the war, in order to plan for the re-opening of Malaya's trade. No one knew what conditions were likely to be in Malaya and Singapore – malaria was bound to be rampant, rubber factory machinery in ruins and the trees probably strangled with weeds and undergrowth. Labour forces would almost certainly have all long before dispersed and, in general, the tasks of restarting the rubber industry and re-activating commerce would be gigantic. The staff at 'Lotus' had therefore been hard pressed completing their detailed planning; and in selecting the best men to accompany the armed forces in the invasion of Malaya.

No one knew, either, what resistance was likely to be encountered from the Japanese.

'Operation Zipper', the invasion itself, in fact proceeded without opposition of any sort. Which was lucky, for the curious choice of muddy Morib as the landing beach would have made the whole force a sitting duck for the enemy, if hostilities had not so dramatically ceased almost immediately before 'Zipper's' arrival.

And now, after so many years of misfortune and disappointment, everything suddenly seemed to be coming right. The members of the Malayan Rubber Estate-Owners' Company and of the Colonial Office, on landing and making their way inland, soon discovered two astonishing things. First was the generally splendid growth of the rubber trees, which had benefited far more from their years of freedom

Packing Dynat rubber for shipment

Guthrie Waugh offices in Singapore

from tapping than they had suffered from enforced neglect and the competition of weeds and secondary jungle; and secondly was the surprising and almost total absence among the remnants of the estate labour forces of that scourge of which they had such good reason to go in fear – malaria. The battle against that dread disease on the estates had, as it now appeared, been won before the war, but time had not been sufficient for that victory to manifest itself before the Japanese came. The clearing of swamps, oiling of streams and the honest work of careful subsoil drainage in pre-war days had beaten the mosquito; and, in spite of all these measures having ceased for four years, the effects during the occupation period had been cumulative. With new machinery already coming out from home and jubilant but emaciated workers rushing back to the estates in hordes to greet their old 'Tuans', it would be no time at all before rubber began once more to pour through the ports of Malaya to all parts of a desperately needy world.

Down in Singapore the British Association of Straits Merchants gazed in wonder at one of the greatest sellers' markets ever seen. From Singapore to Siam, from the borders of China to the farthest islands of South-east Asian seas, everyone was crying out for simply everything; for food, clothing, medicine, shoes, building material, machinery, paper, kitchen utensils, glassware, spectacles, furniture, typewriters, oil, petrol, bicycles, books, motor cars – there was not one manufactured, or one natural, product (except water) in all those lands that could not be sold like hot cakes.

Guthries', as did the other merchant houses, set to with a will; assembled what was left of their commercial staffs in Singapore, Malacca, Kuala Lumpur, Ipoh and Penang; rehabilitated as best they might office accommodation and houses; and began to supply goods of all descriptions to a ravenous Eastern public on the one hand and to produce and export rubber, tin and palm oil to a denuded world on the other.

* * *

In the general optimism of liberation, the despairing cries of Malaya's lately interned administrators were swept aside.

Clear evidence of mental degeneration, this odd and discordant outburst provided an additional reason, if any were needed, for sending these wretched people home with all speed. They were horrible to look at, they had the most extraordinary ideas and their presence was an embarrassment. The British Military Administration (locally known as the 'Black Market Association') was in command and doing itself nicely, whilst Lieutenant-General Sir Harold McMichael from Britain, who had not visited those parts before, interviewed the Sultans of each State and obtained their signatures of agreement to the proposal to form the 'Malayan Union'.

In all honesty it must be admitted that he had little difficulty in obtaining them. Politically, the Malays are not a highly conscious race. It takes time for new ideas to sink in; and time was not given. Also, the Sultans are gentlefolk – some a little out of touch with their people perhaps – but confident in the good faith of Britain and much relieved to learn that their annual Royal Purses were to be guaranteed. Like Sir Andrew Clarke in time gone by, Sir Harold McMichael probably believed that everything had gone off splendidly. If the Sultans had any misgivings, they certainly had not expressed them or shown any such emotion on their faces. And there was no need to consult the population of a million or so British subjects in Malacca and Penang. They would all be bundled into the Malayan Union, lock, stock and barrel, without more ado.

Under these auspices, the advent of the Malayan Union very naturally delighted the Chinese, who at last were to be accredited as 'first class' citizens of Malaya, and who now felt that they had not fought and suffered through the war in vain.

On the other hand, a sense of burning injustice rapidly spread among the Malay population from end to end of the Peninsula. By edict of Britain (the people who had promised to defend them and then failed to do so) they were now to share their home with a horde of foreigners, most of whom did not speak a word of their language. Why were the Malays no longer to be the lords of their own land?

Among the Malay people there is a madness known as 'amok'; a blinding rush of blood to the head in face of insupportable injustice or insult. In these circumstances they kill until they themselves are exterminated, which is the object they seek to achieve. Something a little like this now began to occur in Malaya. Chinese women and children – their menfolk away in search of work or not yet disbanded from jungle camps – were murdered en masse at Parit and Lambor Kanan down the Perak riverside, where they were interspersed among the Malay population. A certain Captain Mohamed Salleh of Simpang Kiri, in western Johore, raised a force known as the 'Parang Panjang' (the 'Long Swords') and ravaged the Chinese villages of Parit Java and Bakri, at both of which places many lives were lost.

An outstanding Malay patriot named Dato* Onn bin Jaffar – a man of unusually balanced and generous mind, who was at that time a District Officer in western Johore – dropped his pen, took emergency leave from the Deputy Resident of the West Coast and, starting at Simpang Kiri, toured the country from north to south; succeeding, by powers of persuasion rare in any man, in quelling the nascent Malay uprising before it had grown completely out of hand.

His method was to bring his people to understand that rioting and warfare could do nothing but harm to the Malay cause. In a desk-full of letters which he had asked the Deputy Resident to clear up for him immediately before his departure ('do please do this for me, keeping aside anything that requires action and burning the rest', he had said) there appeared recurrently the phrase that 'in spite of all apparent evidence to the contrary, the British, I am convinced, are intrinsically a just, well-meaning and decent people. When they understand the mistake they have made they will do their best to rectify this terrible blunder.' By his rapid action and forceful, kindly personality, he succeeded in convincing the Malays that their whole effort must be directed through constitutional channels. The United Malay National Organisation, of which Onn became leader, was the result of his tour – and this soon spread throughout the whole country, canalised Malay thinking and banded the Muslim population into one.

By this time Britain had become deeply concerned over the whole concept of the 'Malayan Union' and, in face of the mounting Malay objections to it, were already showing manifest signs of climbing down. The proposals being formulated by the United Malay National Organisation – and Britain's readiness to listen to them – received wide publicity;

* Dato – equivalent to Sir.

and every Chinese now knew that his promised security as a fully accepted citizen of Malaya was in danger.

A Chinese uproar then at once occurred, led by Dato Tan Cheng Lock* of Malacca, who called together and organised among his people a 'Council of Joint Action'. If the Chinese had not been promised this new status of equality with the Malays in Malaya it would not have mattered so much. But to have been assured of such an advance, and then to have it removed from their grasp in the midst of their jubilation, would cause insupportable loss of face and could never, on any account, be borne.

By now, as a result of the 'Malayan Union', both the Malays and the Chinese throughout the entire Peninsula had been reduced to a condition of seething racial disharmony and blazing anger. Furthermore, Britain had forged another weapon with which it would be belaboured. In 1946 His Majesty's Government had decided that the lot of the working populations of Singapore and Malaya needed to be improved, and could best be so improved by the imposition from above of Trades Unionism. Various expert do-gooders were therefore seconded to the Administration to show the working population the power advantages which could be derived from the mass banding together of the workers.

Having started on the wrong foot in Malaya after the war, Britain's problem was now insoluble. Whichever way it turned there would be nothing but trouble. To continue backing the Malayan Union would force an open uprising among the Malays; and these included the Malay Regiment, the majority of the Police Force and (in the former 'Unfederated States') almost the entire staff of those five States' governments; as well as flatly abrogating every Treaty (except the 'McMichael' one) drawn up with the Malay Sultans since 1875. On the other hand, to rescind the Union and revert to some arrangement more in line with the former treaties, now seemed likely to entail a head-on collision with the Malayan Chinese. In this posture, into which it had so unnecessarily contorted itself, Britain chose the wiser of the only two courses now left open to it.

In spite of violent opposition from the Chinese 'Council of Joint Action', on the 8th of February 1948 the Malayan Union came to an end and was replaced by the 'Federation

* Son of Tan Chay Yan, the pioneer rubber planter of Malacca who had sold 'Bukit Asahan' Estate to form the 'Malacca Rubber Company'.

of Malaya'. By the articles of that Federation, Singapore remained a separate country under continuing Colonial Office tutelage, Malacca and Penang were placed under the Federal government, whose headquarters were in Kuala Lumpur, and the Malays regained their former position as a specially privileged race throughout the Peninsula. Dato Tan Cheng Lock, the leader of the Chinese, told the Federal government that in view of this slap in his peoples' face he could no longer be responsible for their actions; and that only time could tell what their reaction would be. The government did not have long to wait.

In early June there broke out the bloodthirsty politico-racial disturbance that was to bedevil, impoverish, bewilder and divide the entire country for the next eleven years; a war of murders and treachery, of ambushes and jungle camps, that came to be known, somewhat euphemistically, as 'The Emergency'.

CHAPTER 3

PRELUDE TO ANOTHER WAR

But the war was over and the 'Emergency' not yet begun. During this time the great range of estates for which Guthries' were Agents – the closely integrated body known as the 'Guthrie Group' – continued to lead the attack against an entirely new menace that was impending – the war between natural and synthetic rubber.

To understand the strengths and weaknesses of the antagonists in this fresh contest, it is necessary to delve back once more into history.

In 1934 – that is to say, just after the disastrous depression of the early thirties in the price of rubber – Hay had become seriously concerned over the future of the plantations for which he was responsible. Many of the rubber trees on the estates were now of great size; producing the maximum amount of latex of which they were capable from bark much scarred by many years of tapping. Many younger trees, however, planted from seeds chosen from specially high-yielding trees, or with grafted scions in the manner perfected by the Dutch in Indonesia, were yielding significantly larger quantities of latex. In his view, two things should now happen. First of all, although there was a Rubber Research Institute in existence, the Group should set up in Malaya their own rubber research organisation to examine the whole question of the genetics of Hevea Braziliensis, to undertake selective breeding and to investigate applications of other new agricultural techniques. Secondly, an extensive and steady programme of replacement of the old trees should be started immediately.

Cut down the fine trees that might last another hundred years, the life-blood of the estates, and replant them with seeds that would not become even tappable rubber for the next six years? This was madness and must lead to ruination. The majority of the country's hoary old planters, who had tended their plantations like children for thirty years, were convinced that the only way to plant rubber was on virgin soil, freshly cleared from standing jungle.

Hay insisted; and, as had happened before in other fields in the firm's long history, Guthries' had the courage to lead the way to prosperity for all Malaya, by chopping down their old trees in a steady replanting programme continued over the years and, under the untiring direction of 'Sandy' Cranna, their Senior Visiting Agent, to replace them with higher-yielding clones – a step that was to be followed eventually by every estate throughout the country and, later still, by the myriads of small-holders – the owners of five or six acres only. Four to five hundred pounds weight of dry rubber from an acre of mature Hevea was considered a fair annual crop up to 1934. When the new trees came into bearing just before the Japanese invasion, nine hundred to a thousand pounds per acre was not by any means unusual.

Guthries' research station pressed on apace. Not only was selective breeding beginning to show remarkable interim results, but new techniques of 'bud grafting' were being tried out, to produce a composite tree of exceptionally high yield with a good spread of root and a compact head of foliage, so as not to blow over or break in strong winds. Samples of leaf ash from every field of every estate were now being analysed by the scientist in charge, one Dr Walter Chapman, who first applied that excellent system to determine exactly what fertiliser ingredient each patch of soil needed in order to produce the most rubber.

It was Dr Chapman, too, who first brooded upon the fact that local small-holders of rubber sometimes smeared their trees with cow dung immediately below the cut in the bark. They claimed that after this treatment the trees gave more latex. Among the Hindus, cow dung has a semi-sacred connotation, as was widely known; hence this peculiar habit of the local people was generally the cause of smiles among members of the European planting community. But Dr Chapman did not smile. He made experiments and discovered that cow dung contained a substance which stimulated the flow of a hormone in the rubber tree that increased the flow of sap. He eventually isolated the hormone; reproduced it synthetically and manufactured the dressing known as 'Stimulex', which has since then been used throughout the world wherever rubber is grown and which dramatically increased the total output of the 'Guthrie Group' of estates. And that meant reduced costs.

Modern wars cannot be fought without fast transportation of vast quantities of men and materials – and transportation means rubber. Germany could never have started the 1939–45 war, knowing she would be cut off from supplies of rubber, had she not developed a method of producing a synthetic substitute. Although 'Buna', the Axis product, was less elastic than natural rubber and tended to rot in water, it had some advantages over the latter. Scientifically developed, Buna could become a most dangerous rival.

The war went on and America, too, had to produce synthetic rubber in large quantities; and peace found Malaya's rubber plantations facing a new peril. The USA could manufacture an artificial rubber every bit as good as the natural material – except for two things. The first was cost. The second was 'Heat-loss' – that is to say, natural rubber still remained a better conductor of heat than 'synthetic' and so, under conditions of intense stress or friction such as in the tyres of aircraft and lorries, the natural latex from plantations was still preferred.

* * *

The 'Emergency', with its murders and suspicions, its curfews and its restrictive regulations, was a miserable time for everybody, although its effects upon the economies of Singapore and Malaya were not as great as might be supposed. Rubber, tin and palm oil prices, which had been in the doldrums since shortly after the war, surged forward from 1950 to 1954 under the pressure of demand caused by the Korean war; and the undoubted losses of revenue incurred on the estates and mines by reason of the emergency (to say nothing of the sufferings of staff and managers) were, from a commercial point of view, more than offset by high world prices for Malaya's principal export commodities. From the angle of general trade, too, commerce in both countries continued to boom.

The matter of this Malayan 'Emergency' deserves explanation, as it is often misunderstood.

Taking root from the period of the Japanese occupation

of South-east Asia, Malayan Chinese had been divided, as has been mentioned, into two groups; i.e. those who were faithful to their mother country China, now becoming Communist, and those who followed the lead of General Chiang Kai-shek, who was by this time safely ensconced under American protection in Formosa. The latter – the 'KMT' or Kuo Min Tang – led by, but by no means confined to, the respectable middle class core of the Chinese – were in large measure those whose views were represented by Dato Tan Cheng Lock of Malacca, and formed by far the majority of the Malayan Chinese population. Opposed to them – and putting them all greatly in fear – were the Communist guerrillas who had done most of the jungle fighting during the Japanese war. It was these whom Dato Tan Cheng Lock had meant when he warned the government that he 'could no longer be responsible for their actions' – it was these who had hidden their arms in the jungle rather than give them up at the end of the war; it was these who had realised that control of the embryonic Trades Union movement could give them widespread backing – and it was these who now went back to their forest hideouts and formed the backbone of the resistance-movement known as the 'Emergency'.

Whilst all Malayan Chinese were mortally affronted by the 'Federation Agreement', the great majority were prepared to play in with it in the hope of better times. With very few exceptions indeed, it was the minority of indoctrinated Communists (for the greater part externally backed and inspired) – especially the Khehs, that turbulent race whom even China had never quite been able to assimilate and who formed the spearhead of the age-old 'Tien-Ti-Hui' or Triad Society – who now took up arms in the belief that they could obtain sufficient popular support to crush Malay nationalism, supported by weak British imperialism, standing in the way of this rich and fertile land being ruled by the Heaven-born.

Though their actions were the result of an understandable grievance taken far further than the majority desired, they tended to blacken the entire Chinese race in the eyes of the Malays and to inflame a general racial antagonism. Malaya began to come apart at the seams.

After the signing of the Federation Agreement in February 1948, and the resultant outburst of trouble, Sir Edward Gent, the Governor – a brave, perhaps over-idealistic man who had formerly held the 'Malayan' desk at the Colonial Office – was tragically killed on a visit to London in an air collision five minutes before his arrival.

He was succeeded by Sir Henry Gurney, who became High Commissioner of the Federation of Malaya; and during whose time was appointed the first of the two great figures who were to bring order, and at last peace, to Malaya's murderous chaos. This was Lieutenant-General Sir Harold Briggs, who was appointed Director of Operations in 1950. Having carefully discussed matters with District Officers and other administrators 'on the ground' rather than at Federal headquarters, Briggs formulated his now famous 'Briggs Plan'. This scheme was aimed at the complete isolation and starving-out of the jungle fighters, by severing the supply lines between them and the far-scattered Chinese agricultural population of the opened country – an end which was only to be achieved by the physical removal and re-siting of over half a million people throughout the length and breadth of Malaya.

That this stupendous task, entailing the building of hundreds of new villages in areas where they could be guarded (and providing them with schools, shopping centres, dispensaries, police posts and perimeter wire fencing) was completed in under two years – at equally stupendous cost, be it admitted – does much credit to the Administration; and even more to the patience and forbearance of the Chinese. What is not often realised, however, is that this 're-settlement scheme' also included a vast reshuffle of labourers' accommodation on many rubber, tea and oil palm estates. In this work the 'Guthrie Group' of estates willingly played their part and by their drive and co-operation with Government they set an example that was worthy of the highest traditions of the firm.

Estates were the central object of the Communists' strongest and most virulent thrusts, second only to their basic object of countrywide subversion. Indeed, the Emergency started with the cold-blooded murders of a Chinese rubber dealer and three European planters in the Sungei Siput area of Perak. Ever since 1946 the incipient Trade Unions had become increasingly infiltrated by rabble-rousers and by men of violence – the hard core of whom were the Communist jungle fighters of war-time days, as might be expected. Even before the Emergency these were already becoming the planters' principal bugbear. As a result, a body was formed in October 1947 to combat this dangerous state of affairs, known as the 'Malayan Planting Industries Employers' Association', under the guidance of Christopher Dominic Ahearne, as its chief executive, and with Charles Thornton of Guthries' as one of its moving spirits and first Vice-President.

This Association of senior planters and employers had performed an immense work in stabilising the country's labour situation before the outbreak of the armed uprising in June 1948. Immediately after that event occurred, its members were naturally the target of every terrorist's most violent and merciless attack.

At night, and sitting – awake, often alone, sometimes with his wife – in his large dim-lit house among the rubber trees, with ears cocked and rifle loaded, the estate manager or assistant would see the days, the weeks, the months, the years drag by. The treacherous, hit-and-run war went on; and there seemed no hope that it would ever end. But daytime – dawn and dusk – were his main trouble. Distant clearings to be inspected; and he must show no fear. Deadly hollows close to jungle edges – rubber to be sent out down miles of winding road; and pay to be brought up in ill-escorted armoured cars (his own probably, with improvised steel-sheet armour plating). Then ambush – a few shots – and his day was done. Fighting jungle heat and frayed nerves, sticking to their duty against all odds, Guthrie planters – Beard, Boden, Butler-Madden, Hunt, Modder, Mylwahanam, Sergant (from the head office), Ward and Westendorp, as well as a dozen foremen – added their names to the roll of honour of those who had been killed in the service of the firm.

And it was on the wife of a Guthrie planter, Patricia Webber,* that Her Majesty the Queen bestowed the honour of an MBE in recognition of not only her part but the parts which innumerable other wives had played in sustaining the morale of their menfolk.

* * *

Days grew darker in Malaya as the 'Emergency' dragged on. In October 1951 Sir Henry Gurney, the High Commissioner

* The story of Patricia Webber was told in the film *The Plantre's Wife*.

of the Federation of Malaya, was murdered on his way to Fraser's Hill. A detached and benevolent intellectual, he could never be convinced, or at least could never convince the Home Government, of the need for strong measures and the wholesale banishment of Communists in suppressing the uprising. In the ambush, Sir Henry walked out of the car to draw the terrorists' fire from his wife and so was killed. It was an heroic death.

The men who directed the affairs of Guthries' and the other great Merchant Houses knew that there could be no successful outcome to the troubles until the ordinary man in the countryside became convinced that the forces of law and order would win. Then, and then only, would come the flow of information which alone would enable the military forces to hunt down and destroy the terrorists in their hideouts. They exerted all their influence to persuade the British Government that a really dramatic appointment as successor to Gurney would be an opportunity to show that Britain meant business.

Perhaps it was fortunate that by this time the Socialist Government had given place to a Conservative one, for at this critical stage Winston Churchill ordered General Sir Gerald Templer to take immediate command, as High Commissioner as well as Director of Operations.

So came to Malaya the second great figure whose name, together with that of General Briggs, stands out in the history of how that country, first of any in Asia, turned back the tide of Communism and won through at last to freedom and prosperity. Building on the foundations laid by Briggs, Templer's dynamic spirit reanimated Malaya from end to end. A flood of desperately needed finance poured forth to complete the re-settlement of hundreds of thousands more rural Chinese 'squatters'; and the attention that he and his administrators paid to the peoples' needs and hopes went far to win the battle of the 'hearts and minds' of Malaya's population.

At long last the tide had turned.

CHAPTER 4

INDEPENDENCE

If ever two men struck the same note, those two men were Templer and Hay. Sharp tongued, short tempered, forward thrusting, they had no patience either with yes-men or arguers. The only criterion was to do your job, keep your mouth shut, stick to your guns and let the results speak for themselves. If you went wrong, you were out. Templer approved Hay's way of thinking; and especially his foresight in setting up the first scheme ever in Malaya for training local boys to become Assistants, and later Managers, of the Estates. Here was a man who knew what he was doing; one moreover who understood how to ensure that the Guthrie Group of estates would be well received by the new and independent government of the time to come. For Templer was determined that that time should come soon.

Guthries' were wise indeed to initiate the Cadet Scheme for Assistants and Managers, for it was in 1953 that Templer had the courage to insist that elections should be organised and held without delay. The country was to have its own affairs placed in its hands with all speed; and that meant that the planting industry would soon be run by Malayans – in collaboration with the British if they were reasonable, and without them if they were not.

UMNO – the United Malay National Organisation – was now led by Tunku Abdul Rahman Putra, a son of the Sultan of Kedah, who had an intuitive bridge player's sense of the 'run of the game'. He realised that Dato Onn bin Jaffar's theories – sound though they were – would never suit the tempo of the hour. Dato Onn wanted an integration of Malaya's three races on the ground, by the formation of multi-racial village committees. Malcolm MacDonald, the British Government's resident Commissioner-General in South-east Asia, had been steadily at work building up a Communities Liaison Committee and Tunku Abdul Rahman realised that there lay the solution – in forming an immediate alliance between the three leading parties at 'top level' if Independence was to be achieved by peaceful means. This suited Britain well, because early freedom for Malaya would debunk the Communist terrorist slogan, which was now for 'liberation from imperialist dominators'; as well as because a quick grant of independence would prevent the great uncanalised reservoir of goodwill, which had always existed between the two countries, from being needlessly dissipated.

An alliance between the United Malay National Organisation, the Malayan Chinese Association and the Malayan Indian Congress was therefore formed. In 1955 elections were held, bringing the Alliance into power with a mighty majority; and on the 31st of August 1957 – in probably the most gentle 'transfer' the world has ever known – Malaya received its independence.

How much of that warm goodwill had sprung from the years of friendliness – of honest dealing between British traders and planters with the many races of Malaya – from the wealth and development brought to the latter by the commercial man's forcing of Britain's hand to enter the Peninsula in the first place – it has been part of the purpose of this story to tell.

* * *

During the war, with the exception of those owned by The Polymer Corporation in Canada, the plants for development and production of synthetic rubber, which had so materially assisted the Allies to win, had been set up and were owned by the United States Government. It has already been related that in the fields of cost and heat dispersion natural rubber had the advantage over the synthetic product. There then occurred another event which gave yet greater impetus to the chemist and the engineer to produce a material the equal in all respects of natural rubber – the Korean war. The United States Government, so nearly caught without sufficient, still essential, natural rubber in the second world war, was determined not to be caught again and started to buy every pound on which it could lay its hands. The reaction was inevitable. The price soared until it reached over 5s per lb – a level which had not been seen since 1912, and was nearly three times the price at which the synthetic article could be produced. Here indeed was a challenge, for natural's price advantage had disappeared.

When the threat of widespread war receded the United States was to find itself with more than a million tons of natural rubber in stockpile. True to its belief in free enterprise, in 1955 the plants were sold – to manufacturers using rubber as a raw material and to oil companies who supplied the basic ingredients. And now began the real competition between nature's product and that of man.

By this time the price of natural rubber was at a level no more than half the peak it had recently attained and, with the threat of eventual disposal of the vast quantities accumulated in the American and British stockpiles (for Britain too had joined the fashion), natural looked destined to regain its price advantage. The Americans are past masters at reducing cost and science moves quicker than nature – and unless something was done Malaya's rubber industry (together with that of other countries in South-east Asia), from which it was estimated three-quarters of a million breadwinners earned a living, could face extinction – it had happened to Indigo! Moreover, the industrialist who employs 'man-made' rubber in the manufacture of his product knows precisely what he is using. Its chemical composition and physical properties are both known and clearly specified; and its various grades are of regular and unchanging quality. He is therefore able to turn his raw material into an exactly standardised article without first having to test each parcel of such rubber that comes into his hands.

In the case of natural rubber however (in the form in which it used normally to reach the market) he was unable to do this. No two consignments of natural rubber could ever be guaranteed as being identically similar. In spite of the remarkable advances made over the last sixty years in the fields of genetics and of agricultural technique, when it came to the question of processing and marketing, the original procedures had scarcely changed at all. Sheet rubber needed to be 'kippered' or smoked for five or six days and crêpe rubbers air-dried for anything up to four weeks, and then pressed together in clumsy blocks (whose dimensions derived from tea chests of the old East India Company) which were awkward to handle, difficult to store and afforded no protection whatsoever against contamination. By long-standing practice, natural rubber was classified into a large number of 'grades' which gave no indication of the chemical constitution and very little of the properties or the likely performance of any given consignment; these grades being arrived at by a visual examination on the part of the rubber brokers on the basis of what samples from each block 'looked like'. Manufacturers therefore had to test each intake of natural rubber into their factories separately, in order to produce a standard finished product.

Hay knew that, although the price at which rubber was sold was determined in the market place by the inexorable law of supply and demand, costs could be kept under control provided productivity could be increased – and that meant that the same, or a smaller, labour force must work harder to bring in and process the increasing quantity of latex which the continuing replacement of old trees by newer strains could yield. So replanting must be intensified to make up for enforced neglect during the war and the early intensive phase of the 'Emergency'. Modern methods of labour-saving devices must be introduced – for the cost of labour on a plantation made up two-thirds of the total cost of production; drains must be dug by drag-lines rather than by gangs of men; internal roads must be improved so that tankers could take latex to centralised factories with the newest and most economical layout, machinery and handling equipment. Only thus could natural rubber continue to compete in terms of cost when the inevitable drop in price occurred. And so began a drive to alter the way of thinking of all employed on the Guthrie estates – for if natural rubber succumbed to synthetic there would be work for none.

Charles Mann, the senior director under Hay in London, had already led Guthries' in 1950 to produce the latex from the tree in a concentrated form, carefully preserved, meeting a precise analytical, chemical and physical formula and transported in bulk tanks in ships to required destinations. Users knew exactly what they were getting and had no fear of variation in their raw material or finished product. Why could not a similar degree of standardisation be introduced in solid rubbers despite the variations in the exact composition of latex produced by different trees on different soils? If that problem could be solved the natural bias which users

K. M. G. Anderson, chairman of Guthrie & Co (UK) Limited

Sir Eric Griffith-Jones, KBE, CMG, chairman of The Guthrie Corporation Limited

had towards the standardised synthetic material should disappear and nature's product could compete with man's on equal terms of cost and quality.

It was in the year 1961 that Guthries' were once more to assume their traditional position of leadership, by being the first successfully to combat that aspect of this new menace to Malaysia's prosperity.

C. W. Thomson, General Manager of 'Guthrie Latex' in Malaya, was one who had realised that in order successfully to compete with synthetic, Malaya's rubber would have to adhere rigorously to exact and unvarying physical and chemical composition for each grade and be packed in more manageable form.

Encouraged by Sir John Hay, Thomson set to work on some lengths of 'crêpe' rubber and a few 'cup-lumps' with the aid of an ordinary household mincing machine borrowed from his wife, as well as with a small-sized 'drying machine' made from her electric hair-dryer. The successful outcome of this modest beginning encouraged the purchase of a rather larger household mincing machine worked by an electric motor; and this – later hastily reinforced with mild-steel bands to prevent it bursting apart – actually turned out the first five tons of rubber in the new form ever to be placed on the market.

From then on it was a matter of developing to a commercial scale; of designing machines on the principle of a meat mincer but adapted for rubber; of obtaining a wide 'mix' to ensure homogeneity; of testing and modifying dryers; of improving the method of pressing – for a ready market had been established from the moment the first experimental samples had been exposed for sale. The trade name of 'Dynat' to signify the *Dynamic* properties of *Natural* rubber – was chosen.

The factory on a rubber estate where Dynat rubber processing is undertaken bears little or no resemblance to one of even ten years ago, with its electrically controlled and monitored systems, its oil fired drying, its conveyor belts, fork lift trucks, steady hum of ordered activity and, above all, spotless cleanliness. Through the great heat of the dryers and from the ordeal of four minutes of pressure at 3,000 lb per square inch, the transformed rubber emerges in neat translucent blocks of 75 lb weight each, smelling almost like new bread – and the similarity is heightened at the sight of these blocks, each in its own clean polythene wrapping, being loaded onto pallets with the care that one associates with hot loaves.

The Rubber Research Institute had also been working to the same end and announced its own Heveacrumb process a few months after Dynat was introduced. Others have followed, and these new processes, together with the standardisation of properties under the SMR (Standard Malaysian Rubber) scheme, constitute Malaysia's most effective weapon in the struggle of 'natural' against 'synthetic' rubber.

* * *

It was during the troubled 'Emergency' period that two further problems began to occupy the minds of Guthries' Directors.

The first and only business of a Trader is to trade. If the trader subsequently becomes Agent and Trustee for a range of landed properties, then he ceases to be only a trader and something begins to happen to him. If he is perceptive, he finds a cleft growing deeper in his way of thinking. On the one hand, his eyes continue to range the world – they look outward, examining the flow, the coming and going, of trade wherever it may be; and balancing one against the other the possibilities of opportunist revenue from commerce in the world market. On the other hand, as policy-maker for agricultural and mining interests, he is all for permanence, for improvement, for the continued extraction of profit from a fixed and immovable area of soil. Two different thought-processes become required.

In this division of thought, it is not surprising to find that Guthries' trading activities continued to be centred in Singapore (whence the firm had sprung) with branches at Kuala Lumpur, Penang, Ipoh, Malacca and in Borneo and Sumatra, whilst the Agency aspect of its activities had naturally centred on London (whence had come most of the money to finance the plantations and mines) with direct contact to Kuala Lumpur (where was centred the administrative organisation for day to day management of the properties.)

From 1947 to 1954 the commercial side of the firm

flourished amazingly, as has been indicated, but that did not blind either Keith Anderson or Sir John Hay to the fact that British trade with the East was nowadays a very different kettle of fish from the assured position pre-war. The Japanese war had given confidence in Britain a tremendous shake throughout the East. The Malay attitude to the Malayan Union, their immediate reaction to it, the climb-down of Parliament to form the Federation of Malaya and the Communist-inspired 'Emergency', had all been pointers to the ultimate solution.

Not only was Britain morally bound by Queen Victoria's edict to Disraeli to 'bring the peoples of these countries on to the stage where they can govern themselves' – in other words, to grant independence to Malaya as soon as possible – but events in that country strongly suggested that the time to accord independence to it was rapidly approaching, whether the Malayan people were in fact quite ready yet to accept it and use it wisely, or not. Wisdom dictated that Guthries' interests should henceforth become wider spread – and with the portent of the Korean war foreshadowing turmoil in the Far East – geographically wider spread.

Keith Anderson had had some business training before joining Guthries' in 1936; had had a spell 'learning the business' in Malaya and Singapore, whence he returned in the summer of 1939 soon to find himself called upon by the Royal Air Force, on the Reserve of which he was already a Flying Officer with his 'Wings'. Spending four years in Egypt and India, he was fortunate enough to find himself back in England as a Wing Commander and due for early demobilisation when the war with Germany was over. So to 'Lotus' he repaired at the age of thirty-three and busied himself picking up the threads of what had happened to Guthries' affairs and planning for the future. And much there was to do, with the liberation of Malaya imminent and with a very attenuated staff.

Within a few years Anderson was to become successively Chairman of The Rubber Trade Association and Chairman of The Rubber Growers Association – the youngest man to have held that office – but with Hay and Mann there was no lack of talent in Guthries' London office for looking after 'The Estates' and it naturally fell to Anderson's lot to play the major part in policy-making on the Trading side of the business. He moved with speed.

In 1951 Guthries' bought the firm of Cochrane and Milton, operating as dealers in agricultural equipment and builders' hardware in Rhodesia. In that same year they started farming in England to give a basic knowledge for extension of that activity to Central Africa and to be able to set up a service advising the great absentee landlords of Rhodesia. (Alas, for the time being, that enterprise has had to be put into limbo.)

In 1953, as a result of earlier visits by A. F. Taylor and L. L. Cooper, they opened an office in Melbourne to be followed in 1959 by the purchase of F. W. Green and Company, general traders, which gave them a stake in every State of the Australian Commonwealth. Within the decade was to grow a sizeable commercial empire in its own right with interests in cotton spinning, the manufacture of towels, fluorescent lighting fittings, window louvres and roofing materials, as well as considerable trade inter-state and in imports and exports, all playing their part in the tremendous development of that mighty continent.

The London office, too, began to branch out and was soon to own the food importing businesses of B. N. Sexton, Canadian Foods and John Dorell. Shipping and confirming business was expanded to West, Central and East African countries as well as to South Africa, where a new Guthrie company was formed in 1967 – full circle back to old Tom Harrington and his young protégé Sandy Guthrie!

And so the time had come when, after serving as the nerve centre of the firm's trading activities for 148 years, Singapore became inappropriate as the Headquarters and these were transferred to London.

By the end of this story Keith Anderson, from his chair in Gracechurch Street, could survey a worldwide network of Guthrie interests – Guthries' of Singapore and Malaysia (now merged with an off-shoot of the equally famous Eastern House of Jardine Matheson into Guthrie Waugh), Guthries' of Rhodesia, Guthries' of Australia, Guthries' of Canada, Guthries' of South Africa, Guthries' of Nigeria and all the innumerable subsidiaries. True to itself, the old firm, arising like the Phoenix from the flames of war and the smoke of destruction, had taken wings and flown to the ends of the earth.

* * *

The second consideration exercising the minds of the directors of Guthries' arose from the fact that the company, great though it was, was owned by one family and yet effectively controlled a range of publicly owned companies with estates in Malaya, Borneo and Sumatra, far weightier in their combined financial implications than it was itself. By its drive and its foresight Guthries' had given them birth; by its position as their Secretaries and Agents it governed their policy, their purchase of supplies and the exportation and selling of their produce.

But Guthries' did not own them. They were owned by colonels' widows, by parsons and business men, by artisans and country squires, by every man or woman who invested or dabbled in plantation shares on the stock markets. Although they formed what was loosely described as the 'Guthrie Group', and were held in correspondingly high repute, each company was quoted under its own name in the financial columns of the newspapers.

Sir John Hay's whole mind and soul were wrapped up in rubber and 'The Estates' and he had seldom devoted much time or interest to the commercial or trading side of the firm's activities, though as Managing Director in London he retained overall responsibility. In 1950 he had sold back to the Anderson family the one-sixth interest in Guthries' which he had purchased when he first took over after old Sir John Anderson's death twenty-five years previously. He was well aware that Guthries' were the best Secretaries and Agents there were – but that was under his leadership – and what was to happen to this fine edifice the 'Guthrie Group' when he was gone? Its destiny left in the hands of Guthries'? No. There was no one there capable of donning his mantle. Better by far that the 'Guthrie Group' should control its own destiny.

With increasing determination, Hay began to work towards that end, and by 1960 he had convinced the majority of his fellow directors of the various companies which made up the 'Guthrie Group' that they should set up their own organisation to render Secretarial and Agency services, owned proportionately by each of the companies making up the Group, with himself at the head and able to appoint a man of their own choosing to succeed to that position. And so, despite warnings that the move did nothing to solve the problem of succession to Sir John Hay, after long and difficult negotiations on 1st January 1961 the 'Guthrie Group' hived itself off from Guthries', took over necessary staff and premises, and formed a co-operative – Guthrie Estates Agency Limited with a subsidiary, Guthrie Agency (Malaya) Limited – to manage the future affairs of the constituent companies.

CHAPTER 5

THE HAND OF FRIENDSHIP

Malaya was independent. The terrorists' war-cry was now meaningless. The mass of the people knew what the struggle had been about and the needed information flowed in an ever-increasing flood. Armed Communism, from the Thailand border to Singapore, was doomed. Operations by well trained British, Commonwealth and Malayan troops, who now had great experience in jungle warfare, were continued, and by 1959 the last flames flickered out; the 'Emergency' was over.

Unlike the case in so many other countries, whose policies had been to resist political advancement in their colonies, and to deny them the right to ultimate freedom, the British 'business' system of concession and retreat – in other words the age-old trading practice of discussion and compromise rather than the striking of national attitudes – was now to pay good dividends.

In its dealings with a country which had found cohesion originated through the pertinacity and drive of British merchants – from whom it has learned much – Britain was far-seeing enough to protect its investments in Malaya in the only way which had a chance of longevity. Though European planters, traders and industrialists were now to recede gradually from the Malayan scene, British business in the Peninsula could still be safeguarded. The graceful departure of Britain from the control of Malaya turned out to be among the most sensible – as well as among the most enlightened – things that country has ever done; and was, in the charming way that the hand of friendship was received and reciprocated by the Malayans, one which gives equal credit to both peoples.

The first administrative act of the wise little independent country of six million Malayans was to choose to become a member of the British Commonwealth of Nations. The second was to give to Britain, as a residence for its future High Commissioners, the lovely house of 'Carcosa', which had been the seat of successive Chief Secretaries of the old 'Imperialist Dominators'. As K. G. Tregonning remarks in his *History of Modern Malaya*, it 'looked not back: but to the future'.

In Singapore, similar, if slightly slower, political progress was also occurring; and in 1959 that vastly populated City State – with old Thomas Scott's little harbour of 'Tanjong Pagar' now become the fifth largest port in the world – advanced to internal self-government, to be followed in 1963 by full independence when it chose to join its neighbour on the mainland as a member State of the Federation of Malaysia. Two years later it was, however, to break away as an independent republic though still a member of the British Commonwealth of Nations.

* * *

All that is left of this outline of the first hundred and fifty years of British commercial enterprise in South-east Asia – as epitomised by the history of Guthrie and Company – is soon told. There is no need to particularise at this point of time, or to paint in too many details of a picture that has yet to become history.

Sir John Hay remained pre-eminent as the uncrowned king of the rubber plantation industry. In 1947 he had received from Holland's Queen Wilhelmina the high honour of Commander of the Netherlands Order of Oranje-Nassau 'for his services in the cause of world rubber'; and in 1961 the Yang di-Pertuan Agong (or King) of Malaya, conferred on him the title of Paduka Mangku Negara – equivalent to yet another knighthood. But at the beginning of 1961 he was an old man, shortly to celebrate his seventy-eighth birthday and, alas, the schism from Guthrie and Company was but a part of the last unhappy chapter in the life of this remarkable man. Within two and a half years it became apparent to a majority of his colleagues on the board of Guthrie Estates Agency that Sir John, then over eighty, had no intention of relinquishing the helm and providing the necessary succession and that his methods were alienating the loyalty of the key staff. Four out of the six directors on the board resigned and the dispute became public, leading to much acrimony. As is its wont, the City of London, led by the big Institutions, stepped in to find a solution. After months of patient negotiation under the guidance of Lord Cromer, Governor of the Bank of England, it was agreed that Sir Eric Griffith-Jones, KBE, CMG, should join the Guthrie Group, taking over the Chairmanships of the more important companies as Sir John retired from them. On the 27th May 1964, Sir John Hay died and with him an era which he had dominated for forty years.

And so there came on to the scene another figure with a major part to play. Eric Griffith-Jones had been born in Singapore in 1913 and many of his forbears had made their impact on the history of that city. He was a great great grandson of Mr Blundell, who had been Governor at the time of the currency tangle, as described earlier. He was a grandson of Howard Newton, one of Singapore's best known Municipal Engineers (after whom Newton Road and Newton Circus were named) and his father, Oswald Griffith-Jones, was an outstanding Singapore sportsman – a brilliant cricketer and rugger player. With such a background it is not surprising to find Eric practising, soon after he became a barrister, as an Advocate and Solicitor in the Straits Settlements. Then to the Colonial Legal Service as Crown Counsel, from which position he was forcibly removed, as a Captain in the Volunteer Force, by the Japanese to work on the Siamese Railway where he was in company with many Guthrie men.

After release from captivity, Eric Griffith-Jones continued working in Malaya in various posts in the Colonial Legal Service until transfer to Kenya as Solicitor General in 1952, becoming Attorney General three years later. Deputy Governor in 1961, he was Acting Governor several times covering, just prior to entering this story, the occasion of the formation of the first Government of Kenya with an unofficial political majority, when he swore in, as one of two joint Chief Ministers, Jomo Kenyatta who subsequently became Kenya's first President. For his manifold services to his Sovereign, Sir Eric was knighted in 1962.

It has been Sir Eric Griffith-Jones who, in the short space of six years, has welded all the rubber and oil palm interests which had been the 'Guthrie Group' into the giant Guthrie Corporation, largest owners of such plantations in the world. It has been he who set the trend for that giant to branch out by acquiring industrial concerns, based in the United Kingdom, which use rubber – natural and synthetic – in large quantities so that the men on the plantations can learn new technologies and new methods of preparing and modifying what Nature so bountifully provides for Malaysia's prosperity.

And there we must leave the story of Guthries' until some new chapter comes to be written, as it surely will be, with the leadership of Keith Anderson and Eric Griffith-Jones to follow the six with whom this story has been mainly concerned.

> There were wonderful giants of old, you know.
> There were wonderful giants of old.
>
> . . .
>
>   For all of we,
>   Whoever we be,
> Come up to the giants of old, you see!*

Let this tale be read as typifying, in greater or less degree, all the many long-standing British businesses in South-east Asia who, over the years, like Guthries', have also 'Stood for Truth'.

* First and last lines of a Harrow School song.

APPENDIX A

NOTE ON THE FAMILY OF GUTHRIE

The name of 'Guthrie' is an old one in Scotland; one of the fables of its origin being that it harks back to Guthrum the Dane, to whom Alfred the Great granted the northern part of Mercia by the Peace of Wedmore in AD 878.

A certain 'Guthrie' was Chief Falconer to Malcolm Canmore when that King had his palace at Forfar about the time of the Norman Conquest.

In 1290 it was a 'Squire Guthrie' who brought the unfortunate William Wallace back to Scotland (and his subsequent death) from the Court of Philip IV of France.

During the fourteenth and fifteenth centuries the Guthries flourished, becoming 'King's Barons' (i.e. feudal vassals holding their lands immediately from the Crown, though not possessing titles of nobility); no less than sixteen of whom – all Guthries – being alive at one and the same time in the county of Angus during the reign of James the Second of Scotland.

Upon that king's death through the bursting of a cannon at the siege of Roxburgh, a certain Sir David Guthrie (one of the four sons of Alexander Guthrie of Kincaldrum) received from the widowed Queen the appointment of Lord Treasurer and Comptroller of the Royal Household. Thenceforth Sir David was considered the head of the Guthrie clan and from him descend the present owner of Guthrie Castle and also the offshoot thereof with whom *The Traders* deals.

Sir David Guthrie was granted the Barony of Guthrie by King David II of Scotland; and in 1469 King James III issued his Royal Warrant empowering Sir David to build the said castle and an 'iron Yett' upon the banks of the river Lunan, where (much smothered by later 'Improvements' and machicolated 'Victoriana') they may be seen to this day.

Sir David's son, Sir Alexander Guthrie, married a daughter of Lyon of the nearby Glamis Castle (an ancestor of Her

Majesty Queen Elizabeth the Second) and fell at Flodden with his own son Sir David and three of his brothers-in-law, William, David and George Lyon – whence arose the Lament

> I've heard them lilting at the ewe-milking,
> Lasses a'lilting before the dawn o'day,
> But now they are moaning on ilka green loaning.
> The flowers of the forest are a'wede away.

The Guthries could never keep out of trouble; and during the religious arguments of the sixteenth century they were up to their necks in it. It was a Guthrie who, together with Norman Leslie, was charged with the 'treasonabil slauchter' of that Richelieu of Scotland, David Beaton, 'Cardinal Archbishop of Sanct Androis', the Chancellor, for engineering the Catholic marriage of Mary, the daughter of James V with the French Dauphin. Fond as the Scots were of France, they had a mind to manage their own affairs.

Shortly after this it was no less than Alexander Guthrie, Burgess of Edinburgh, who was cited as guilty of the 'vyle, treasonabil slauchter of the umquwhile David Riccio, their Majesties' Secretary, committed in their Majesties' presents within the Palace of Hailleraid House'. The Guthries would make poor Mary Stuart behave, whether she would or no.

In the light of these and 'sundry uther such abhominabil crymes' (as the register of the Privy Council remarks), the mere slaying, on the highway between Brechin and Dundee, of one Patrick Gardyne by William Guthrie of Ravensby, third son of Guthrie of Guthrie, may virtually pass unnoticed – more especially as Gardyne of Gardyne got his own back by assassinating Alexander Guthrie of Guthrie (his own cousin) ten years later.

The Guthries have always been most reasonable and they will go to any lengths to battle the rest of the world out of its extraordinary pig-headedness. About the year 1638 four members of the family 'were in the ministry', as they say in Scotland, of whom the most famous was James Guthrie, Minister of Lauder (later known as the 'Martyr') who was the first to sign with his life blood the 'Covenant' that bound all those who assembled together to worship God to do so in their own way. Known to Oliver Cromwell as the 'man who would not bow', James became such a problem to Charles II that he was finally condemned to death by hanging, for having committed many treasonable acts against his Majesty and His lieges, but was at the same time given every possible opportunity to walk out of prison a free man. James, however, persisted in being hanged and preferred martyrdom to liberty. In a dying speech which should ring in the ears of Scotland for a thousand years (but alas does not) he said that he would 'not exchange this scaffold for the fairest palace or the mitre of the greatest prelate'; and, after adding that 'if he had been otherwise minded he might have been no prisoner', assured his hearers that he 'durst not redeem his life with the loss of his integrity'. A bystander remarked that 'Our minister had a great power of matter' and that 'he grat and swat and spat like mischief'. After the hanging, his head was struck off and set over the 'Nether Bow', his estates were confiscated and his children deprived of all rights. His name stands on the Martyrs' Monument in Greyfriars' Churchyard, Edinburgh.

A later manifestation of the same spirit induced the Reverend Thomas Guthrie, DD (born at Brechin in 1803, the son of 'Banking' relatives of the Alexander of *The Traders*) to express such forceful views in support of the 'Free Church of Scotland' as to embarrass the authorities and result in his 'banishment' to Loch Lee – where he delivered a series of open-air sermons long remembered for their eloquence and power. He was the great apostle of the 'Ragged Schools' (Charity Schools) of Scotland, in connection with which his name is of wide renown.*

The 'Alexander Guthrie' of *The Traders* descends from the Guthries of Guthrie Castle through the Guthries of Pitforthie, David Guthrie of Cookston, Alexander Guthrie of Kincraig and Alexander Guthrie (his father) of the farm of Burnside, in the parish of Menmuir, near Brechin.

That such stubborn and turbulent blood could mellow to form an assiduous and patient man of business in little over a hundred years, is perhaps due to the four generations of hardworking farmers who were Alexander's immediate ancestors.

* A fine statue of him, with his arm round the shoulders of a trusting urchin, stands in Princes Street, Edinburgh.

APPENDIX B

THE VARIOUS SITES OF GUTHRIES' OFFICE IN SINGAPORE

An impression exists that the office of Messrs Guthrie and Company in Battery Road, Singapore, is built on the original site leased by Alexander Guthrie. This is not so.

Grants 48 and 407 Boat Quay, dated 1827 and issued in the name of Alexander Guthrie, concern portions of land some 300 yards further inland along Boat Quay than the present site. By the middle of the nineteenth century neither Grant remained in the name either of a Guthrie or of the firm of Guthrie and Company; both having been subdivided as shop lots etc among many owners.

The firm of Guthrie and Company was by 1850 leasing office and godown accommodation from Mr Alkaff along Collyer Quay, on a site which was later cleared of the old building and rebuilt by Mr Alkaff to become the Arcade. Guthries' remained in occupation of that building until at least 1905, as it was from the tower above the office on Collyer Quay that Mr A. E. Baddeley, later the firm's manager, saw (according to an account written by him) the Russian Fleet under Admiral Rostjestvensky sail past to its utter destruction by Admiral Togo in the Straits of Tsushima.

Shortly after the death of James Guthrie in 1900, his widow, Sophia née Fraser, made over to Guthrie and Company certain lands along Battery Road inherited by her from her father and leased to Messrs McKerrow and Company; and it was upon these lands that Guthrie and Company built their office when Alkaff decided to pull down his office along Collyer Quay and build the Arcade.

In 1950 Guthrie and Company sold the site to The Chartered Bank (of India, Australia and China, as it then was) to enable that bank to expand its premises; and have since remained tenants.

APPENDIX C

NOTE ON THE 'AFRICAN' OIL PALM AND ON GUTHRIES' RESEARCH WORK AT CHEMARA, JOHORE

'Elaeis Guineensis', the African oil palm, is a member of the tribe or sub-family of palms known as the 'Cocoinese'. At full growth 'Elaeis' is a palm about thirty or forty feet high, with a heavy head of fronds and a massive trunk. On this latter the petioles of past seasons' fronds adhere for many years, to form a pattern not unlike that of a pineapple. The fronds, dark green in colour, are of great size and these consist, as is usual in palms, of a yellow midrib along which sprout out the horizontally-opposed leaflets at regular intervals of an inch or so. In that other member of the 'Cocoinese', the ubiquitous coconut palm of the East, these leaflets, coiffured to perfection and exquisitely parted by the midrib, endow the slim coconuts with an air of graceful ease as they lean their sleek heads against the tropic wind, 'as elegant as women – and as vain'. In Elaeis, however, the fronds are so arranged that every second or third leaflet juts off from the midrib at a more or less acute angle upwards, to produce a strangely tousled effect to the foliage as a whole. With its 'fir-cone', or pineapple-like, trunk (in whose cracks ferns often take root and grow to considerable size), its large bundles of orange-coloured nuts and its rebellious head of tangled hair, Elaeis is thus an interesting rather than a beautiful tree – and one that looks (as indeed it is) an intruder into the poised and polished Orient from some barbaric land.

In past time the oil palm seems to have adventured (probably in the ditty-box of a seventeenth-century sailor) from Africa to the island of Reunion and to Amsterdam; and from these two places four nuts, or some incredibly small number of that sort, are said to have been the progenitors of all the vast proliferation of Elaeis throughout the East. It was certainly from Reunion and from Amsterdam that the Dutch first brought these trees in the mid-nineteenth century to Java – where their descendants flourished exceedingly and furnished 'Mynheer' with many a fine ornamental avenue to grace his Eastern country home.

The value of Elaeis to mankind's economy has been known in Africa from time immemorial. The oil palm produces a profusion of hard-cased nuts, each one about the size of an elongated bantam's-egg, in heavy bunches that may weigh up to half a hundredweight each; and it continues to do this through all seasons from the fourth or fifth year of its life. When boiled and crushed, these nuts produce two excellent forms of edible oil in large quantities, one from the flesh under the outer husk and one from the kernel of the nut itself.

In the East Indies, commercial interest in the African oil palm was aroused shortly after the first four nuts were planted in the Botanical Garden at Buitenzorg (now 'Bogor') in Java in 1848: and trial plantings of nuts from the Buitenzorg 'Economic Garden' were well established in various Dutch East Indian territories by 1878. From that stage on, the story becomes a trifle complicated.

Ornamental 'avenue' palms were in considerable evidence in Sumatra between 1880 and 1900; the Lake Gardens in Kuala Lumpur possessed good specimens by 1905 and from the 'avenue' oil palm of Sumatra came the nuts at Rantau Panjang in Malaya which in turn produced the first oil palms to be planted at Tennamaram Estate in Selangor in 1917.

Meanwhile, the 'avenue' oil palms in Sumatra had already grown, by as early as 1911, into several full-scale oil palm estates in that island – notably a large property in the east coast 'Deli' district near Medan called Marihat Baris. It was from this Marihat Baris estate in Sumatra and from Tennamaram estate in Selangor that the nuts were purchased to plant up the small estate near Kluang in Johore that later became the nucleus of 'Elaeis Estate' and it was these too which were planted in due time on all the other plantations which were formed into the large group known as 'Oil Palms of Malaya', as recounted in *The Traders*.

Up to that time the oil palms throughout the East had been of one general variety – this being a tree that produced a nut with a thick hard shell, known, from its local origin of Marihat Baris estate in the district of 'Deli', as the 'Deli-dura'.

From about 1924 onwards, Guthrie and Company (together with other planters of the African oil palm) began to improve this 'Deli-dura' strain by selecting, for the purposes of cross-breeding, trees bearing nuts with the greatest amount of flesh and (more important) with the thinnest shells. Nuts were selected from an estate in Malaya known as 'Elmina', which had been planted up in 1920 with nuts from Tennamaram estate; from the Malayan Government's Agricultural Station at Serdang in Selangor, which had been planted with nuts from the Kuala Lumpur Lake Gardens in 1922; and from Dutch sources at Marihat Baris, where an official breeding programme had been initiated in that same year.

A central research station named 'Chemara', set up by Guthries' thus came naturally into being at the estates in Johore, where experimental cross-breeding from many different places was now being undertaken. As a result of this practical work of research, the 'Deli-dura' strain was greatly improved over the years.

But elsewhere an entirely new event was occurring. As from 1922, in Africa – at Yangambi, in the Garden of the National Institute of Agronomy of the Belgian Congo, to be exact – research work was proceeding along completely different lines. Among the wild 'Elaeis' palms growing in their natural state in Africa, a curious 'sport', or eccentric, among the oil palms was at times observed; this being an apparently normal oil palm whose nuts, instead of coming to maturity, fell off when half grown. What was particularly interesting to note, however, was that these aborted nuts had no shells at all.

This variant, named by scientists the 'Pisifera', often occurred in the neighbourhood of palms with exceptionally thin shells, which therefore furnished a high oil-yield. In 1933 Ringoet introduced quite a range of Pisifera, as well as of these thin-shelled palms (called the 'Tenara' variety), into his research station at Yangambi, and there he and his assistant Beirnaert began to cross-breed Tenara with Tenara in an attempt to produce a permanent strain of high-yielding palm. Unfortunately, however, the progeny of these crosses invariably resulted in approximately one-third being the normal type thick-shelled 'Elaeis' known in the East as the 'Deli-dura', only about one-third the high-yielding Tenara and one-third the nut-dropping Pisifera. The origin of the useless Pisifera would therefore appear to be explained; but how to create a permanent strain of 100 per cent high-yielding Tenara remained a mystery.

It was not until after further research at Yangambi that in 1940 Beirnaert and Vanderweyen were able to publish a paper (Bulletin Agric. Congo Belge, 31; p95) showing that the original thick-shelled 'Dura' palms, when crossed with 'useless' Pisifera, produced nothing but 100 per cent of the much-sought-after, high-yielding, thin-shelled Tenara. Pisifera, therefore, for the first time, became recognised as the vital male element in the creation of the new 'thin-shelled' oil palm. When the Japanese war closed down upon the Eastern world, H. M. Gray at Guthries' Chemara research station in Johore was already in close touch with the Congo regarding this important discovery.

Immediately the war was over, the work of Beirnaert and Vanderweyen began to have an immense impact on the whole theory of oil palm breeding. One of the first acts of H. M. Gray on his return from the war was to send to the Belgian Congo for pollen of the Pisifera for cross-breeding with his Deli-dura; and equal credit must go to him for his foresight in taking this step (and thereby initiating the great oil palm improvement work throughout the Orient) as well as to the National Institute of Agronomy of the Belgian Congo for supplying the pollen freely as a generous gift. The nuts produced by this 'Pisifera × Deli-dura' cross-breeding in Johore were planted out – as the first thin-shelled, high-yielding 'Tenara' to be created in Malaya – in 1949. From that moment, a new future opened for the oil palm industry in the East.

H. M. Gray – the introducer into Malaya of the advance discovered by Beirnaert in the Congo – left on retirement in 1951; to be followed by Mr Arokiasamy, who successfully carried on Gray's genetical crossing programme unaided until 1954, when Dr Eric Rosenquist took over. During Dr Rosenquist's tenure of office as Director of Research at Chemara until 1961 (when he left to take over Guthries' Rubber Research station at Seremban) the production of Tenara palms by cross-breeding Deli-dura with imported pollen of the Congo Pisifera was much intensified; to the point (which is perhaps the step for which Dr Rosenquist is chiefly remembered) where it became sound policy for Guthries' to establish a Pisifera plantation of their own purely for the production of pollen.

The research work at Chemara – and especially this new development, the local production of Pisifera pollen – were together sufficient to attract the interest of all oil palm companies throughout Malaya; as a result of which the Malayan Agricultural Department, on Dr Rosenquist's advice, organised a co-operative oil palm breeding scheme in 1955; to be followed in 1959 by the formation, between Unilever of the Congo and Guthries' of Malaya, of a breeding and general information 'exchange programme'. From this increasingly close interchange of data and physical material there grew, as a natural next step, a 'Consortium' between Guthries', The Dunlop Company, Harrisons and Crosfield and Unilever, who set up the Oil Palm Genetics Laboratory under Dr Harden to ensure that the next and succeeding generations of planting material available in Malaysia would compare with anything available anywhere in the world.

AUTHOR'S ACKNOWLEDGEMENTS

The research and writing of *The Traders* has been a demanding undertaking, but it has also been an enjoyable and rewarding experience. My thanks are therefore due to my old friend and wartime shipmate John Craig, the managing director at one time of Guthrie & Co (Singapore) Limited, who suggested that I write this book to celebrate his company's sesquicentenary in 1971. I was thus brought in contact with Trevor Walker, the chairman in Singapore, whose unfailing good humour and help I can never sufficiently acknowledge.

I continued my research at Guthries' Head Office in London, where I received every possible kindness and assistance from the chairman of Guthrie & Co (UK) Limited, Keith Anderson, and from John Stafford, Maurice Gulliford, Miss Swain and many others. Messrs Hester, Mann, Peterkin and Cooper, all recently retired from the company, generously helped me with their reminiscences. While in London I gathered much useful information from the Guildhall, Somerset House and the India Office Library. In addition, I acknowledge the assistance received at this time in correspondence with the Cape Archives Department in Cape Town.

My researches into records of the Guthrie and Scott families were greatly aided by the following: Lord John Forres of Glenogil, himself a member of the Guthrie clan on his mother's side; Colonel and Mrs Carnegie-Arbuthnot of Balnamoon, whose helpful intervention enabled me to visit Guthrie Castle; Mr Euan Guthrie of Edinburgh, who gave me invaluable information regarding the famous Dr Guthrie DD of the 'Ragged Schools', of which he is now the lifetime governor; Colonel Leslie Gray-Cheape of Carse Gray, grandson of James Guthrie and Suzanna, who supplied useful details of his grandfather's life; Mr W. C. Shiell, a grandson of James Guthrie and his second wife, who permitted Mr Walter Kauffman to photograph the portrait of Alexander Guthrie which appears as the frontispiece; Major R. McNair

Scott, grandson of Thomas Scott, who also supplied details of his grandfather's life; Jock and Joy Hunter, who invited me to stay at *Auchenreoch*, Thomas Scott's house near Edzell which they now own; Miss Smith of Montrose Library, who was always helpful; Mr A. O. Small, the Town Clerk of Brechin, and Mr 'Davy' Sharpe, who both recounted fascinating anecdotes of the Guthrie and Scott families; Mr Kenneth Drummond-Hay of Montrose, who took many excellent and useful photographs.

I was fortunate to obtain personal information concerning Sir John Hay from his son Mr Ian Hay. I am further indebted to him for permitting Mr Walter Kauffman to take the photograph of Sir John's portrait which appears in this book. I was also glad to meet Mr Nesbit Hay, Sir John's brother, and Mrs Gibson, who was Sir John's secretary for many years, and I am grateful to both for their co-operation.

On returning to Singapore and Malaysia, I received considerable assistance from Professor K. G. Tregonning and Professor N. Sherry of Singapore University; Mrs Hedwig Anwar of the Singapore Library; Mr Alfred of the Singapore Museum; Mr Armstrong of the Singapore Government Land Office; the Singapore Port Authority; Mr Wee Kim Wee, editorial manager of the *Straits Times*; Simon and Percival Aroozoo, descendants of Guthries' chief clerk in the late nineteenth century; Mr Peng Seng Wee, the photographer; Dr F. R. J. Verhoeven, chief of the Malaysian Archaeological Department; Messrs Bayne, Crawford, Saker, Howarth and Jones, who gave helpful information on Guthries' Malaysian interests in rubber and tin; Mr John Drabble, who allowed me to use his treatise on the Malayan rubber industry, without which I would certainly have made many serious errors – any that still occur must be attributed solely to me. During this period, I received much help in correspondence with Lord Marchwood concerning Sir John Anderson's life in Singapore at the turn of this century, and from Sir Laurence Hartnett, Director of Ordnance Production in Australia during the last war and one time engineer to Guthries', who gave me a unique insight into the company's affairs in the nineteen-twenties.

My humble thanks go to the friends who read the draft and made helpful suggestions, and my sincere gratitude is due to Mrs Loo Carter, who typed and re-typed the book with accuracy, patience and understanding. Finally, my sincere thanks go to all those whose spontaneous kindness and friendly assistance made this task so pleasurable. To acknowledge fully so much generous help is impossible in the space available, and so I can only hope that a general expression of my gratitude and deep appreciation will be acceptable and that, for all of them, 'in black ink my love may still shine bright'.

SJOVALD CUNYNGHAM-BROWN
Penang,
Malaysia

REFERENCES

HEIC Ships' Logs in the India Office Library, 1750–1835.
The Statistical Account of Scotland. Sir John Sinclair. 1793.
Penang Government Notices, 1786–1819.
Singapore Government Notices, 1820–1835.
Strait Settlements Government Gazettes, 1835–1941.
Straits Times Archives, Singapore: Singapore Free Press, Straits Times, Penang Gazette, Straits Echo.
Hansard's Parliamentary Debates, 1803–1888.
Parliamentary Papers, 1889–1942.
Hansard, 1943–1946.
Memoir of the Life and Public Services of Sir Stamford Raffles. Lady Raffles. 1830.
The Eastern Seas; or Voyages in the Eastern Archipelago in 1832, 1833 and 1834. G. W. Earl. 1837.
British Settlements in the Straits of Malacca. T. J. Newbold. 1839.
The New Statistical Account of Scotland, Vol XI. Ministers of different Parishes. 1845.
Journal of the Indian Archipelago. J. R. Logan. 1847.
Papers relating to the Indian Archipelago. J. R. Logan. 1847.
Journal of the Royal Asiatic Society.
A visit to the Indian Archipelago in HMS *Meander*. H. Keppel. 1853.
A descriptive Dictionary of the Indian Islands and adjacent Countries. Crawfurd. 1856.
Memorials of Angus and the Mearns. Andrew Jervise. 1861.
Straits Calendar and Directory, 1861, 1871, 1873.
Our Tropical Possessions in Malayan India. J. Cameron. 1865.
Autobiography of Thomas Guthrie, DD and Memoirs. David and Charles Guthrie. 1876.
Singapore Thirty Years Ago. G. Norris. 1878.
Manners and Customs of the Chinese in the Straits Settlements. J. D. Vaughan. 1879.
Angus and Forfarshire, the land and people. A. J. Warden. 1885.
A History of Currency in the British Colonies. R. Chalmers. 1893.
The Life of Sir Stamford Raffles. D. C. Boulger. 1899.
Malay Magic. W. W. Skeat. 1900.
An Anecdotal History of Old Times in Singapore. C. B. Buckley. 1902.
British Malaya. An Account of the Origins and Progress of British Influence in Malaya. Sir Frank Swettenham. 1907.
One Hundred Years of Singapore. W. Makepeace and Others. 1921.
One Hundred Years of History of the Chinese in Singapore. Say Ong Siang. 1923.
Papers on the Ethnology and Archeology of the Malay Peninsula. I. H. N. Evans. 1927.
Personalities of Old Malaya. C. Baxendale. 1930.
The Opium Clippers. Basil Lubbock. 1933.
Handbook to British Malaya. R. L. German. 1935.
Triad and Tabut. Mervyn M. W. Wynne. 1941.

The History of Rubber Regulation, 1934–1943. Sir A. Macfadean. 1944.
The Chinese in Malaya. V. Purcell. 1948.
Malaya's First British Pioneer. H. P. Clodd. 1948.
The Green Torture. Robert Chrystal. 1949.
The Malays, a Cultural History. Sir R. Winstedt. 1950.
Yap Ah Loy. S. M. Middlebrook and J. M. Gullick. 1951.
Raffles of the Eastern Isles. C. E. Wurtzburg. 1954.
Realms of Silver. Sir Compton MacKenzie. 1954.
Western Enterprise in Indonesia and Malaya. G. C. Allen and A. C. Donnithorne. 1957.
Prince and Premier. Harry Miller. 1959.
British Intervention in Malaya, 1867–1874. C. Northcote Parkinson. 1960.
British Malaya 1824–1867. L. A. Mills. 1961.
Nineteenth Century Malaya. C. D. Cowan. 1960.
A History of Modern Malaya. K. G. Tregonning. 1964.
Malaya. J. M. Gullick. 1964.
Pickering, Protector of Chinese. R. N. Jackson. 1965.
Malaysia, Selected Historical Readings. John Bastin. 1966.
Raffles. Morris Collis. 1966.
Conrad's Eastern World. N. Sherry. 1966.

Singapore University Academic Exercises, Theses and Dissertations (1947–66)

Abdul Rahman bin Abdul Jalal: Tin mining in Selangor, 1874–1895. BA (Hons) 1954.
Aminuddin bin Baki: Debt-slavery in Perak. BA (Hons) 1951.
Bachan Singh: A history of tin mining in Perak, 1896–1928. BA (Hons) 1960.
Bogaars, George: The Suez Canal and the Singapore trade. BA (Hons) 1951.
Bogaars, George: The Tanjong Pagar Dock Co, Ltd, 1864–1905. MA 1952.
Chelliah, Tha-rumaratnam: War in Negri Sembilan, 1874–1875. BA (Hons) 1955.
Cheong, Weng-eang: German interest in the Malay Peninsula, 1867–1909; BA (Hons) 1960.
Chia, Henry Soo-boon: Island trade of Singapore, 1946–1955. BA (Hons) 1958.
Chu, Tee-seng: The Singapore Chinese Protectorate, 1900–1941. BA (Hons) 1960.
Doraisingham, Manonmany: Colonel Orfeur Cavenagh, Governor of the Straits Settlements, 1859–1867. BA (Hons) 1961.
Goh, Keat-seng: Piracy in the Straits of Malacca, 1867–1877. BA (Hons) 1960.
Hong, Eu-ngoh: Larut to Kinta; a study of tin mining in Perak, 1874–1895. BA (Hons) 1952.
Hooi, Christopher Liang-yin: Piracy and its suppression in Malayan waters, 1800–1867. BA (Hons) 1957.
Ishak bin Pateh Akhir: Selangor district administration between 1874 to 1888. BA (Hons) 1957.
Jalleh, William: Disorders in Selangor before 1874. BA (Hons) 1955.
Khor, Eng-hee: The public life of Dr Lim Boon Keng. BA (Hons) 1958.
Kumaraguru, Visagaperumal: Rubber in Malaya, 1914–1941. BA (Hons) 1962.
Lian, Hock-bang: A study of tin mining in Selangor, 1875–1896. BA (Hons) 1961.
Lim, Lena Uwen (Cheng): British opium policy in the Straits Settlements, 1867–1910. BA (Hons) 1960.
Lim, Leong-bee: The introduction of the rubber industry, Perak, 1895–1910. BA (Hons) 1953.

Lo, Wai-fun: The Transfer of the Straits Settlements from the Indian Office to the Colonial Office in 1867. BA (Hons) 1957.

Loh, Wen-fong: Singapore agency houses, 1819–1900. BA (Hons) 1958.

Menon, Vila-sini: The Singapore houses of agency, 1900–1940. BA (Hons) 1958.

Mosbergen, Rudolf William: The Sepoy Rebellion: a history of the Singapore Mutiny, 1915. BA (Hons) 1954.

Navaratnarajah, Ponnudurai: The introduction of rubber into the state of Negri Sembilan, 1895–1910. BA (Hons) 1957.

Ng, Siew-yoong: Chinese Protectorate (1877–1900). BA (Hons) 1955.

Ngui, Dawn chon-oi: The early growth of the rubber industry in Selangor, 1895–1910. BA (Hons) 1954.

Ong, Chin-boo: A short study of the Malayan depression, 1929–1934. BA (Hons) 1958.

Ong, Tiong-whatt: Farquhar's administration of Singapore, 1819–1823. BA (Hons) 1959.

Rajah, Thavamani Devi: John Crawfurd, Resident of Singapore, 1823–1826. BA (Hons) 1959.

Retnam, Eric Selvaretnam: The trade of Singapore, 1869–1896. BA (Hons) 1961.

Seah, Yun-khong: Rioting and internal security in Singapore, 1819–1911. BA (Hons) 1956.

Soh, Eng-lim: Tan Cheng Lock: his leadership of the Malayan Chinese. BA (Hons) 1959.

Soh, Jenny: Tin mining in Selangor, 1896–1914. BA (Hons) 1961.

Tan, Boon-lin: The Chinese in the Larut Wars, 1861–1874. BA (Hons) 1955.

Tay, Seow-huah: The history of the Singapore Police Force, 1819–1889. BA (Hons) 1956.

Thio, Eunice: The Singapore Chinese Protectorate – events and conditions leading to its establishment, 1823–1877. BA (Hons) 1952.

Tiwary, Ram Awadh: Raffles at Singapore. BA (Hons) 1959.

Tong, Teck-ing: Opium in the Straits Settlements, 1867–1909. BA (Hons).

Veloo, Saminathan: The Tanjong Pagar Dock Board, 1905–1913. BA (Hons) 1959.

Visvanathan, Ramalingam: Riots in Singapore, 1900–1940. BA (Hons) 1959.

Wan, King-cheong: Coffee planting in Selangor, 1880–1900. BA (Hons) 1954.

Wang, Sophia: Thomas Braddell. BA (Hons) 1959.

Wong, Ellen: The Singapore Harbour Board, 1913–1941. BA (Hons) 1961.

Wong, Lin-ken: A study of the trade of Singapore: 1819–1869. MA 1956.

Documents in the possession of Messrs Guthrie and Company Limited of Singapore.

Documents in the possession of Messrs Guthrie and Company Limited of Kuala Lumpur.

Documents letters, photographs and family records in the possession of Mr Ian Hay, of Woodrising Hall, Norfolk.

Guthrie Family Tree in the possession of Lord Forres of Glenogil, Angus, Scotland.

Documents and books in the possession of Mr Aroozoo of Singapore.

Naval records and other documents from Whitehall.

INDEX

Abbreviations. AG – Alexander Guthrie ; JG – James Guthrie; EIC – East India Company; FMS – Federated Malay States; S – Singapore; SS – Straits Settlements; mh – main heading

1746
IG MT
STO·PRO·VERITATE